THE REMARKABLY REFRESHING TALE OF
THE BEER THAT CONQUERED THE WORLD

THE
HEINEKEN
Story

BARBARA SMIT

P
PROFILE BOOKS

First published in Great Britain in 2014 by
PROFILE BOOKS LTD
3A Exmouth House
Pine Street
London EC1R 0JH
www.profilebooks.com

10 9 8 7 6 5 4 3 2 1

Typeset in Minion by MacGuru Ltd
info@macguru.org.uk

Printed and bound by
CPI Group (UK) Ltd, Croydon, CR0 4YY

A CIP catalogue record for this book is available from the British Library.

ISBN 978 1 78125 360 1
eISBN 978 1 78283 113 6

The paper this book is printed on is certified by the © 1996 Forest Stewardship
Council A.C. (FSC). It is ancient-forest friendly. The printer holds FSC chain of
custody SGS-COC-2061

Contents

Prologue

On a drab winter's day several years ago, the head office of the Franzen Hey & Veltman (FHV) advertising agency just outside Amsterdam was in a state of unusual agitation. Two of the agency's directors, Giep Franzen and Tejo Hollander, were peering nervously out from the hallway through the drizzling rain, watching an unusual convoy glide up to the entrance.

At the back of the middle vehicle, a huge armoured Bentley, sat Alfred 'Freddy' Heineken, the man who held the Heineken beer empire in his hands. His limousine was sandwiched between the heavy cars of the 'boys' who accompanied the brewer ever since he had been kidnapped in 1983. The previous day three of them had thoroughly inspected the FHV building, searching the room where Freddy was to view two proposed adverts and even checking the projector for potential firing devices.

The team at FHV had prepared the forthcoming pitch down to the last detail. They didn't waste much time on introductory presentations because they knew that Freddy couldn't be bothered to listen to them. On the eve of such nerve-racking events, it was the guest list that topped the agenda. 'From experience, we knew that Freddy liked to make a show of his power by taking shocking decisions. And the bigger the audience, the more irrepressible the urge', one of them explained. 'So the trick was to keep the invitation list as short as possible.'

Although many hard-boiled entrepreneurs walked through the agency's corridors, Freddy's twice-yearly visits always made the ad-men jittery. They esteemed the mercurial tycoon highly for his instinct for advertising and his creativity. 'It never ceased to amaze us. Inevitably and instantly, he always picked the best lines', said Marlies Ponsioen, a former Heineken account manager at FHV. But Freddy's disciples also knew that his unpredictable mood swings could be devastating.

Allan van Rijn, the man who directed FHV's Heineken adverts at the time, knew precisely how Freddy and his ad-men operated. He explained that in preparation for Freddy's visits 'the receptionists all had their hair done, the mess was cleaned up and the managers wore their best three-piece suits. After all, their mortgages were at stake. Then Freddy stepped out of his limo with a crumpled suit and he walked straight through all this bullshit.'

Freddy himself liked to recall that his legendary affinity with advertising was inspired by a school trip to the Philips lighting and electronics group in Eindhoven. 'They didn't sell light bulbs; they sold light', he explained. Since he returned from an eye-opening two-year traineeship in the United States in his early twenties, the grandson of Heineken's founder had meticulously constructed the brand's identity so that it appealed to consumers throughout the world.

As planned, the diminutive tycoon arrived early in the afternoon. After a couple of handshakes in the hallway, he was ushered into the plain meeting room on the first floor of the FHV offices, which had a projector concealed behind a one-way mirror on one side and a screen on the other side.

As the lights went out and the curtains were drawn, all those present turned discreetly to Freddy Heineken and anxiously scrutinised the deep grooves in his bulldog-like face. The slightest tension on his lips, the merest hint of a frown – even the way he puffed at his seemingly never-ending ultra-light cigarette – could be an omen of a forthcoming disaster. After all, Heineken was one of the most avidly watched accounts in advertising, and Freddy ruled over it with the tyrannical edge that characterised his entire leadership.

Since he had regained his family's majority share in Heineken in his mid-twenties, Freddy ruled over an efficient brewing group that made a crisp lager. This he transformed into a brewing group with an unrivalled international scope, all the while keeping watch in an almost paranoid fashion over the sprawling business, and the brand's reputation in particular.

Few outside the Netherlands realised that Heineken was the name not just of a beer but also of the uncrowned king of the Netherlands – an extravagant yet utterly ordinary billion-aire, who could be both irresistibly charming and outrageously vulgar. Reviled by some, he was hailed by others for turning a relatively bland beer into an iconic global brand.

Freddy had a few strict rules for success. Only in the United Kingdom did Heineken deviate from its recipe – in more ways than one. Yet even there Freddy Heineken was much lauded for supporting a whimsical advertising campaign that became iconic and placed Heineken at the forefront of the Lager Revolution.

FHV and Heineken's advertising staff had spent about three months and 1.2 million guilders on the commercials to be screened by the magnate. Replicating an earlier concept, they consisted of short, fast-cut film fragments accompanied with fitting soundbites – for instance, there was a glass of beer that whooshed across a bar to the sound of a roaring engine.

'Again, Mr Heineken?' Franzen inquired gently when the reel stopped. Because normally, when Freddy liked the commercials, he smiled contentedly and asked to watch them again. But this time the chairman looked hideously under-whelmed. 'Not funny at all', he grumbled – and that, in Heineken's vocabulary, was tantamount to a death sentence. 'It was like a volcano erupting in our faces', said one of the participants. 'There was stunned silence. All of us turned white. We knew it would have been completely pointless to protest.'

The shocked ad-men only found out several weeks later what it was that had offended Freddy: a short sequence with two dogs smooching under bar stools. It was meant to be a little edgy, but in retrospect even the director acknowledged that Heineken had been right. 'Before the presentation Freddy had probably had a drink in a bar in Amsterdam with Joe Bloggs', said Van Rijn. 'He knew the guy who handled the projector at the agency even better than the directors. That way he could tell, without fail, how the general public would react.' As often in such cases, the dust quickly settled. The shot with the drooling dogs was edited out, and the adverts were used. Again Freddy Heineken had got his way, and with the briefest of comments.

Over the previous years Heineken had made headlines for reasons ranging from his eye-catching billionaire toys and adventures to his royal friendships and spectacular kidnapping. But when it came to his company, Heineken proved relentless and utterly consistent. He was the man behind the extraordinary story of Heineken, made of adventurous deals, clever marketing and just the right amount of froth.

1

All or Nothing!

Alfred 'Freddy' Heineken, the Dutchman who built up the brand after the Second World War, often acknowledged that his fortune started with his family name. Had there been a computer program to think up ideal beer brands, it might well have come up with 'Heineken'. Like many other popular beers, the name has three syllables, sounds friendly and has a Germanic ring to it that brings to mind ancestral brewing traditions. Small wonder, since the Dutch beer's name is German.

The name can be traced back to Bremen, the Hanseatic port city in northern Germany. Well established in the town, the Heinekens boasted their own coat of arms, split by a vertical line with a lily on the right-hand side and an open hand on the left. But in the eighteenth century several Heinekens settled in the Dutch Republic, a country famed for its prolific trade as well as its progressive attitude to science and religion. Two generations later, the immigrants had made it to Amsterdam, where they ran a prosperous and very Dutch business: Gerard Adriaan Heineken, the brewery's founder, was the son of a butter and cheese trader.

In the mid-nineteenth century, when Gerard was growing up, Amsterdam appeared to be in a state of advanced decay. Crumbling houses and the overwhelming stench that rose from the canals spoke to the decline of a city that, just two centuries earlier, had been one of the most buoyant ports in Europe. Since then, the sea trade that had made Amsterdam rich had been taken over by the English and the French. Fuelled by the Industrial Revolution, England, Germany and the United States underwent huge economic expansion that left the Netherlands behind. The four Anglo-Dutch wars between 1652 and 1684 had drained finances and further undermined Amsterdam's influence. Almost half of the city's people were registered as indigent and destitute.

The Heinekens lived in relative comfort. The cheese trade had been deftly built up by Gerard's grandfather and expanded with equal drive by his father, Cornelis Heineken. The household became even more affluent when Cornelis married Anna Geertruida van der Paauw. A plump widow, she brought to the marriage two children and the fortune amassed by her previous husband's family in West Indies plantations.

Cornelis and Anna went on to have four children. Their second, Gerard, born in 1841, was their first son. At this time epidemics ravaged Dutch towns, and only three of the family's children made it to adulthood. They were brought up to honour hard work, and Gerard grew into an industrious young man, 'with a sense of adventure and a good heart'. When his father passed away in 1862, Gerard, then just twenty-one, could easily have spent the rest of his days living from the family fortune. Instead, he left the cheese trade to other family members and searched for a way to make his own name. In June 1863 he spotted a brewery for sale not far from the family home. Gerard quickly organised a meeting with two of the brewery's directors, and that same evening he wrote an urgent letter to his mother asking for her financial assistance.

Den Hoyberch (The Haystack) had once been a prominent brewery – among the largest in the Dutch Republic – but it had been in sharp decline for several decades. Gerard knew little about brewing, but he was certain that he could revive the Haystack's fortunes. So he proposed taking over the brewery entirely. 'All! Or nothing! Otherwise it would be a waste of time!' he wrote to his mother.

Anna Geertruida had her own reasons to provide her son with financial support. Towards the middle of the nineteenth century gin had become the Dutch drink of choice (as it had in London). It was causing unsightly spectacles in Amsterdam and misery for hundreds of Dutch families. Every Sunday morning, as she set off to church, Anna Geertruida had to negotiate the gin-soaked drunkards who stumbled around the streets swearing. If her son managed to produce a clean and reliable beer, he might encourage drinkers to relinquish their destructive liquor.

With his mother's support, Gerard Heineken pursued negotiations for the takeover of The Haystack. The brewery was formally registered as Heineken's property on 15 February 1864, when Gerard established Heineken & Co.

Gerard Heineken's faith in the prospects of The Haystack pointed to remarkable optimism, because the brewery was in a parlous state and brewing was often an unrewarding business. The production of beer required substantial financial investments, while at the same time the chemical processes involved were little understood, making the results unpredictable.

The Haystack dated back to June 1592 – a time when beer was the people's drink, used to wash down breakfast, lunch and dinner. Relatively cheap, in the Netherlands beer was not only drunk by adults at a rate of about 300 litres a year, but also by children (the country's budget included tax revenues based on consumption of 155 litres per year for each child less than eight years old). This had much to do with the insalubrity of medieval water: it was pumped from the ports and canals, which also functioned as open sewers. Brewing methods were not especially clean either, but the heating process eliminated at least some of the germs. In those days, there were scores of tiny breweries in brewing towns such as Gouda and Delft.

In the seventeenth century, however, hundreds of such family outfits ran dry, as former beer drinkers switched to wine. 'Even the brewers drank wine when they congregated to discuss the downfall of their business', one historian lamented. This decline accelerated towards the end of the seventeenth century, when the Dutch discovered jenever, a sort of gin, as well as coffee and tea. While distilleries sprang up, hundreds of breweries like The Haystack drowned.

Gerard must have inherited some of the family's trading acumen. He had barely settled in his office before he sent out scores of letters to clients and relations. Brimming with self-confidence, Heineken not only pledged to supply a clean and safe brew but also promised to take back any batches that turned sour. Almost instantly, Gerard's beer started spreading like yeast gone wild. Just twelve months after the takeover, annual sales of The Haystack's beers had roughly doubled to 5,000 barrels.

Gerard was exporting a few batches to France and the Dutch East Indies, the Dutch colony that would become Indonesia, but he chiefly strove to establish Heineken's reputation in the Dutch beer market. A forward-looking young man, he was particularly interested in new techniques that would allow his workers more control over the brewing process. The invention of the thermometer in 1714 and of the hydrometer (a device for measuring a liquid's relative density) in 1780 had made brewing more scientific, and brewing was industrialised in the second half of the nineteenth century, with steam power used to heat mixtures of malt, water and hops.

Gerard was eager to use all of these technical advances in a much larger brewing plant that would be able to produce a greater volume of beer as well as house these novelties. Less than two years after he acquired The Haystack, the fearless brewer acquired a plot of land in the outskirts of Amsterdam (now the Stadhouderskade, in central Amsterdam, where the Heineken museum stands).

When the Heineken brewery was inaugurated in 1867, workers predicted the demise of hard liquor: 'No longer shall intoxicating spirits be our people's drink. No, Holland's beer shall always accompany our dishes, either large or small.' The imposing red-brick building was geared towards a fast-growing market. The use of a star on the labels of beers made by Heineken probably dates back to that year, when Gerard opened an establishment called De Vijfhoek ('The Pentagon'), with a star hung above the entrance.

As Gerard still lacked brewing expertise, he recruited a German head brewer, who joined Heineken & Co. in 1869. Wilhelm Feltmann Jr stirred the brew with stubborn dedication, but he could be equally intransigent with his colleagues. In a letter to Feltmann, Gerard even expressed the hope 'that you will moderate your short temper and not throw any employees out of the window'. Feltmann's impulsive attitude later triggered explosive conflicts in Heineken's board, but the improvements brought about by the German brewer bolstered sales and proved invaluable. Gerard was equally relentless when it came to sales.

It was at this time, while he was working hard to establish

the brewery, that Gerard met Lady Marie Tindal, the descendant of a long line of military officers originating from Scotland. Mary, as she liked to be known, owed her title to her grandfather on her father's side. A man of Scottish origin, Ralph Dundas Tindal was elevated to the rank of Baron de l'Empire on the back of military services rendered to Napoleon. Mary's father, Willem Frederik Tindal, was a cavalry major and a prominent member of the royal entourage. The young woman grew up playing with the princes. However, her father's friendship with Queen Sophie, the spouse of King Willem III, cast dishonour on the entire family when an inquiry found that the two had been a little too close.

Her father fled to Mexico, leaving Mary behind in Amsterdam. Since her mother had passed away a year earlier, the fifteen-year-old Mary was left alone to take care of five younger siblings. They were taken in by childless cousins and sent to boarding-school. Mary then moved in with her guardian, Willem van der Vliet, becoming a lady companion to him and his wife.

It was probably there that Gerard met this pretty young woman with a will of her own. Van der Vliet was against the marriage, so Mary travelled all the way to southern France to get approval from her father, who had settled there after his return from Mexico. Gerard and Mary's wedding, in April 1871, was lavishly celebrated in The Pentagon, a pavilion in the fields behind the brewery.

Like their British counterparts, Dutch breweries at the time mostly sold dark and cloudy, ale-type beers. They were known as top-fermented beers because they fermented at the top of the brewing vessel, forming bubbles and thick foam. The problem was that this exposed the brew to all sorts of microscopic organisms, which could spoil it entirely. Bavarian monks worked out that, if they fermented at colder temperatures, some of the yeast sank to the bottom of the vessel. It took much longer than top-fermenting, but the beer was lighter and more consistent. This lengthy maturation inspired the English name 'lager' for this sort of beer: *lagern* is German for 'to store'.

The bottom-fermenting beers rapidly spread around Bavaria in the second half of the nineteenth century, and they were avidly tried by Dutch drinkers as well. The growing thirst for 'Beiersch bier' became embarrassingly evident during an international fair held in Amsterdam in 1869. The stand erected by Heineken & Co. was almost deserted, while visitors were queuing up to taste the clear Bavarian beer served up by a competing Dutch brewer. Sensing that bottom-fermenting beer was more than a passing fad, Gerard immediately sent Feltmann to investigate bottom-fermentation in his home country. A few months later Heineken switched to lager-brewing.

It was around the same time that Gerard Heineken started turning out a beer that bore his name. Scores of guests tasted the brew in February 1870 in The Pentagon, the pavilion often used by Heineken for parties and receptions. A reporter described it as 'a full-bodied, clear, particularly tasty drink that appeared to combine the good qualities of Viennese beer and Belgian beer'.

The Bavarian 'lager' made by Heineken and other brewers was still quite dark. Just a few years later the Bohemians staked their own claim to brewing fame with a much lighter take on bottom-fermenting beers. It came out of Plzeň (Pilsen), a small town in Bohemia, using pale malting techniques and lager yeast smuggled from Bavaria, along with local water and hops. 'Pilsner' was just as stable as Bavarian beer, but much lighter in shade and with a crisp taste. It's this beer that Britons call 'lager', but Europeans more accurately describe it as 'pilsner'.

Demand for the beer surged, but Heineken struggled to deliver, leaving a gap in the market that De Amstel rose to fill in 1872. Two years earlier three wealthy families had started building a huge brewery on the banks of the River Amstel. It dwarfed the Heineken brewery, which could be spotted in the distance. Once the Amstel barrels started rolling out, competition suddenly heated up in the Dutch beer market. Amstel had enormous capacity, and it deployed unusually aggressive tactics to secure sales.

To hold its own, Heineken & Co. urgently needed another brewery. Since Heineken was unable to finance the construction alone, he struck a deal with Willem Baartz, the man behind the competing d'Oranjeboom brewery in Rotterdam. The friendly rivals struck a partnership that would enable Heineken to build its own brewery in Rotterdam. Heineken was the largest shareholder, with 166 shares, amounting to about 70 per cent of the capital; Baartz held 20 per cent, and his friend Hubertus Hoijer had 6 per cent. The company was formally established in January 1873 as Heineken's Bierbrouwerij Maatschappij (HBM) N.V.

As Gerard had predicted, sinking yeast turned the Dutch beer industry on its head. This was because it required large-scale investments that only the brewers with good financial resources could afford. One of the difficulties of lager production was that it required cool storage. While the Germans could 'lager' their beer in caves, the Dutch had to build cellars and keep their beer cool with ice. In harsh winters, ice could be harvested from the Amsterdam canals, but in milder seasons they had to have ice blocks shipped all the way from Norway at considerable cost.

Always on the look-out for new inventions and scientific developments that might prove useful, Heineken and Feltmann found the solution to this problem: an artificial ice-making machine invented by the German engineer Carl von Linde. Heineken bought one of the first prototypes in 1880. Producing about 1,000 kilos of ice per hour, this not only cooled Heineken's beer but also enabled HBM to run a lucrative ice trade. But the real breakthrough in modern brewing came with the discovery of pure yeast. Until then, many batches of beer had to be thrown away because they were affected by 'diseases' that caused bitterness or acidity – seemingly at random.

The French bacteriologist Louis Pasteur was crucial to this discovery. Pasteur had made his name by explaining how diseases such as rabies and chicken cholera spread, and by developing the first vaccines. But when France got embroiled in a war with Prussia in 1870, it seems that Pasteur decided to undermine Germany's brewing industry by producing detailed studies on beer and sharing the outcome with all brewers – except the Germans.

Pasteur persuaded the managers at the Whitbread brewery in Chiswell Street, London, to buy a microscope and settled down to study the micro-organisms at work in the brewing vessels. He wanted to explain the hitherto mysterious brewing process and investigate the damage caused by bacteria. Published in 1876 in *Etudes sur la bière*, the Frenchman's findings amounted to a huge breakthrough. They explained fermentation as a process in which yeast cells split sugar into alcohol and carbon dioxide, and provided advice on destroying bacteria in fermenting beer. This enabled brewers to avoid random spoilage and extended the shelf life of their beer, thereby allowing it to be shipped much further.

The Carlsberg laboratory in Denmark built on these

discoveries to carry out equally important research for the entire brewing industry, and it was Christian Hansen, head of the Carlsberg laboratory, who isolated the first single-cell lager yeast culture. Based on Pasteur's findings, the scientist identified and removed 'bad' yeast cells that caused beer to spoil. Heineken was among the few brewers sufficiently rich to open their own laboratory, in Rotterdam. It was the second brewery known to cultivate its own strain of pure yeast. Hartog Elion, one of Pasteur's disciples, was hired to create the irreplaceable ingredient of the Dutch beer: Heineken's A-yeast.

Heineken's effervescent sales and Gerard's involvement in many organisations, ranging from soup kitchens to artistic societies, turned him into a prominent citizen of the Dutch capital. His group of friends were among the enterprising men who invested in the city, funding bold constructions and canals. They contributed to many influential projects, supporting economic as well as social progress.

The Heinekens started building a sumptuous mansion opposite the breweries, Villa Heineken, complete with a winter garden and a huge wine cellar. But the brewer was apparently less fortunate in his marriage, which long failed to produce any children. The couple became the target of pernicious rumours suggesting that Mary was rather too close to Julius Petersen, a friend of the Heineken family. A former jockey, this short and stocky man was one of the pillars of Amsterdam society at the time. 'Piet' was admired for his intelligence, and was particularly eloquent on the topics of music and horse-racing, the latter being one of Mary's favourite occupations. Gerard, Julius and Mary spent many evenings together and even travelled to Brussels together to celebrate the couple's wedding anniversary.

Mary Heineken-Tindal and Julius Petersen's closeness became a subject of yet more malicious whispers in Amsterdam after the arrival of Henry Pierre in April 1886, about fifteen years into the Heinekens' marriage. For several years Gerard managed to keep them out of print, but in 1890 they appeared in a venomous pamphlet, *Achter de Schermen* ('Behind the Scenes'):

> A few years ago Piet received warmest congratulations from his friends. After fifteen years of marriage his friend Mary had given birth to a healthy boy. Our friend's joy and pride knew no bounds. On the other hand, it is rumoured that some people saw Mr Heineken that day and did not recognise him. It was whispered that the man himself, when he looked in the mirror, discovered an enormous pair of horns on his forehead.

The scandal that erupted didn't end Gerard's friendship with Petersen, nor did it affect his beer business. Heineken was still thriving when his leadership abruptly came to an end on 18 March 1893. That morning, at eleven o'clock, Heineken was preparing to address the company's shareholders 'when he suddenly collapsed, without letting out the slightest sound', as one reporter noted. He was fifty-one years old.

The convoy of horse-drawn carriages that brought Gerard Heineken to his final resting place, the Zorgvlied cemetery in Amsterdam, was watched by 'hundreds of people'. Heineken was praised as a pioneering industrialist, as well as a generous sponsor of the arts.

Feltmann, who made an emotional speech at Heineken's

graveside, quickly recovered his wits. He apparently courted Heineken's widow, Marie Tindal, in an attempt to persuade her to sell her majority in HBM, and set his son up as a potential successor. The widow, however, had a will of her own. Although Feltmann remained technically in charge of the breweries after Gerard's death, Lady Tindal proved a tough opponent. Both feared and respected, she became known at the breweries as 'Her Majesty'. Far from selling out, she demanded that the directors surrender their own shares, so that she could redeem shares pledged by her late husband as collateral for his debts. Heineken remained a family affair.

The rumours about Henry Pierre Heineken's paternity re-surfaced predictably enough less than two years later, in January 1895, when his mother married Julius Petersen. As Henry Pierre grew up, some pointed to a 'striking physical resemblance' between Henry Pierre and his stepfather. 'Gerard Adriaan was a tall, slender gentleman with sharp features, while Henry Pierre inherited Petersen's square face and stout allure', said a former Heinekeen employee. The boy was close to the man he called 'Father', and particularly enjoyed the mornings they spent playing the piano together with four hands.

Mary Tindal resolutely backed Petersen by appointing him as a director and later chairman of HBM, although he had no track record in brewing or any business other than horse-racing. Meanwhile she ran the household with the same authority she had displayed in the brewery. Henry Pierre was educated the military way and made to stand to attention at the dinner table. If she ever dreamed of turning the boy into an army general, however, Mary was quickly disillusioned. When his stepfather died in 1904, Henry Pierre enrolled in chemistry studies. He obtained his doctorate in July 1914 and joined the Heineken breweries three months later.

Over the next three years the impatience of this dapper heir, with his thin moustache and slicked-back hair, triggered a clash of generations within HBM's management board. The old guard first attempted to restrict Henry Pierre's influence by confining him to the laboratory. To impose his will, Heineken sometimes resorted to unorthodox negotiating tactics. When the master brewer opposed the modernisation of the brewery's steam boilers, for example, Henry Pierre summoned a group of directors and locked the door behind them. Sliding the key in his pocket, he coolly declared that he would only release them when his proposal was approved. Eventually, Henry Pierre triumphed. Both the master brewer and the company's chairman departed in 1917, allowing Heineken to jump into the saddle.

At a time when brewing still required a mixture of human and scientific input, Henry Pierre's interest in chemistry was quite practical. The quality of the beer had been recognised beyond the Netherlands, earning a Diplôme de Grand Prix at the World's Fair in Paris in 1889 (something still mentioned on Heineken labels).

Yet even Heineken could not uphold the quality of its beer when war broke out. By 1917 it had become so tricky to import barley from central Europe that Heineken was forced to brew with rice, sugar and tapioca flour. In a fit of despair, Henry Pierre even ordered tests using flour from tulip and hyacinth bulbs. In these devastating years Heineken's production more than halved, from 429,000 hectolitres (each hectolitre equalling 100 litres) in 1916 to 182,000 three years later. Yet Heineken recovered swiftly. The signing of the armistice ushered in an era of almost effortless, unbridled growth: in 1921 it recorded profits of some 2 million guilders and it paid about 28 per cent of all Dutch beer levies – a reliable indication of its market share. Two years later the company was undeniably the Dutch market leader, with an output of 498,000 hectolitres.

Throughout the 1920s Heineken tightened its grip on the Dutch beer market through a string of small takeovers and careful investments in property. At the same time, the company started working on serious international expansion. Undermined by unreliable agents, technical hiccups and armed conflicts, the brewery's exports up to this point were negligible. But by the late '20s, the market was ready for a fresh offensive, and Heineken was sitting on a suitably heavy war chest.

Apart from exports, Henry Pierre set his sights on Stella Artois, already one of the largest breweries in Belgium. However, he was not all that picky: when Stella's chairman politely declined his takeover offer, Heineken laconically inquired about the address of the next target on his list, the Brasseries Léopold in Brussels. Heineken's first foreign acquisition was settled with the Damiens family in 1927. It was also under Henry Pierre's formal chairmanship that Heineken managers established long-lasting ties with partners in the Far East, the West Indies and the United States.

If Heineken needed any justification for this expansionist drive, it was amply provided by the economic crisis that gripped the Netherlands in the 1930s, which sent beer consumption crashing to just 14 litres per person in 1936. Thanks to its foreign investments, Heineken pulled through these dire years without large-scale cut-backs and redundancies. Henry Pierre even set up a special support fund for impoverished employees, which was largely financed by donations from the chairman himself. The advanced employment policies earned Heineken the nickname of The Red Brewery: as early as 1923, Henry Pierre had introduced a premium-free pension scheme for all employees with an income of less than 4,000 guilders.

⊙

Many Heineken managers at the time regarded Henry Pierre as a strange, melancholic character. 'He seemed to live in another world', one of them said. His hard-headed mother had pushed him into the brewery and continued to watch over him until her passing in Lucerne in 1932, but Henry Pierre threw himself more eagerly into his artistic hobbies. 'Business didn't interest him very much', his son Alfred Henry said many years later. 'He would really have preferred to play music tucked away in a small attic.'

In April 1919 Henry Pierre had married Carla Breitenstein, the sumptuous daughter of an Amsterdam merchant. When the marriage was celebrated in Aerdenhout, an elegant resort about half an hour's drive east of Amsterdam, Carla was only eighteen, while the thick-set groom was thirty-five. Mary Francesca was born three years into the marriage, in April 1922, followed by Alfred Henry in November the following year. A second son, Robert Felix, was born less than four years later, in June 1927.

The children were brought up with all the comforts afforded by their father's inheritance, travelling around Europe and even to the United States. However, the atmosphere in the Heineken home was uneasy. 'Everybody in our home seemed lost', Freddy said years later. What unsettled the three siblings above all else was the acrimony between their parents. Freddy conceded that the relationship 'did not work' and that 'it was not much fun'.

Henry Pierre increasingly isolated himself with his music. One former Heineken executive remembered that the chairman even asked his colleagues to stay away from cafés on the Rembrandt Square in Amsterdam, because he often sat there anonymously, playing the piano. More publicly, Henry Pierre Heineken became chairman of the famous Amsterdam Concert Hall in 1934. According to his son, he not only subsidised it but also performed as a pianist.

At the same time, Henry Pierre regularly went on drinking binges. He was often spotted in the Amsterdam social scene, where he delighted guests with his *esprit*. Then, as the relationship with his wife deteriorated, the brewer allegedly became known as 'the hundred guilders man', because he rewarded prostitutes generously.

Exposed to the marital skirmishes in their home, the Heineken children all went their own way. The Protestant couple's daughter, Cesca, converted to Catholicism and became an adept cello player. Their youngest son, Robert Felix, tested his skills as an illusionist, performing at children's parties under the stage name of 'Robini'. As for 'Fred', he had turned into a boisterous and unruly pupil.

After he was expelled from the Hervormd Lyceum in Amsterdam South, after just one term, 'due to a poor performance and domestic circumstances', Freddy was sent to boarding-school in 1937. He was apparently appalled by the austerity of the residence in Bloemendaal, a small town west of Amsterdam: he said he only agreed to move in on the condition that he would be allowed to refurbish his room with curtains, walls- and bedcovers all in the same shade of grey. But perhaps Heineken did exaggerate a little when he recounted that he had to fight for his meals. 'I learned to sneeze on my plate so that nobody would pinch my food', he claimed.

Despite appalling school reports, Fred did finally get his school-leaving certificate. Teachers predicted that Fred might turn into a bright leader. 'He won't let anything or anybody get in his way, he follows his own path', read his final report. But in the meantime, the leadership of the Heineken breweries had been entrusted to another promising youngster.

2

Bier soll sein!

With his warm smile and large ears, Dirk Stikker wielded an unassuming brand of charm. He obtained leadership almost unnoticed and often got his way without even appearing to try. It was said that he could get hard-boiled European heads of state such as the German chancellor Konrad Adenauer on his side with just a wink across the long meeting-room table.

Stikker was one of the architects of Europe's post-war reconstruction, and served as a Dutch foreign minister in the late 1940s and as secretary-general of NATO in the early '60s. Yet when he turned up at the White House for talks with President Harry Truman, he said correspondents were still more inclined to ask him about the welfare of the Heineken breweries, which he led more or less formally for nearly ten years. The diplomatic talent as well as the integrity and wit that made Stikker such a successful statesman after the Second World War had been a fabulous asset for Heineken during those ten crucial years, when the breweries rushed to spread their beer in international markets and struggled through the German occupation.

Stikker hailed from the northern Dutch town of Groningen, where his father ran a small bank, and he was often plagued by ill health. After his law studies he joined the Twentsche Bank, one of the country's most important financial institutions at the time, rapidly climbing the ranks in the early 1930s. When he received a tip that Heineken was after a board member, Stikker wasn't interested – that is, until he started studying the brewery's finances. 'Such a balance sheet has, no doubt, never been seen before or since', he wrote in his memoirs. 'The resources of the firm were so large, its affairs so complicated, and its reserves against debtors so high that accounts receivable appeared as a liability.' He became convinced that, if Heineken made full use of its assets, it would have the resources to develop on a much larger stage.

The wily banker was ignorant of all things brewing when he joined Heineken's executive board in 1935. Yet he quickly became the man in charge, particularly when it came to international affairs. Henry Pierre remained formally at the helm until 1940, but Stikker rapidly came to function as Heineken's informal chairman.

Although the brewery was the clear leader in the Dutch beer market, Stikker aspired to much more than that. As the political situation became increasingly unstable in Europe in the build-up to the Second World War, the Heineken brand made an advance on international markets – a move with which others have yet to catch up. Admittedly, Stikker was not starting entirely from scratch.

At a time when travels to Asia and the United States still required several weeks at sea, Pieter Feith regularly packed his suitcase for long and often uncomfortable voyages. He was sent by the Heineken brewery to seek out brewing interests in far-flung places, which would enable Heineken to crack international markets before their rivals reached them.

Heineken had already been exporting beer on a small scale when it was still The Haystack, sending consignments of bottled beer as far as the Dutch East Indies. The trade was later picked up by the Heineken brewery's plant in Rotterdam, a busy port. The company continued to dispatch a few crates here and there, mostly to France and Britain, but Heineken's export drive started in earnest when the department was taken over by Pieter Feith in 1928. Shortly after his appointment, in 1929, Feith embarked on a particularly important journey to study investments in the Dutch East Indies. Sales there were weak as Heineken refused to compromise on quality by using alternative ingredients that would have made the beer cheaper and more durable. The company intended to build a brewing plant in Surabaya, a large city on the eastern side of Java, the most heavily populated island in the Indonesian archipelago.

When he got there, Feith was badly disappointed: the site he had picked for the construction of the Heineken brewery had already been claimed by another investor. This time Feith had been just a few weeks late. However, his trip to the Dutch East Indies was not in vain: it brought about a lasting partnership that laid the foundations for its expansion in the ebullient Asian beer market.

As the dispirited Feith made his way back to Amsterdam, he stopped over in Singapore, where he bumped into John Fraser and David Chalmers Neave. These two Scottish gentlemen were partners in a Singapore printing business and once earned a living by peddling English-language Bibles. But more interestingly for Feith, Fraser & Neave had also set up the Singapore and Straits Aerated Water Company in 1883, a small lemonade factory on Battery Road. They agreed to expand into beer by setting up the Malayan Breweries Limited (MBL) with

Heineken. Almost three years after this encounter, in 1932, their brewery in Singapore started producing Tiger Beer.

While Heineken and Fraser & Neave supposedly contributed to MBL on equal terms, the roles were clearly split. Heineken dealt with the technical aspect of tropical brewing, entrusting sales to the lemonade traders. The former Bible-sellers rapidly turned Tiger into a best-selling lager around South-East Asia. The local knowledge of these partners was a huge asset for the tie-up, but then so was Heineken's ability to turn out a stable lager in almost any climate. Heineken's laboratory and technical department in Rotterdam boasted what was probably the most advanced knowledge of brewing technology at the time. While guarding Heineken's A-yeast, its chemists worked to adapt the formula to various conditions and tastes. Technicians were regularly detached to foreign breweries to instruct them on the latest advances. This ensured that Heineken and other beers owned by the brewery reached the market in perfect condition, regardless of their location.

The partnership with Fraser & Neave turned out to be one of Heineken's most significant moves. But in the meantime, the company accelerated its foreign expansion with an investment that got its beer flowing in several continents at a stroke.

Among the assets not being fully exploited by Heineken were shareholdings in two of the investments firms that were most active in the beer business in the 1930s. One was Sofibra (Société Financière de Brasserie), an investment firm based in Zurich, which had interests in breweries as far afield as Egypt, Morocco and Indochina. It was established by René Gaston-Dreyfus, a French banker. He obtained a diploma in brewing and made

it a speciality for his Paris-based bank, R. Gaston-Dreyfus &
Cie, to invest in brewing assets. The other was Interbra (Société
Internationale de Brasserie), a Belgian investment group with
activities in France and Belgium as well as the Belgian Congo
and Angola.

With his track record and contacts in banking, Stikker
was the right man to try and tighten Heineken's grip on these
assets. A few months after his move to Heineken, he heard that
the Banque de Bruxelles wanted to divest its majority stake
in Interbra. He quickly struck up a partnership with Gaston-
Dreyfus and Swiss bankers. Before the year was out, the Dutch,
French and Swiss partners had agreed to purchase the majority
of Interbra shares from Banque de Bruxelles.

The tie-up started off with an uneasy gathering in Brussels,
where Banque de Bruxelles informed the other shareholders
about the sale of its majority package. 'Jews and foreigners!'
the appalled Belgians cried out. Stikker was then subjected to
a merciless grilling by Léon Verhelst about Heineken's intent-
ions with the Interbra package. The former chairman of the
Stella Artois breweries, Verhelst was an imposing personality
dubbed 'The Pope of Brewers'. As Stikker admitted, the inter-
rogation placed him in 'acute discomfort', because 'none of
us even had a clear idea of what we had bought'. But once he
returned to Amsterdam, Stikker realised that the transaction
was well worth the anguish. 'In due course when everything
was sorted out and rearranged, Heineken emerged having
made its new acquisitions practically without cost and working
on a worldwide scale', he wrote.

On the back of this transaction, Heineken held substantial stakes in breweries in ten countries. Many of them were
located in former French or Belgian colonies, from Dakar to
Saigon and Léopoldville (now Kinshasa). Such dealings with

the investment firms also enabled Heineken to acquire the Nederlandsch-Indische Bierbrouwerij (NIB), with the brewery built on Feith's chosen site in Surabaya.

Stikker then went about folding these disparate interests into a more integrated entity. It was established in the Netherlands as the N.V. Koloniale Brouwerijen Cobra, and its records were centralised at Heineken in Amsterdam. Heineken owned about 52 per cent in the partnership, while the rest was equally split between Gaston-Dreyfus and Robert Lambert, another banker. In practice, the interests were supervised jointly by Stikker and Gaston-Dreyfus, who turned out to be both meticulous and hyperactive. He forged personal relationships with brewery managers around Asia and Africa, detailed in warm letters and French travel reports to Stikker. On his own travels for Cobra, the Dutchman acquired insights that would serve his political aspirations. He worked with Arab farmers in Palestine as well as Chinese middlemen in the Middle East and politicians in the Dutch East Indies. Along the way he witnessed abundant corruption and brutality: Egypt's finance minister in 1938 was shot dead just seconds after leaving the table where he'd shared drinks with Stikker.

The patchwork of interests held by Cobra changed over the years as the partners closed some breweries and opened others. They agreed that any of their foreign brewing investments would go through Cobra. However, Stikker and Gaston-Dreyfus struggled to safeguard their manifold brewing interests as the war broke out.

For all his insanity, there was one madness that Adolf Hitler did not dare commit: to deprive his troops of their favourite thirst-quencher. 'Bier soll sein!' ('There must be beer!'), the tyrant decreed, and he thus guaranteed the survival of a brewing industry in the occupied Netherlands. Leagued in a joint brewing organisation, the Dutch brewers not only managed to prevent closures but were also able to pass on information to Allied intelligence units.

German troops began the invasion of the Netherlands on 10 May 1940. The Dutch surrendered only five days later, after German bombers had devastated Rotterdam. The Netherlands were placed under the supervision of Reichskommissar Arthur Seyss-Inquart, a meticulous Austrian Nazi who epitomised the thorough, bureaucratic approach to the occupation. Thousands of Dutch men were drafted as labourers.

It was Stikker's foresight and cunning that saved the Dutch brewing industry from ruin during the occupation. In the late 1930s he had carefully studied Hitler's pamphlets and was aware of the threat posed by the Nazis. He lobbied to create a strong collective organ that would protect the breweries in the event of an armed conflagration: the Centraal Brouwerij Kantoor (CBK) was formed on 18 September 1939, three weeks after the outbreak of the war in Europe. In the same effortless way that he had become the boss at Heineken, Stikker matter-of-factly assumed leadership of the entire Dutch brewing community.

Among the many regulations introduced by the German rulers, the members of several German organisations were entitled to a share of the beer production in the Netherlands. In principle, each of the soldiers stationed in the country should receive a ration of at least two litres of beer per week. The explanations circulated by the CBK indicated that the deliveries were to apply to all units of the Wehrmacht, the SS and the police.

Stikker said that the Dutch brewers used 'every conceivable excuse and stratagem' to persuade the German occupants that beer deliveries should be jointly handled by all the Dutch brewers. 'There are situations in which the better part of wisdom is not to behave like the underdog one is', observed the diplomat, and he apparently played his part with remarkable talent. The CBK was appointed as the sole authorised purchaser of raw materials for brewing. It received an allotment of grain that was spread among all the brewers to prevent forcible shutdowns and the seizure of copper tubs. Employees at Dutch brewing plants were classified as 'indispensable', so that they would not be rounded up and sent off to labour camps. At the same time, by supervising the supplies Stikker could get his hands on very useful information. Since it was unlikely that any of the soldiers would refuse their beer ration, he could tell almost exactly where the German troops were stationed.

'We then tried to pass on this information to England', Stikker wrote later. 'I know we succeeded, because I was once summoned by the German official handling brewery affairs and told by him – to my combined delight and dismay – that "our sources in London inform us that our troop dispositions in the Netherlands are known to the enemy through deliveries of beer".' Thinking ahead, Stikker had warned the Germans in evasive terms about the potential dangers of the arrangements. When he was confronted with the leaks, Stikker feigned incredulity. He reminded the Germans that he had pointed to this potential issue and argued that he could hardly be held responsible for a leak in an organisation that numbered at least seventy people. He coyly suggested that the Germans might want to take over beer deliveries themselves, but he was well aware that they had a few other things to worry about. They reluctantly agreed to stick with the centralised production and distribution.

The purpose of the CBK in the war years was to ensure the

survival of the breweries and to preserve the *status quo ante bellum*: the Dutch brewers should emerge from the occupation as they entered it. The centrally purchased resources were allocated to the breweries on the basis of pre-war turnovers. For the first two years most of them fared well because beer sales nearly doubled during the occupation. While beer production was increased by deliveries to the German troops, the rise chiefly came from the increase in beer consumption that followed the closure of many distilleries.

Dutch brewers had also drawn lessons from their predicaments during the previous war. In the 1930s they developed barley cultures in the southern province of Zeeland, which enabled them to keep up production even when they were cut off from their usual supplies in central Europe. Nevertheless, from the third year of the occupation, shortages forced Heineken and other brewers to halve the strength of their beer. At the height of the wartime suffering in the occupied Netherlands the breweries were permanently on the verge of collapse. During the Dutch famine of 1944, known as the 'Hunger Winter', an estimated 22,000 perished due to a German blockade that cut off supplies of food and fuel. People would scour the countryside for a potato or tulip bulb to take the edge off their hunger. It was a particularly cold winter, and fuel was in extremely short supply. Thousands of Heineken barrels were reduced to ashes.

Staying afloat was difficult enough during the occupation, but Stikker's commitment went further. Throughout the war both the Amsterdam and the Rotterdam plants were used as soup kitchens. During the Hunger Winter, employees could feed their families on rations of porridge distributed by the breweries, and the support fund set up by Henry Pierre Heineken served to help those worst affected by the occupation.

Stikker also risked his own life by getting involved personally in resistance activities. His private secretary brought him in contact with the German officer Gerhard Wander, who described himself as a member of an anti-Hitler group in the Luftwaffe. Through this German contact Stikker got his hands on false documents and petrol that enabled him to drive around the Netherlands freely in the company's Chevrolet. Under the cover of business activities, he established contacts with foreign resistance movements and other patriotic business and trade union men.

Importantly for the Dutch breweries, Stikker's German sources often let him know in advance when the occupants prepared requisitions of labour. When an SS general travelled from Berlin to inspect the Rotterdam plant, Stikker arranged that only women and invalids should go to work that day. 'The SS general was impressed at our ability to keep going with only these workers, and all our able-bodied men at the Reich's disposal', Stikker recounted.

Towards the end of the occupation, in September 1944, he also risked immediate execution by providing financial support to railway strikers in Amsterdam. They had responded to a call from Radio Oranje, the illegal patriotic broadcasting unit in London, on the day that Allied troops began their Operation Market Garden offensive in the Netherlands. Stikker diverted money from a fund for closed-down companies and transferred it to the strikers. With the help of friendly bankers Stikker moved funds from one false bank account to the other, thus outwitting German inspectors. The money was provided by the resistance, but Stikker 'legalised' it by signing cheques that were supposedly intended for the funds and were cashed by the strikers instead.

Later it emerged that Heineken's Rotterdam plant was used

by the Binnenlandse Strijdkrachten, one of the Dutch resistance groups in Rotterdam. To kill time towards the end of the occupation, those who hid in the building apparently helped themselves generously to the available stock. As one witness noted, they hung around the office 'in an inebriated state'.

The fate of Heineken's interests in foreign breweries during the war was uncertain. As the war spread, Stikker was often unable to obtain news from Cobra's operations. The company's interests in the Dutch East Indies were affected by the Japanese occupation, and for many months Stikker could not even make contact with his two partners, René Gaston-Dreyfus and Robert Lambert.

While Lambert escaped to the United States, Gaston-Dreyfus stayed in France. In August 1939 he was drafted by the French army as an artillery captain. Gaston-Dreyfus agreed to resign as a Cobra director in November 1940 – as required under the rules of the occupation, because he was Jewish. The fees owed to him from May that year were subsequently claimed by the German authorities in the occupied Netherlands. However, contact became much more sporadic after Gaston-Dreyfus moved to Marseille, in the then unoccupied south of France. He reported in December 1941 that his bank was in liquidation, which was 'extremely painful'. From Marseille, Gaston-Dreyfus sent a few more detailed letters to Stikker. But from March 1942 Cobra's French partner apparently vanished. The silence became so worrying that Stikker sent an envoy to investigate in Marseille. It turned out that, shortly after his last epistle to Stikker, Gaston-Dreyfus had fallen out with the French 'Verwalter' who was supervising him. He 'disappeared in prison for five months', the envoy reported. 'Owing to the intervention of friends, he was released, but he was rapidly picked up again and interned in the infamous Fort Cisteron prison. He was released after several more months, more dead than alive.'

Meanwhile, Stikker had become embroiled in tricky exchanges with the German authorities about ownership of Cobra, because of regulations that required the handover of 'enemy assets'. Stikker appears to have adroitly managed to befuddle and delay the bureaucratic process, so that the ownership remained unchanged.

Like most other Dutch people, the Heinekens remained in the occupied Netherlands, ignoring Stikker's insistent pleas for them to emigrate. They are not known to have engaged in any major political activities, either of collaboration or for the resistance, and they were not among those worst affected by the deprivations of the war. Those bleak years were nonetheless marked by much anguish and suffering for the Heineken family.

Henry Pierre became increasingly absent from the breweries during the war. He formally handed over his chairmanship of the board to Stikker in 1940 and appeared to retire almost completely. When German tanks invaded the Netherlands, Freddy Heineken was still at school in Bloemendaal. He said he got in trouble on several occasions because he ignored the restrictions of the occupation. At one point he was picked up by German officers, he said, 'because I was driving around on a motor bike with false papers and gas that I had stolen from the German navy'.

Heineken said that, during his detention in the local police station, he was told he would be executed. He was then driven to the Oberkommandantur in Haarlem, 'in the side-carriage of a heavy BMW bike, with two heroic gentlemen of the local police sitting on the bike itself'. Several days later Freddy was released unharmed.

Once he had left school in 1942, Freddy had another run-in with the German authorities, when they came to seize two illegal radios that had been reported at his undercover address in Wassenaar. Freddy had ignored the occupiers' order to hand over such radios. Fortunately he was absent when the police came calling, and his landlady was ordered to bring in the radios within two days.

To avoid forcible enrolment in German labour camps (the fate reserved to many able-bodied young men in the occupied Netherlands) Freddy was employed by the breweries as soon as he had finished school. He sweated alongside Allard Stikker, one of the chairman's sons, in Heineken's laboratory in Rotterdam. The two youngsters commuted together from Wassenaar, with false identity papers and a motor bike. 'Fred was just one of the boys. He hauled sacks of barley, cheerfully, and never worried about getting his hands dirty', said Anton van Gulik, another laboratory employee. (Unlike Heineken and Stikker Jr, he was eventually placed on a list for the labour camps.)

In an interview several decades later Freddy Heineken admitted that he had been unaware of the resistance activities in the brewery. 'The secret was very well kept', he said. 'I only realised what was going on the evening of the Liberation.' Heineken said that he then met a Canadian general and chatted with him for a while. 'At some stage I said that I had to go home. How do I get there, because I don't have any transport? This general says to me, "Go and ask the resistance, they'll sort it out. Here's a note", and on that note, he had written the address of the brewery in Rotterdam.'

Freddy further claimed that he had acted as a messenger for the resistance. 'In Rotterdam, I got notes on my desk that said: this and that German post has been reinforced with twenty people, so make sure you deliver an extra forty litres of that disgustingly thin stuff every week. I passed these notes on to someone from the resistance, who in turn transmitted them to London.' When this was discovered, Freddy said he had to seek refuge in Kasteel Zuylenstein, then the home of Phlip van Alphen, director of an Amsterdam advertising agency. He said he stayed there with Henk Timmer, a former Dutch tennis champion.

It's still not clear whether Freddy Heineken did have any direct contact with the resistance movement. The company's official chronicle states that it was his task to organise contact with the German administration over beer deliveries. However, it appears that Freddy mixed up a few facts. Timmer squarely denied ever hiding with Heineken and a former employee of Kasteel Zuylenstein remembered Freddy only as a holiday-maker. 'Freddy just stayed there as a guest for a couple of days', said the property's gardener at the time. 'I was asked to build a shelter for the mayor under the roof. Had there been any other people hiding in the castle, I would have known.'

The last months of the occupation were marred by tragic family events. Freddy's younger brother Robert Felix, an aspiring magician, spent the first months of the occupation in the guest-house of Wilhelmina Bladergroen on the Van Eeghen-straat in Amsterdam. She provided shelter to several Jewish boys, as well as to youngsters with family troubles. Robert, who was known at the breweries as a more amiable youngster than his older brother, was thereby kept well out of the Germans' way. But he contracted a devastating form of cancer: he became blind only weeks after malignant cells were detected behind his eyes, and his face became badly mis-shapen. Robert Felix Heineken died on 15 July 1944, aged seventeen.

Following Robert's death, and with his marriage becoming increasingly acrimonious, Henry Pierre frequently withdrew to play the piano and drown his sorrows. The Heinekens formally split immediately after the Liberation. Carla Breitenstein entered a second marriage in April 1946, in London, with Wilhelm Cnoop Koopmans, a former secretary of the Amsterdam Stock Exchange. She then moved to Madrid, where Cnoop Koopmans was named ambassador.

Parading through Dutch streets, victorious Allied troops unleashed scenes of jubilation all around the country. Hundreds of thousands of grateful citizens lined the pavements and cheered from their windows to welcome the Canadian, American, British and Polish soldiers who had liberated the northern part of the country in May 1945. The Dutch were shaking off five years of violence and deprivation at the hands of their German occupiers. Beer flowed abundantly in those days, but their thirst was rapidly quenched, and beer consumption rapidly declined again.

While Heineken started to rebuild its business in the Netherlands, Stikker headed to London to organise beer deliveries to the Allied troops in Asian countries where the fighting had yet to end, and where Heineken had some capacity. He found out through the War Office in London that there had been only limited damage to Cobra's interests. Heineken's Indonesian brewery had been forced to turn out beer for the Japanese occupants, but the apparatus was intact.

Stikker wisely advocated that Heineken should throw all its resources into the reconstruction of its foreign business. 'Stikker realised he had to get moving right away', said Ben ter Haar, a Heineken board member at the time. 'To put it bluntly, the entire offensive was based on the argument that Heineken should re-establish its brand in the international market before the Germans had a chance to get back on their feet again.'

German breweries such as Beck's and Löwenbräu, Heineken's most credible rivals in the wider international beer business, lay in ruins – sometimes literally as a result of Allied bombings. Most of their foreign assets had been seized, and their export trade was crippled by a military embargo as well as the devastation of the German economy. The Danish breweries Carlsberg and Tuborg, which had shown ambitions for international expansion before the war, were focusing on the European market at this point. The wider international market was there for the taking.

An opportunity to hit back at German brewers had already presented itself during the war. Beck's Brewery was the owner of Archipelago Brewing Company (ABC), the makers of Anchor and Diamond beer in Singapore. ABC was the leading rival for Malayan Breweries, the company owned by Heineken and Fraser & Neave in Singapore. The ABC business in Singapore was seized as enemy property during the war and acquired in 1941 by Heineken and Fraser & Neave. They helped to fulfil Winston Churchill's promise that there should be beer for the Allied soldiers who were still stationed in Asia and preparing to recapture Singapore. Deliveries of beer to British and American troops would account for up to 20 per cent of Heineken's exports in the next decades.

Throughout the mid-1940s Stikker's audacious line of thinking fuelled a ferocious debate at the highest level of

Heineken's management. Johannes Honig, the board member who handled domestic sales, argued that the breweries should be concentrating on the Dutch market. Like most other breweries in Europe, Heineken had to reconstruct every aspect of its business, from workforce and supplies to demand. It was struggling to get hold of the most rudimentary ingredients, and the Dutch economy had been all but destroyed by five years of occupation. The export trade was fragile, as the war had just illustrated, and Heineken needed all the resources it could get to reaffirm its leadership in the Netherlands. Still, even the stubborn Honig was unable to counter the argument put forward by Stikker and Ter Haar that the post-war conditions would enable Heineken to grab the international beer market by the throat.

At the same time Stikker got entangled in a running battle with René Gaston-Dreyfus and Robert Lambert, the two other shareholders in Cobra. The tension was partly caused by Stikker's growing irritation at Gaston-Dreyfus, who was slowly recovering from his wartime ordeal. Even the banker's appearance annoyed Stikker. 'He looked uglier than ever', Stikker reported after a post-war meeting. 'Memories of his enormous nose had somewhat faded away, and he has kept the disgusting habit of fumbling at this extraordinary piece of facial furniture with his hands and his handkerchief. He looked a little thinner, older, and worn out, while in negotiations he appears to have lost part of his energy and his self-confidence.'

The relationship almost completely broke down when Stikker and Gaston-Dreyfus travelled to Egypt at the same time in early 1947, and held separate talks with their contacts without themselves meeting. Stikker became convinced that Gaston-Dreyfus was plotting to make more investments in Egypt behind his back. Gaston-Dreyfus apparently accepted in his own name an option to acquire a majority stake in the Crown Breweries in Alexandria. 'Your acceptance option majority Crown without consultation unacceptable for me', read Stikker's furious telegram. 'Have informed Lambert [...] collaboration between us now impossible.'

Although the two men managed to rebuild a working relationship, the rift exposed diverging interests. The Heineken chairman argued, quite rightly, that the joint company's future was meaningless without Heineken's brewing expertise, and he complained about the lack of input from the other two shareholders, who were based in Paris and New York. Tired by the squabbles, Gaston-Dreyfus agreed to transfer his shares to Lambert in 1948. A few years later, in 1954, Lambert surrendered his shares as well. Pulling all the Cobra strings, Heineken then had complete control of a network of breweries spread over four continents.

These breweries formed a crucial part of the strategy mapped out by Stikker, which was two-pronged. On the one hand, his successors led a frantic export drive, which established Heineken's reputation as a premium beer. But at the same time they also continued to build on Heineken's foreign network of brewing plants, which gave Heineken a foothold in far-flung markets. The standard national beers turned out by these breweries served to elevate the status of imported Heineken – the real thing – thereby preparing the ground for the segmentation of the local market through the introduction of Heineken, which could be sold with juicy margins.

As the export offensive got under way, Heineken employees in Rotterdam found themselves running a veritable beer armada.

The atmosphere in the noisy packaging and shipping halls matched the industrious reputation of the port city, where it was said that shirts were sold with the sleeves already rolled up. Labourers spent their days covering the necks of export bottles with bundles of straw, gluing labels and filling the wooden and cardboard boxes, which became a fixture in the Rotterdam harbour.

The office of Sjef Annegarn, the manager of Heineken's purchasing department in Rotterdam, was filled with stacks of supplies, from cardboard to crown caps. While he struggled to find all sorts of packaging, his worst headache was the shortage of bottles, which affected the entire brewing industry. In the late 1940s Heineken was so desperate for bottles that it even collected them from the sea bottom in the Dutch Antilles. Bottles of all sizes, shapes and colours, which had been thrown overboard in harbours by partying cruisers, were dredged from the water. They were then stuffed into sacks, shipped to Rotterdam and tediously sorted in the brewery.

It was during these years that Heineken built up a lucrative beer business in Africa. About half of the profits from the brand's exports in the early '50s were derived from that continent. In former British colonies such as Ghana and Nigeria, Heineken leaned on the Liverpool merchants Eastwood & Sharples, who peddled anything from bed frames and shoes to Courvoisier cognac and flour. Rudy de Man, former Heineken export manager, said that Norman Eastwood and Bill Sharples behaved like archetypal colonial merchants. The two gentlemen were 'a stereotype of the conservative true Brit, sporting thick long-johns and bowler hats in the blasting African heat'.

But Heineken's most prominent partner from 1946 was the United Africa Company (UAC), an arm of Unilever, the Anglo-Dutch giant, which sold everything from margarine to detergent. UAC's African trade and plantations then represented up to half of Unilever's profits, and roughly a quarter of its turnover. It traded local products such as palm oil and cacao beans all over the world, while marketing salt, flour and metalware in the African market. After the war it was rumoured that Unilever was planning to construct floating breweries along the African coast. Instead, Heineken and Unilever teamed up to establish Nigerian Brewery Ltd (NBL).

As dictated by Heineken's strategy, NBL started in 1949 by brewing a local brand, Star lager. Five years later it was the most avidly drunk lager in the region and NBL could not fill its vessels fast enough. So from the late '50s Heineken and UAC built a string of other regional breweries. Another prominent brand sold by the company in Africa was Primus, brewed by the former Brasserie de Léopoldville in the Belgian Congo (later the Bralima brewery in Zaïre and then Democratic Republic of the Congo).

Oddly enough, the international department was also allowed to make a dark beer under the Heineken brand for the African and West Indies market. With Malta Heineken, as the product was called, the Dutch markets hoped to piggy-back the huge African demand for Guinness, another UAC partner. The Irish stout was marketed to African men with the argument that it was good for them, 'and your wife knows why'.

The frothy rise of the export business led Heineken to open a third production plant in the Netherlands, in 1958 in the southern town of Den Bosch. About once a year each of the distributors got a visit from one of the young managers in the team of Melchior Weymarshausen, Heineken's export chief. Most of them spent about half of their time travelling the world to spread the green bottles. One of their main tasks was to make sure that, from Tahiti to Puerto Rico, the distributors would respect Heineken's premium positioning – and that they should never, ever, compromise on quality.

Clear and relatively simple, this strategy proved utterly efficient, and it was later adopted by other brewers with their eyes on international expansion. There were only a few countries where it did not apply. By far the most important of them was the United States, where an avuncular importer turned Heineken into the champagne of beers.

3

The Dutch Beer King of Manhattan

From morning until night the burly Dutchman Leo van Munching paced the streets of Manhattan with packs of 'the world's finest lager beer', throwing all his zest into a tireless battle to outsell competing imports. Along the way he came up with beer-selling antics worthy of burlesque Broadway performances.

Van Munching's most famous technique was to storm into a restaurant, stride confidently to the bar and loudly demand a Heineken – knowing full well that it was not served in that establishment. As heads turned and the bartender timidly proposed another imported brand, Van Munching would cry out, feigning outrage and disbelief. Fortunately, the publican would get a chance to set this straight when a Heineken salesman walked into the bar, only a matter of hours after Van Munching's performance, carrying with him a pack of the precious beer and a contract proposal.

Even the importer's German-born wife, Mia, was recruited as a marketing ploy. 'Leo would leave a case of Heineken in a restaurant during the day and return in the evening for supper with his wife', said one witness. 'All dressed up and jolly, they made a spectacle of ordering their Heineken beer, loud and clear. They made an enormous fuss – as if they were ordering a bottle of champagne to celebrate some big event.'

These and other such theatrical tactics were the preamble to a remarkably smooth and well-targeted pitch. Van Munching never attempted to compete with leading American lager brands such as Blue Ribbon from Pabst and Budweiser from Anheuser-Busch. Instead, he figured out that Heineken should be sold as an import – for those who had taste and could afford a European beer. It was all in the label on the distinctive green bottle: 'imported from Holland'.

This strategy dictated that Van Munching focused on upmarket restaurants and bars, such as the Waldorf Astoria Hotel, Jack Dempsey's restaurant and the New York Athletic Club. 'Snob appeal is much stronger in the United States than anywhere else', explained Van Munching. 'When they wanted to show off, they needed something that was imported.' And for the privilege of holding a green bottle, many were prepared to pay nearly 50 per cent more than the price of their American beer.

The indefatigable efforts of the Dutch baron turned Heineken into the most popular European beer in the USA. The tag earned Heineken millions of guilders as well as a reputation that proved invaluable to build up its business in many other markets.

The impetuous Dutchman from small-town Harderwijk had started learning about the beer business in the early 1930s, while he was working as a steward at the Holland America Line, a shipping line based in Rotterdam and operating between the Netherlands and North America. Van Munching's job on board mostly consisted of providing freshly tapped beer and entertaining conversation for almost any class of passenger. But once they had all disembarked, Van Munching went out to explore the city. He rapidly built up contacts with restaurants and business people in New York, where he spotted a frothy business opening.

Van Munching kept turning up at the Heineken breweries in these years to outline his plans. As the steward exaltedly explained to Pieter Feith, then still in charge of the export department in Rotterdam, there was a market for Heineken in the United States, starting with the better restaurants in New York. And Van Munching put himself forward as the right man to bring Heineken into the US market.

Three centuries earlier, the Dutch had introduced their beer to the country when they settled in New Amsterdam (later New York). An influx of German immigrants in the middle of the nineteenth century washed ashore hordes of beer drinkers as well as brewers who had become acquainted with bottom-fermenting beers. Just as they had across Europe (with the exception of the UK), these beers quickly conquered the United States. Among the arrivals were brewers such as Jacob Best, whose son-in-law Fredrick Pabst gave his name to one of America's largest breweries. Another was August Krug, whose widow married Joseph Schlitz and inspired another best-selling lager. They both settled in Milwaukee, Wisconsin, turning it into the American beer capital.

But the man who would become the most famous of these German immigrants in the US beer industry was Adolphus Busch, who made it all the way to St Louis, Missouri. There he married the daughter of a local brewer, Eberhard Anheuser. The beer made by Anheuser was apparently so ghastly that the *American Mercury* claimed 'St Louis rowdies were known to project mouthfuls of it back over the bar.' Busch fixed that by studying beer production in Bohemia. He apparently took inspiration from the medieval town of České Budějovice and its German name, Budweis, for his own beer brand, Budweiser.

Hundreds of small American breweries sprang up in these years. While the entire country recorded just 132 breweries in 1810, the number soared to 1,269 forty years later and reached a peak of 4,131 breweries, making 9 million barrels in 1873. The spread of bottled beer in the next decades favoured those who could invest in scale and brand-building. Anheuser-Busch, Pabst and Schlitz led the way.

However, the outbreak of the First World War prompted anti-German reactions that damaged the brewers and supported calls for the prohibition of alcoholic beverages. 'We have German enemies across the water', said one dry politician. 'We have German enemies in this country too. And the worst of all our German enemies, the most treacherous, the most menacing, are Pabst, Schlitz, Blatz and Miller.' Protestant moralism was whipped up by movements such as the National Prohibition Party, the Women's Christian Temperance Union and, most virulent of all, the Anti-Saloon League. Their propaganda depicted ragged parents and abandoned children, while supporters of the 'wets' were described as 'the most unprincipled, the most unscrupulous and the most Satanic forces possible to consider'.

The agitation and shrewd political manoeuvres paved the way for the adoption of the Eighteenth Amendment and the Volstead Act, which defined all beverages containing more than 0.5 per cent of alcohol as 'intoxicating' and a danger to society. The taps were turned off in January 1920. Proponents of Prohibition claimed that it substantially reduced unhealthy behaviour and contributed to the economic prosperity of the '20s. On the other hand, opponents argued that the Great Drought barely reduced drinking – the ban just led to the rise of bathtub gin sales and racketeering.

For several years it was Al 'Scarface' Capone who pulled the most powerful strings in the American beer business. While about half of the country's breweries went out of business, the Italian gangster thrived on Prohibition, with half a dozen plants turning out real beer and thousands of illegal drinking dens. The most inventive legal breweries survived on so-called 'near beer' – malt beverages containing less than 0.5 per cent alcohol, mineral waters, fruit juices, dairy products and the odd delivery of yeast to Capone's gang.

By the early '30s it had become undeniable that Prohibition was unworkable. Franklin D. Roosevelt and the Democrats committed themselves to Repeal. When they won the election in 1932, Pieter Feith was advised that Prohibition would be lifted rapidly. While American brewers merrily began to fill their tanks again, several European brewers made a dash for the American coast. Feith embarked on the *Statendam* passenger ship in March 1933 with a small shipment of Heineken barrels and crates. The Dutch beer was heading safely towards the coast at midnight on 7 April, as thousands of America's beer drinkers were getting smashed to mark the end of Prohibition in nineteen states.

The shipment reached Hoboken, in New Jersey, just a few days later, on 11 April 1933 – ahead of all Heineken's rivals. The crates of Heineken were netted from the ship precisely one week later, and welcomed by gasping beer drinkers and even *The New York Times*. 'The first legal shipment of imported beer in thirteen years arrived Tuesday', the newspaper reported on 14 April. But a few weeks later some of that beer would have to be tipped into New York harbour: the end of Prohibition came with prohibitive import duties, and the government still only allowed beer with an alcohol content of 3.2 per cent. Few were prepared to pay extra for such a watered-down brew.

Pieter Feith figured out that Heineken would need a persuasive and persistent salesman to get the beer into American bars. Fortunately, on the way over to New York on the *Statendam*, he got to know a steward who turned out to be just the right man: Leo van Munching, the young man who repeatedly turned up at the brewery in Rotterdam. The weeks at sea gave Feith plenty of time to appreciate the enthusiasm of his compatriot, his fluent English and his gift of the gab. A few months after Feith's return to Rotterdam, in September, Leo van Munching was picked as the man to promote Heineken in the United States.

This time Leo van Munching purchased tickets on the Holland America Line for his entire family. It was to be a one-way trip: Van Munching bid farewell to the Netherlands in December 1933 and settled in New York with his wife, Mia, and their two children, Leo Jr and Anne. There was another passenger on the *Statendam* – Captain Krol, a former captain of the Holland America Line who had been asked to establish Amstel beer in the United States.

As it turned out, Captain Krol was back on the sea after only a few months. He just gave up and returned to Amsterdam, reporting that the American market was impenetrable. In the early years Leo van Munching may well have been tempted to give up too. The bank to which he entrusted his savings went bankrupt, and so did several of the agents he contracted to sell Heineken beer. 'I think that, in the '30s, my father regularly considered giving up', his son admitted much later. But Van Munching persisted.

After two years Van Munching had persuaded around a

hundred New York bartenders to stock Heineken. Selling one case at a time, he knew the bar map of Manhattan like the back of his hand. He said he canvassed the market 'with a lot of impudence and courage'. Van Munching was mostly competing against German brews such as Beck's and Würzburger, Bergendorff and Löwenbräu. Owing to an abundance of small American breweries and hefty import duties, beer imports still only amounted to a trickle. They made up less than 1 per cent of the entire American beer market.

Until the mid-1930s virtually all of Heineken's outlets could be seen from the roof of the Empire State Building. This was hardly surprising, though, as even the largest American breweries lacked national distribution. To prove that Heineken had the potential to spread its wings nationwide, Van Munching started exploring the Midwest, a region with a great tradition of beer and mafia. In Chicago he met the owner of an Irish restaurant who claimed he had served the Dutch brew throughout Prohibition by smuggling it from Nassau in the Bahamas.

The restaurateur introduced Van Munching to a trade union boss, who in turn arranged for a local trader to test the market during a ten-day canvassing tour. With Van Munching trotting humbly at his side, this trader obtained contracts in every outlet they visited. 'Only much later did it become clear to me how they operated', said Van Munching. 'He always said: "Neil sent me. Would you like to try this beer?" Much later I discovered that Neil was his brother, and one of the most powerful gangsters in Chicago.'

Distribution expanded again when Heineken teamed up with Austin, Nichols & Co., a weighty New York-based wine and liquor business. Led by Tom McCarthy, this firm was an agent for the Pabst brewery, the largest in the United States. With offices in New Jersey, Illinois and Florida, its operations extended well beyond New York. Austin Nichols could open the doors of hundreds of bars for Heineken. The firm agreed to take up Heineken as part of its assortment in April 1936, after import duties had been halved a year earlier.

Another breakthrough came in 1939, when Van Munching persuaded Heineken to make a flashy contribution to the New York World's Fair. He wanted to establish Heineken as *the* premium quality beer, 'The Peer of Beers', with a pavilion that underlined the brew's Dutch origin as well as its quality. The ensuing extravaganza, 'Heineken's on the Zuiderzee', was built on the stream that wriggled through the fairgrounds. Featuring a life-size windmill complete with a ground-floor bar and a replica of the fishing harbour at Harderwijk, the pavilion was crammed with Delft ceramics. Heineken sold about 10,000 hectolitres at the fair – and more importantly in the long term, the brand gained invaluable recognition.

Van Munching continued to build on the rewards of the Fair until Pearl Harbor made it impossible. Since he could no longer export from the Netherlands during the Second World War, he arranged for Heineken beer to be shipped to the United States from the Surabaya plant in the Dutch East Indies. But when this alternative supply route was cut off by the Japanese, he was totally deprived of merchandise. He started selling wine. Then he offered his services to the Dutch Ministry of Shipping, and until the end of the war he assisted the Dutch Seamen's Home and the Dutch Officers' Club.

The relationship between Heineken and Austin Nichols soured during the war owing to a feud between Leo van Munching and Tom McCarthy. Feith was told that McCarthy nearly starved Van Munching during the war, giving him only half of his authorised salary while Austin Nichols was thriving. So when beer deliveries could be resumed after the war,

Van Munching pleaded in favour of an improved deal. Over lunch at a fish restaurant in Amsterdam it was agreed that Van Munching would have the market to himself. He had two years to prove that this was the best strategy.

Van Munching borrowed $150,000 and set up his own firm, Van Munching & Co. (VMCO), in 1946, together with his business partner Ralph Carter. 'That was the amazing thing about Van Munching', said Ben ter Haar, Heineken's former export manager. 'He told Heineken "give me the contract" and he got it. Then he needed dollars and he got them. He had something that made people believe in him somehow.'

At this stage Van Munching was impatient to get the beer flowing in Manhattan again, but his nerves were stretched for another six months, as the Dutch breweries found themselves at the centre of a public outcry. Furious editorials pointed out that the Americans were depriving themselves of much-needed grain to feed hungry Europeans, only to see it shipped back across the sea in the shape of expensive beer. Unable to justify this traffic, the Dutch government itself prohibited beer exports to the United States in April 1946, leaving Van Munching empty-handed again. It took several months of political kowtowing to quell the fury, but then there was no stopping the uncrowned 'Dutch Beer King of Manhattan'.

When he travelled to New York to observe Van Munching's business in practice in 1948, Ben ter Haar could hardly believe what he saw: Heineken's green bottles were in almost every appealing bar and eatery in Manhattan. The Dutch export manager was hugely impressed by the importer's achievement and amused by his sales blurb. 'Van Munching was hugely talented and genuinely enthusiastic about the product', said Ter Haar. 'When he went around selling the beer, he emphasised perfectly Heineken's appeal. "Your pub needs a little extra from abroad and that's Heineken", he used to say.'

Those who had run the American alcohol business during the thirteen years of Prohibition had tended to stick around after Repeal, which meant the beer trade sometimes required guts and plenty of cash. A salesman who started working in New York in the '50s said he received a salary of $60 a week but he was given an additional $600 to $800 each week 'to spend in the trade'.

Leo van Munching was able to build lasting relationships with bartenders because of his rakish personality and by offering steadfast support. He was friendly with many at the Manhattan bartenders' union, run by another Dutchman. If ever bar owners complained, he inundated them with free beer. And he wheedled bar staff with the unorthodox 'crown cap premium' – a bonus for each bottle of Heineken sold. Another former export manager who was once invited to a pub crawl with Van Munching, Rob van Duursen, said he was greeted with hearty 'Hi Leos' in twenty-six of the thirty premises they checked out (supposedly) at random.

Van Munching's effort to beat the competition was rigorous and uncompromising, especially when it came to Amstel. The premium-priced Dutch beer was far less of a threat than German brews such as Beck's and Löwenbräu, yet Heineken's importer took radical steps to eliminate Amstel from Manhattan. 'Van Munching believed that the market was too small for two Dutch brands, because American publicans liked to stock only one German beer and one Dutch', said Sibe Minnema, the Netherlands-based Heineken manager in charge of the United States. 'Thousands of Amstel bottles were emptied in the gutters of

New York', he said, after Van Munching instructed his agents to 'look out for Amstel, clean it up and dump it'.

John Elink Schuurman, Amstel's export manager at the time, mildly understated Amstel's feelings when he said that Van Munching's hardball tactics 'were not always appreciated'. He described how Van Munching imposed Heineken as the leading Dutch import beer by 'thrashing' Amstel. 'Van Munching walked the streets from one outlet to the other with a couple of corpulent agents and whenever he spotted Amstel on the shelves, he purchased the entire stock', he said. 'Then retailers were told in no uncertain terms that they'd better stop pushing Amstel.' Such tactics established Heineken as the Netherlands' leading beer export to the United States, accounting for 90 per cent of Dutch beer exports.

Until the late '40s, Van Munching's operation in the USA was barely profitable. However, the company's sales and profits gradually improved as Van Munching deployed a strategy described as 'overall presence'. He set up what no other importer had managed to build at the time: distribution that covered the entire country. As part of this strategy, in 1953, Leo Jr was sent out to supervise the company's business in Chicago and, later, California. Such coverage was complicated by strict regulations, which varied from state to state. Van Munching had to sell through a raft of regional agents, instead of delivering directly to bars and grocery stores. These agents often offered at least one of the largest American beer brands and then took up Heineken as a premium brand to complement their assortment. Unlike most other brewing companies, Van Munching made sure that distribution was closely watched over by his own men. The way it worked was that he employed 'missionary' men who tagged along with his distributors' salesmen. They were not allowed to solicit orders, but they still went on the rounds along with the salesman to talk about Heineken, and to make sure that the brand was displayed or tapped in the right way. The 'right' way meant consistent and uncompromising quality. 'They always wanted to impress on the public that Heineken was something classy', explained George Kahl, a former VMCO manager.

To set Heineken apart from its German rivals, Van Munching continued to push the 'Dutchness' of the beer. He showered publicans with kitschy Dutch ornaments such as ceramic statuettes of a pipe-smoking farmer and conspicuous windmill displays. As well as the predictable blondes in bathing suits, advertising posters featured young Dutch farming couples in traditional dress, windmills, tulips and Friesian cows. With annual orders of up to 25,000 pairs, Leo van Munching Jr claimed VMCO also became the largest single costumer for Dutch clogs. Van Munching offered a single clog to each of his clients and, to counter theft, he had the left and right clogs shipped separately.

However, most American drinkers still thought Heineken was a German product. A study conducted by the breweries embarrassingly revealed that pitching Heineken as a Dutch beer was a complete waste of time because the average US punter was unashamedly ignorant of European geography: one of the baffling answers recorded in the brewery's questionnaire was that 'Holland is the capital of Copenhagen'. Confusion was further heightened by the fact that Americans often referred to immigrants from both the Netherlands and Germany as 'Dutch'.

In the late '50s Van Munching changed strategy, embarking on large-scale advertising campaigns, with the slogan 'Heineken tastes tremendous'. Heineken's US sales started to take off, and Van Munching grew to be the brewery's largest customer. They called him Heineken's unofficial fifth board member.

◉

When Leo van Munching travelled to Amsterdam, about once a year, Heineken rolled out the red carpet. For a few nerve-wracking days the entire export department was on its toes, bending over backwards to please him with boat trips to Volendam and luncheons at The Old Dutch, his favourite eatery in Rotterdam. 'Van Munching was like a bear with a sore head, but we all felt that he could make or break Heineken', said one of the brewery's export managers. 'Quite frankly, everybody was flat-out terrified of the guy.'

As a result, when VMCO's contract with Heineken was about to expire, in 1959, Van Munching found himself in a position to negotiate an extravagant deal. The negotiations lasted more than a year, punctuated with much legal wrangling. Oscar Wittert van Hoogland, then Heineken's chief executive, wanted to tighten the brewery's control over the organisation by acquiring part of the company, but Van Munching would have none of that. He enlarged his own stake in VMCO to become the majority shareholder, and he did not intend to let Heineken meddle either. Anxious not to anger Van Munching, and perhaps a little intimidated, in September 1960 Heineken offered him a fabulous deal: it would safeguard his exclusive right to import Heineken into the USA, then the biggest beer market in the world, not only for his lifetime but also for the lifetime of Leo Jr. The only thing that Heineken got in return was an assurance about the sales trend.

Van Munching later acknowledged that he was extremely fortunate to get away with the cast-iron deal. 'Freddy Heineken meant nothing at the time, otherwise I don't think he would have let this happen', he told a Dutch reporter. And Sibe Minnema, who was partly responsible for the outcome of the talks, as the export manager in charge of the United States, admitted sheepishly that 'this concession with its far-reaching consequences did not earn me the warmest of praise in later years'.

4

Our Young Friend

Alfred H. Heineken, the impetuous son of the brewery's largest shareholder, was a bit of a nuisance. On the one hand, Freddy had grown prematurely streetwise during the occupation, and it could not be ignored that he would inherit the family's stake in the company. On the other hand, the Heinekens' influence on the brewery had diminished since Freddy's father, the absent-minded Henry Pierre Heineken, had delegated the running of the breweries to Dirk Stikker and Pieter Feith. Freddy's lack of formal business education strengthened some of the managers' inclination to sneer at 'our young friend'.

Shrewdly, Heineken's board recommended that Freddy should be sent to the United States, where he could learn about advertising techniques unknown in the Netherlands. 'We were very eager to get rid of him', said a former board member. 'What else could we do with the lad? He knew nothing and had no inclination to study. He was a particularly awkward problem.'

In a letter with a snide undertone, one elderly board member wrote that Freddy would do the company a great service by learning about marketing. So the brewery asked Leo van Munching, their importer in the United States, to teach 'little Freddy' the ropes of the beer trade. Freddy was offered an annual salary of $6,800, which some of the managers in

Amsterdam thought 'exorbitant' but which he regarded as stingy. In any case, after the restrictions of the war years, the curious twenty-three-year-old was unlikely to turn down the offer, and in April 1946 he boarded one of the earliest transatlantic passenger flights in Shannon, Ireland.

To begin with, Freddy was taken in by Leo van Munching, his wife and two children, who were a little older than the Dutch youngster. Anne Wilsey, the importer's daughter, recalled that the special Dutch guest was treated 'like one of the family', and she came to regard him as 'a second brother'. As instructed by the managers in Amsterdam, Van Munching still kept Freddy on a tight rein and impressed on him that he had to prove himself. He would have to sell one case at a time, just like Leo and his son had done.

Freddy was wise enough to take his assignment seriously. For about two years he learned exactly what it took to flog an expensive and unknown beer brand to American customers. At first, he wore out his soles on the pavements of Manhattan. Later he drove around with packs of Heineken beer loaded in the boot of a second-hand Buick.

When he moved out of the Van Munching mansion, Freddy said he stayed at the Astor Hotel on Times Square. He grumbled that he 'lived in a rotten hotel room with a monthly budget of $350' and 'got to know all the Chinese restaurants where you can have a meal for 55 cents'. He supplemented his wages by trading in second-hand cars. 'It went wrong sometimes, and then the Buick had to go back to the bank', he said.

In April 1947 Freddy was appointed sales promoter for Heineken on the West Coast and moved to California. Further away from Leo van Munching's watchful eye, it seems Heineken enjoyed his freedom even more than in New York. Ter Haar, the former export manager, who visited the youngster while on a business trip, observed that Heineken resided in 'a very comfortable penthouse in Los Angeles and painted the town red'.

It was in California that Freddy spent much of his second year in America, and it was here that he met Martha Lucille Cummins. Two years younger than Freddy, Lucille was a descendant of early nineteenth-century Irish immigrants who had established their name in the whisky trade. Lucille's grandfather 'Artie' Cummins ran the Willow Springs Distillery in Nelson County. Her uncle Arthur J. Cummins established the Cummins-Collins distillery in Athertonville. Her father, Charles Warrell Cummins, was registered as a distillery employee.

The charming young woman had probably left Kentucky for the excitement and bright lights of the city. According to Freddy, when he met her, she was working as a model in Los Angeles. He was instantly seduced by her grace, unpretentious intelligence and 'Marlene Dietrich legs'. Despite his well-groomed appearance, immaculate suits and slicked-back hair, Freddy seemed an unlikely match for the aspiring, twenty-three-year-old Lucille. And she had never heard about Heineken beer. Still, he liked to say that Lucille accepted his marriage proposal during one of their first nights out, after lending him a $50 note to settle the restaurant bill. 'That was exactly what was great – that she liked the poor and unknown Freddy', he told *NRC Handelsblad* many years later. Their wedding was hastily registered in New York in August 1948, and a few days later they were aboard a boat to the Netherlands.

When the twenty-four-year-old Freddy returned with his bride, he knew the ropes of the beer business, but he still had to learn the basics of corporate finance. This time it was the Nederlandsche Handel-Maatschappij that was entrusted with the youngster's tutelage. This institution, the oldest component of the future ABN Amro bank, was closely linked to the brewery. The bank's chairman, Baron Collot d'Escury, had been a member of Heineken's supervisory board since 1930.

Freddy's junior position at the bank's headquarters in central Amsterdam was not exactly stimulating. 'I was so American-ised by that stage that it took me a while to get used to the idea of sorting out small credits for the branch in Loon op Zand', he said. It may have been this boring occupation, however, that reversed the aspiring brewer's fortune.

While Freddy Heineken always underlined 'Papa's contri-bution to the international expansion of the breweries, he also acknowledged that his father had almost ruined the family by 'giving away' the majority of his shares in the N.V. Heineken's Bierbrouwerij Maatschappij (HBM) and letting other managers and members of the supervisory board build up their private stakes in Cobra.

Mary Tindal had secured the family's capital after Gerard's passing, and when she died in 1932, the brewery was still in family hands. Six years later, in 1938, Henry Pierre still held 62.4 per cent of the shares when he agreed to float the company on the stock exchanges of Amsterdam and Rotterdam. The offering in January 1939 of 2,000 shares was vastly over-subscribed. After that transaction Heineken was left with just 49 per cent of the company's capital. He did not bother to issue priority shares because he heard the government was about to impose tax rules that would be unfavourable for such shares. That never occurred, but Heineken was still faced with huge tax bills, levied by the government to help finance reconstruc-tion. When the company increased its capital by issuing more shares, Heineken was unable to take up his full allotment. In 1940 his stake was diluted to 45 per cent and it was further reduced after his divorce.

Freddy Heineken was well aware of the situation while he was in the United States. In a letter to his father, written from Seattle in 1947, he made it clear that he wanted to regain family ownership of HBM, the company behind the Heineken brand. 'Due to the various things that have occurred in recent years, such as the divorce from Mum and the large amount of money that the tax authorities got their hands on, your interest in HBM has been considerably reduced compared to the percentage that Otie [Mary Tindal] had. There is nothing you can do about that, circumstances were to blame. My intention, however, is to try during my lifetime to ensure that the majority of HBM shares are returned to the family', he wrote, describing it as 'a matter of pride'.

When he returned from the United States, Freddy Heineken realised that regaining ownership might be even harder than he had envisaged. His father's financial situation was 'a frightful mess'. Advisers 'claimed that all the capital had gone' and his 'father was sitting there quite forlorn'.

In February 1949 Freddy found out that Henry Pierre had divested some of his personal shares in Cobra as well – and he smelled betrayal. Harry, as Freddy's father was called by the other directors, had agreed to sell 90,000 guilders worth of Cobra shares to eleven members of Heineken's management and supervisory board. The problem was that the shares had been sold at a rate of 170 per cent, well below their estimated worth of 300 per cent. The largest package went to the director Jan Emmens. Three other large chunks were purchased by Johannes Honig, a board member, Pieter Feith and Baron Collot d'Escury.

Freddy suspected that the managers had unashamedly taken advantage of his father. Freddy rushed to seek advice from Stikker, who had left the brewery a few months earlier to join the Dutch government, and had described the deal as 'a swindle'. Freddy wrote in February 1949 that he was 'incensed' that his father had not offered the Cobra shares to him or his sister, Cesca, who had inherited from 'grandma Petersen'. But most of all, Freddy was outraged that his father might have been fleeced. 'As far as I am concerned, if Pa was hoodwinked, and I know just as well as you do what an easy trick that would be, then something will have to happen, even if it has to come to blows', he wrote. Freddy approached Stikker 'not so much as a former HBMer, but as my uncle Dirk. You are the only person whom Cesca and I can trust.'

As Freddy dug further, he found yet more evidence that the directors might have taken advantage of Henry Pierre. Over lunch with his father, Freddy heard that Henry Pierre had only agreed to the Cobra deal because he understood that his Cobra shares would go to HBM. Henry Pierre would never have gone along at this price, had he been told that his Cobra shares would be split and bought privately by Heineken managers. Stikker openly attributed the incident to Henry Pierre's distracted nature and lack of interest in business. While he was still at Heineken, he noted that he and his colleagues had 'often discussed how easy it would be to force Harry into transactions which would be favourable for the managers and unfavourable for him'.

The Cobra deal had been discussed in detail with Henry Pierre on three occasions, and he had been warned that the price didn't reflect the true value of Cobra, so in April, Freddy Heineken had to back down and accept the buyers were not at fault. But his fraught relationship with the management made it all the more important for him to build up his share ownership rapidly. To muster the required funds, he bought a Jaguar and bluffed his way into banks and pension funds. His own share of the company amounted to about 20 per cent of the capital. He placed that in a holding company that he established in 1950, HBBM, along with the shares he amassed on the stock exchange.

Freddy went on to acquire control of the share package that was allocated to his sister. A former board member said that the deal around Cesca's shares was sealed informally between Freddy and his father: in return for the package, the brewer promised to take care of Cesca's financial welfare.

As he amassed more shares on the stock exchange, Freddy said he tested the loyalty of every single Heineken manager and supervisory board member. He unmasked those who bought shares behind the family's back by indirectly offering them HBM share packages at attractive prices. Since the shares came with debts, he used shares as collateral to get loans, and loans to get more shares. The tricks were remarkably gutsy, especially coming from a youngster whose only asset on paper was his name, but Freddy was patient, and he had nothing to lose.

Freddy Heineken joined the supervisory board of HBM when his father stepped down, as a delegate member in March 1951. A few months later, the youngster asked to be appointed to the same position as his father had held. It would have given him some prerogatives, such as the right to attend directors' meetings. Other board members were against it.

Freddy asked again in February 1953, and again the management board was unfavourable. As Feith explained, the board would only consider it 'once he has proven in practice that he is prepared and able to adjust to the style and working methods of HBM, instead of the opposite, and to use his position of power reasonably and first and foremost in the interest of HBM'. As a gesture of goodwill, the Heineken heir was allowed to attend all management board meetings.

A few months later, Freddy Heineken no longer had to ask for permission. He had finally secured the majority of HBM's shares, all under his personal holding company, HBBM. Freddy savoured his triumph in 1954 by strutting into Johannes Honig's office and informing him that he would be leaving for a six-week holiday. Then, just as he was leaving the room, Heineken added: 'I almost forgot to tell you something. As of yesterday, I have a majority shareholding in this company.'

Ironically, it was the family behind the competing Oranje-boom breweries that tipped the scales in Freddy's favour. The Hoyer family had been involved in Heineken's business since 1873, when Gerard Heineken sought investors to finance the construction of his Rotterdam brewing plant. They had long ceased to be active in HBM's management, but they kept their shares of the company and gave Freddy decisive support by agreeing, in 1954, to bundle their stake with his package. Dik Hoyer, one of the family's heirs, said there had been only one reason for the family to back Freddy: they were struck by the young man's quick wit and most impressed with his bravado.

From the beginning of October that year Heineken was appointed as a management adviser, with a salary of 30,000 guilders per year. Heineken later described the outcome of his many years of financial juggling as the crowning glory of his working life.

Several sources said that, once he had stepped down from all his duties at the Heineken breweries, Freddy's father rapidly sank into 'deep unhappiness', squandering his money on alcohol and women. Personal records indicate that Henry Pierre briefly had a more formal relationship, when he married again in January 1948, aged sixty-two. His bride was Jeanne Suzanne Berthier, and the marriage was formally recorded in a posh district of Paris. However, the same records indicate that she died in Paris just over a year later, in June 1949, aged just fifty-one.

While Freddy's mother resided in Spain with her husband, Henry Pierre Heineken led a lonesome life in Amsterdam. A former neighbour said he often returned to his flat on the Appololaan in the early hours of the morning in a pitiful state. 'It was making an awful lot of noise because the porter often had to haul Heineken inside and to drag him up the stairs', he said. He died in May 1971 and was buried in the Zorgvlied cemetery, with his mother, Marie Tindal, and her second husband, Julius Petersen.

⊙

After the family's heritage had been secured, Freddy and Lucille Heineken started indulging in the privileges of the wealthy few. Several decades later, Freddy said he hated to be called a playboy. 'I hate this word. What is a playboy? Someone who does bugger all. And I don't fit the profile at all. I work my arse off', he said. To a large extent, that was true. Freddy applied himself to Heineken with the sort of passionate commitment unlikely to be matched by outsiders. Yet in his 'wild years' Freddy hardly discouraged associations with the exuberant son-of-a-rich-man type.

In fact, he amassed all the paraphernalia of an unrepentant playboy. In the garage of his green-tiled villa in Noordwijk aan Zee, the Dutch beach resort, he kept an entire fleet of vehicles. It comprised a Facel Vega and a Mercury Cougar with a folding steering wheel, as well as collectors' items that he imported from the United States through the brewery's transport department.

Freddy was most proud of his Alfa Romeo Zagato 1934 and his minuscule 'Willam'. The brewer spotted this oddball vehicle in the French beach resort of St Tropez and bought it for the equivalent of 3,000 guilders in Paris. 'Delightful. You can park it in between two cars, in a space of about one and a half metres, with its nose against the pavement. It's the most ridiculous car I've ever seen', he said.

In the 1950s he obtained a pilot's licence, which enabled him to spend many afternoons hovering above Europe in private jets. In 1960 Freddy even created a private air navigation company, N.V. Sportair Amsterdam, with a capital of 100,000 guilders. It had at its disposal a Jodel aircraft, a single-engine two-seater, and Heineken later bought a Piper Comanche, an American four-seater. Its call sign was 'PH-RED', as in 'Fred'.

Former guests fondly remember the bashes thrown by the couple at their house in Noordwijk. Two architects were contracted to design the Heinekens' boomerang-shaped home, called De Ark ('The Arch'). Like the couple's splendid villa in Cap d'Antibes, in the south of France, it was said to be fitted with all sorts of architectural gadgets, such as a downstairs bar with a glass partition that enabled visitors to watch the legs of swimmers in the adjacent pool.

On the Riviera, Freddy treated his guests to Mediterranean cruises. He once owned a seaworthy Caravelle, worth an estimated 450,000 guilders, as well as several other boats. He could embark from his domain, La Garoupe, which stretched from the mansion's terrace to the beach, at the bottom of a lush peninsula. One of the property's swimming pools was said to be fitted with a plastic sheet just one inch below the surface, so that Freddy could surprise his guests by seemingly walking towards them on the water.

It was Freddy's reputation for gallivanting with long-legged women, however, that cemented his reputation as a playboy. Freddy himself made little effort to hide his interest in women, which he often expressed with startling vulgarity. He dallied around Amsterdam with insouciante young women and openly admitted that he did not take his marital vows all that literally.

Lucille Heineken opted for a low-profile existence. Those who met her were invariably impressed by her grace and personality, but she never visibly interfered with the Heineken business. When Lucille attended parties, she moved around discreetly, sipping on a glass of sherry. She preferred to go riding on the beach at Noordwijk and let her husband lead his own 'social' life.

Still, all this frivolity never quite distracted Freddy from his commitment to the family firm. Although some former staff remember that the company's owner was often notable for his absence during those early years, he rapidly built up credibility by inspiring an in-depth reform of Heineken's image. With undeniable instinct and consistency, he led the meticulous construction of one of the world's most recognisable beer brands.

Heineken already had a 'publicity department' in the '40s, which was set up to persuade consumers that Heineken beer had become drinkable again after the war. They contributed to a collective campaign by the Dutch beer industry with the slogan

'Beer Is Best Again'. But it was Freddy Heineken who supposedly introduced advertising at the brewery upon his return from the United States, by sticking a piece of paper with the words 'advertising department' on the door of an empty office.

Freddy guided the department's efforts. He had grasped the importance of advertising while travelling around the United States: 'I had seen the future. I had seen how refrigerators, television and supermarkets were changing beer-drinking habits in the US. And I knew they would have much the same impact in Holland', he told *Fortune* magazine.

Then in his mid-twenties, Heineken enjoyed the creative side of advertising, but he had also learned that the message had to be simple and consistent: it was useless to tell consumers that Heineken was tasty, fresh and smooth if it didn't at least look that way. So he started by updating the beer's packaging, to make it more appealing.

Until the late '40s Heineken's bottled beer was most likely to be packaged in shabby timber boxes that bore the brand name in rough black print. The bottles themselves were adorned with a whole palette of labels: grey, red, green, blue, oval, rectangular, dominated by Heineken's trademark red star and the upper-case Heineken name.

In 1947 the brewery's publicity commission started by harmonising the font of the Heineken brand name on its bottles and switching it to lower case. Freddy applauded: 'I realised that when I signed my own name, it looked friendlier than the Heineken on the beer bottle, which was set all in capitals', he explained long afterwards. 'Heineken in upper case has eleven vertical lines – far too many to be read easily – and the name was spread all around the bottle. It was useless.'

The red star was another controversial feature. It had been used for many years to distinguish the beer bottled at

Heineken's own plant from the Heineken beer sold by dedicated bottlers. Some managers feared that the red star would hamper Heineken's international expansion, because it was invariably associated with Cuba and the Soviet Union. Heineken considered replacing it with a windmill or a haystack but ultimately decided to use a smaller, less conspicuous star.

The brand's identity underwent a string of seemingly insignificant changes in the early '50s. For a start, it was decided to remove the apostrophe and the 's' in the brand name 'Heineken's'. Consumer research had revealed that many identified the brand as 'Heinekes', and Freddy figured out that shortening the name would save him millions in electricity bills for neon signs. He spent hours working out the difference. Meanwhile, the 'e' in the lower-case version of the name was tilted slightly upwards, giving birth to Heineken's famous 'smiling e'.

To this day, the origin of these graphic adjustments remains a subject of controversy in Dutch advertising circles. But according to one designer who worked with Heineken at Claessens, a graphic design agency based in Hilversum, the 'smiling e' was not the fruit of any creative genius – it was adopted after an almost scientific study. 'It's ironic that Freddy Heineken should describe the "smiling e" as one of his brainchildren. It was actually born on these premises. But what the heck, it's pretty flattering for an agency when a client is so proud of a job that he wants to reap the praise for it', he said.

Freddy Heineken himself admitted that the birth of the 'smiling e' had been preceded by a long period of labour: 'We had scientists looking through microscopes for days to work out the right degree of tilt for the "e". Too far one way it looks sad, too far the other and it is crazy. If you look at it now, it smiles at you.' At the same time, he made the 'n's and 'k's look 'fat and friendly', to give an impression of 'hospitality'.

Freddy's biggest packaging coup, however, was the adoption of green as Heineken's trademark colour. The tycoon later reckoned that 'you didn't have to be a genius to work that one out', but at the time he had needed all his persuasion powers to impose the shade. 'They thought I was out of my skull', said Heineken. 'But I always kept in mind that consumers are very conservative about what goes into their stomachs. I predicted that green would become a universal symbol for nature and safety, long before the environmental lobby told us so.'

The next step, in the '60s, was to modernise the corporate identity of the brewery with a new logo for the neon lights hanging outside the pubs as well as a whole array of accessories, from beer mats to bicycle racks. The black bar under the brand name was one of Freddy's suggestions, as part of the visual identity. 'The advertising department fiercely opposed this absurdity, which looked like a funeral frame on a coffin. But the boss created what we at Heineken called the "black-bar culture", by dictating that this should feature on all of the brewery's promotional tools', said Wim Bouman, a former advertising employee.

Freddy and his aides also worked on the corporate logo. After weeks of work, the advertising team came up with the two red half-circles around the black bar, which would enter the brewery's advertising history as 'the Heineken kiss'. It was tested extensively by the agency handling Heineken's account, which organised trials in cinemas, asking the audience to assess the impact of the logo in various shapes and colours. Finally, in 1964, the red and black logo was inaugurated during a meeting of about twenty advertising experts, including Freddy Heineken, in a pub in Loenen aan de Vecht, fitted with all the artefacts in the Heineken kiss-style. By the mid-'60s Heineken had thus established a worldwide brand identity strong enough to withstand several decades of intensive cultural changes – a rare feat in corporate history.

Somewhere along the line somebody came up with the slogan 'Heerlijk, Helder Heineken' ('delicious, clear Heineken'). This alliterative line, still used to identify Heineken in the Netherlands today, became such a legend of Dutch advertising that even national newspapers conducted in-depth investigations to trace its author. Freddy Heineken claimed responsibility, but this has been disputed by many other would-be advertising geniuses.

To the frustration of Heineken's staff, Freddy had a complete lack of respect for hierarchy in advertising matters and a habit of meddling in the department's affairs, often upsetting carefully mapped-out strategies. Despite this, all those involved agreed that Freddy's inspired commitment was a blessing. It not only provided advertisers with almost bottomless budgets but also helped to establish Freddy Heineken as an ebullient and creative personality in Dutch business – a useful publicity tool in itself. This was an image Freddy cultivated – even his adopted name ('Freddy with a "y" and why not?') served to make Heineken friendlier.

5

Gulping Down Amstel

On Monday 26 August 1968 about twenty of Amstel's managers were summoned to the board room of the brewery's Amsterdam head office, with its sand-blasted windows which opened onto the Mauritskade and a plaster goddess protruding from the ceiling. The four members of Amstel's executive board had important news. Yet as they spread around the table, the other employees were entirely unprepared for the blow that was to hit them.

His voice still shaking with anger, several decades later, a former Amstel executive recalled: 'The four gentlemen told us in a jovial manner that they had sold the Amstel brewery to Heineken. "We are very happy to inform you that we have struck an excellent deal," they said. All of a sudden, our number one enemy had become our owner. It seemed so sickening that one of the people in the room actually vomited.'

The formal merger put an end to an ambiguous relationship that lasted almost exactly a century. On the one hand, the two breweries had competed head-on in the Dutch market and beyond. On the other hand, their managers had sealed a number of collaboration agreements over the years, to make sure that the fight would stay clean and affordable for both parties. During the war the two breweries had discussed plans to share resources and profits and end an era of 'superficial courtship and hidden combat', as Heineken put it, but the talks had dragged on without result.

Asked to explain Amstel's ultimate defeat, Freddy Heineken shrugged. 'We were the sober ones', he jibed, hinting at the Amstel managers' careless spending, as well as their alleged consumption at work. (The unofficial rule was that Amstel employees weren't to start drinking before eleven o'clock in the morning.) Others were more diplomatic, but it is clear that Amstel's leadership had made the takeover easier for Heineken by committing a string of almost laughable errors.

As in many other European countries, the beer market was entirely transformed in the Netherlands in the 1950s, as consumers started to change their habits. Instead of heading for the bar to quaff a few after work, Dutch men increasingly spent evenings in a home equipped with a television set and central heating. Friends who dropped by could be treated to chilled beers stacked in a brand-new refrigerator.

All of this had huge repercussions for the beer business. It became increasingly clear that the brewers would have to adjust their distribution, as well as their entire marketing approach. While they previously dealt mostly with bar owners, they suddenly had to negotiate with fast-growing grocery companies – and start talking to consumers.

Until the late '40s Dutch brewers pumped nearly all of their beer into the market through the taps in bars and restaurants. The consumer was hardly relevant: it was bar owners who picked their brands, and only the most pedantic drinkers would go out of their way to find an establishment that served a specific beer. So the brewers' game consisted chiefly in greasing bar owners. A few sunshades weren't enough: bar owners were more likely to ask for discounts or cheap loans, with the odd carpet thrown into the bargain. Brewers occasionally made informal arrangements to avoid an escalation in such requests. But when agreements were breached, unleashing full-blown competition, bar owners could throttle brewers with financial demands that siphoned off the largest share of their profits.

Selling beer at the time was a jolly affair, as the breweries' agents spent their days buying rounds for regulars and staff. Yet the job required a lot more than a resilient stomach: a Heineken report titled 'The ideal profile of the on-premise representative' stated that a beer agent should have 'tact and self-control', should 'master the art of listening' and should be 'mentally and physically balanced'. Perhaps more importantly, he should 'have a good sense of humour'. If those really were the most important skills to sell beer, Heineken's agents must have been hilarious: Heineken was served in more bars than any competing beers, and some who were tied to other brands still sold Heineken under the counter.

Heineken was the first of the major players in the Dutch beer market to start selling their brew outside bars. Pieter Feith drove industry-wide changes by organising separate distribution to sell Heineken to the grocers. He set up Heineken's Store Committee and assigned it to write a report on distribution to grocers. When it started to circulate at the brewery in 1947, 'Our Beer at the Grocer's' was met with consternation. It wasn't so much the move into retailing as the approach advocated by Feith that stirred ill feelings: instead of working with the brewery's established distributors, Feith wanted to assign the take-home market to specialist wholesalers.

When they heard of the plans, the beer distributors were up in arms. They argued that the contracts they had sealed with the brewers gave them an exclusive right to sell their partners' beer in a specific district regardless of the packaging. They wanted a chance to prove that they were able to service the retailers as well as the bars. Yet Feith apparently decided to ignore their pleas: his team quietly sealed exclusive contracts with wholesalers covering about 8,000 stores, roughly a third of the country's entire retail network. All hell broke loose towards the end of February 1948, when it became clear that Heineken would start delivering beer to retailers through wholesalers about three months later. They were equally aghast to learn that Amstel was moving in the same direction.

Leagued in the Dutch alliance of beer and soft drinks traders, the BBM, the irate distributors vowed to respond with 'the most drastic of counter-actions'. The BBM drummed up support among distributors to set up their own beer production and sales unit, but only a minority were prepared to invest. They then established a list of brewers who pledged to respect their contracts with distributors, published in a pamphlet titled 'Know Your True Friends'. And finally, in August 1948, they threatened to go on strike.

This desperate rebellion never really worried Feith. The Heineken breweries made concessions that apparently enabled the distributors to test their skills in the retail sector, but the BBM's battle never stood a chance. By the mid-'50s the distributors had given up their campaign and wholesalers had firmly established their grip on the off-premise sales network for bottled beer. Heineken could quietly dismiss the entire stand-off as 'a storm in a beer glass'.

Feith's overhaul of distribution and accompanying organisational adjustments came just in time to take advantage of sweeping social changes that led to a boom in the take-home market. Almost negligible in the late '40s, the retail trade swiftly came to account for more than half of the Dutch market. It stimulated the entire market, which soared from a paltry 10 litres per capita in 1949 to 45.4 litres in 1968. As elsewhere in Europe, drinking habits were transformed by increased standards of welfare, as well as the addition of televisions and refrigerators in Dutch homes. Until then, bottles of beer had often been kept cool in a bucket, placed under a tap of running water. They had to be consumed quickly, and housewives purchased only a few bottles at a time. Refrigerators meant that the beer could be stored at home for much longer. There was no excuse for not having a few bottles at hand when the neighbours called.

This market shift also required an entirely new marketing approach. All of a sudden, consumers had to make their own decisions in the stores, based on price and taste as well as brand recognition. Branding and packaging became a lot more important: all the changes driven by Freddy to make the brand look more appealing and recognisable took on their full impact with the rise of the take-home market.

The market's transformation prompted Heineken to change both the message and the target of its advertising. Until the end of the '40s Heineken ads pointed to the beer's popularity in bars with the slogan 'Heineken, het meest getapt' ('Heineken, the most tapped beer'). But throughout the '50s and '60s former advertising managers estimate that about 80 per cent of the brewery's budget was invested to encourage home consumption, with the slogan 'Gezellige mensen halen Heineken in huis!' ('Friendly people have Heineken at home!').

Since market research had shown that women did most of the buying, the campaign's target was predominantly female. Its underlying message was that housewives would create a welcoming atmosphere in their homes and keep their husbands happy by purchasing Heineken. No doubt the resulting print ads would have infuriated even the least fervent of feminists in later years: they showed docile housewives presenting a bottle of Heineken to their husband as he settled down in his armchair to read the newspaper, and neat couples sharing a beer with neighbours, the women crouching at their husbands' feet.

The early television commercials reinforced this message – and were equally patronising. Women with little pearl necklaces and neatly pinned-up hair showed exactly how to serve a bottled beer. 'Hold the glass sideways and pour gently', it advised. Such commercials were much more costly than the print ads of the previous years, which worked in the favour of the larger brewers. But as televisions entered more and more Dutch households, these commercials had the potential to reach millions of people.

This upheaval had a decisive impact on the balance of power in the Dutch beer market. Heineken's efforts to conquer the take-home market paid off. While nearly all of the country's other brewers were weakened by the radical transformation of the Dutch beer industry in the '50s and '60s, Heineken enjoyed a period of strong growth. And while Dutch annual beer consumption more than quadrupled to 45.4 litres per capita in the two decades leading up to 1968, Heineken's market share climbed from 21.7 per cent to about 39 per cent.

Amstel, although it had moved into grocery stores early, along with Heineken, was unable to keep up with the pace set by the market leader. After nearly a hundred years of unabated rivalry, Amstel ultimately bowed to Heineken's supremacy.

The proximity between Amstel and Heineken's brewing plants meant that the two breweries were in close contact, but also highlighted how different their management approaches were. The behaviour of Amstel's pompous, chauffeur-driven managers was a permanent source of entertainment for their Heineken counterparts. Visitors to Amstel's headquarters were greeted by a white-gloved butler who served refreshments on a silver tray. More damaging for the brand, Amstel's noble heritage encouraged a complacent, unrealistic business approach. 'In a nutshell, Amstel always lacked Heineken's vision', admitted Elink Schuurman, the board member.

Part of the problem in the early days was that Amstel was strongest in the weakest segment of the market. While the rising popularity of lager accounted for most of the beer market's growth, Amstel had long thrived on Oud Bruin, a darker, bitter beer. Bar owners, then the breweries' main customers, soon noticed the difference: light and refreshing, Heineken's lager could be consumed in large quantities. Heavy and sweet, Oud Bruin was a one-glass affair.

Even with its lager, a product of undisputed quality, Amstel never attained the same popularity as Heineken. This was partly because Amstel's leadership deemed the average beer drinker unworthy of the brew. Guus Avis, then Amstel's advertising manager, sighed: 'The board was adamant that our beer should not compete directly with Heineken. "Amstel is too sophisticated to deal with the drinking masses", they said. This may have been a noble approach but obviously wasn't the best strategy for selling torrents of beer.'

A brand identity study indicated that Amstel drinkers were regarded as impeccable gentlemen who quietly enjoyed their beer – just the one – in the evening. By contrast, Heineken drinkers were seen as the loud and unsophisticated punters, 'the sausage and mash crowd', said Avis. Unfortunately for Amstel, that crowd generated much more attractive turnovers than the 'impeccable gentlemen'. By threatening to switch to the more lucrative Heineken, bar owners could demand outrageous favours, which squeezed Amstel's profit margins. Amstel's financial resources, which were already drained by large investments abroad, became increasingly tight.

The problem was, as Gregor Frenkel-Frank, the man in charge of Amstel's advertising campaigns, put it, that 'when you thought of Amstel, you thought of beer. But when you thought of beer, you thought of Heineken.' In terms of brand, Amstel realised that Heineken held a monopoly on 'cosiness', while Grolsch, Amstel's other main competitor, played on 'tradition'. Amstel fought back, launching a campaign in 1967 that presented Amstel as the beer for tough guys, based on the pleasure of savouring an Amstel beer after a hard day's work or other supposedly 'manly' activities. The slogan: 'Dit is de man, dit is z'n bier' ('This is the man, this is his beer').

Despite these efforts, and a sustained rise in production, the brewery's profitability was desperately low compared with Heineken's: with roughly the same number of employees, it yielded only half of its rival's turnover. Weary and dispirited, Amstel's board stated in 1968: 'Our position is like that of an army fighting along a wide battle front. Any attack on that battle front means casualties on our side.'

Merger talks had been rife among the largest Dutch brewers since the '50s. Yet the radical shake-up of the Dutch beer market in the late '60s was triggered by outsiders. As part of an all-out trend towards concentration in European business, two foreign breweries bought their way into the Dutch market. In December 1967 Allied Breweries, of the United Kingdom, bought Oranjeboom in Rotterdam. Six months later, the Stella Artois breweries of Leuven, Belgium, gulped the Dommelsche Bierbrouwerij.

But it was Allied Breweries' second bid that ultimately drove Amstel into Heineken's arms. In the third week of August 1968 it was announced that Allied would be taking over De Drie Hoefijzers (The Three Horseshoes), the only sizeable piece left to take in the Dutch market, with a share of about 10 per cent. Having already acquired Oranjeboom, the British then controlled 20 per cent of the Dutch beer market. If the Britons were also to swallow Amstel, with a market share of 18 per cent, they would directly challenge Heineken's leadership – with an equal market share of about 38 per cent.

Carel van Lookeren Campagne, Heineken's Dutch commercial director, was driving to Amsterdam when he heard the news about the takeover of De Drie Hoefijzers on the radio. 'The thought of such a challenge hit me so suddenly that I bumped into the car in front of me. Luckily, I got a lift into Amsterdam with a Heineken truck. When I arrived at the head office, I immediately asked my colleagues whether they had done the sums too. They said "yes", in a state of mild excitement. Freddy was already there', he recalled.

Nerves were also showing on the Mauritskade, where Amstel's leaders had gathered. 'Egberts [the chairman of the management board] said the time had come to sell to Heineken. But Plantenga [the chairman of the supervisory board] told Egberts he would be fired on the spot if he walked over to Heineken. And indeed, one and a half hours later, Freddy was at the Amstel headquarters. That made a lot of difference to the price of the transaction.'

The deal was concluded at amazing speed. Initiated on Friday 23 August, it was worked out in its entirety over the weekend, during talks in Huize Cronenburgh, the stately home of Oscar Wittert van Hoogland, then Heineken's executive chairman, on the River Vecht. The close relations between the two boards, which had been holding regular talks for several years before the merger, certainly made things easier. Besides, both breweries were in a hurry.

Although Heineken's board was chaired by Wittert van Hoogland, the deal was clearly orchestrated by Freddy Heineken, who was by then the company's majority shareholder and a member of its executive board. 'We knew exactly what was happening at Amstel, perhaps even better than they did themselves', he said. 'Everything had been prepared on our side. When the time was ripe, all we needed to do was to put the papers on the table.' Freddy's inside knowledge was partly based on contacts with disgruntled Amstel shareholders, who repeatedly pleaded with Heineken to rescue their investments.

Amstel's chairman, Egberts, and his colleague Elink Schuurman were easily convinced. On the other hand, Heineken faced emotional resistance from the other two board members. Rein van Marwijk Kooij, in charge of production at Amstel, was a descendant of one of the brewery's founders who had inherited a large share package. He was one of those who held the belief that Amstel could never be defeated, simply because it produced the tastiest brew. Piet Kranenberg, in charge of domestic sales, was another passionate rebel. Yet the alternative to the Heineken deal, selling to a foreign brewery, was even more revolting in their eyes.

On Tuesday 27 August, the news of the 'merger' between the country's two largest brewers was splashed across the front pages of the national dailies. *De Telegraaf* featured a picture of a smiling young Freddy with the caption, in bold, 'Dit is de man' ('This is the man') and a red-and-white Amstel logo under the headline 'Dit is z'n bier' ('This is his beer'). Other symbolic shots showed the two chairmen, Wittert van Hoogland and Egberts, merrily sharing a beer, and two bottles (one Heineken, the other Amstel) tipped upside down in a single glass.

The Heineken–Amstel alliance signified the birth of a new brewing force that controlled about 60 per cent of the Dutch beer market and rivalled some of Europe's largest players. Together, the two breweries boasted an estimated turnover of about 450 million guilders. They produced some 425 million litres of beer annually, and had a combined workforce of roughly 4,500 employees. They also accounted for about 70 per cent of total Dutch beer exports.

Speculation about a forthcoming deal had been rife on the Amsterdam stock exchange since the takeover of De Drie Hoefijzers. The price of Amstel shares had shot up, as investors understood that the brewery would play a pivotal role in the final distribution of the cards. And in the end Heineken share-holders benefited handsomely as well, with a capitalisation dividend paid in shares and cash. As Freddy Heineken said, with a touch of irony: 'I didn't do too badly myself.'

Although the deal was consistently presented as a merger, it was clear that Heineken, being almost twice the size of Amstel, would call the shots, and the integration was sometimes painful. Some Heineken and Amstel agents continued to compete. Others were appalled when Heineken defaced the proud Amstel building in Amsterdam – removing the emblems and the Amstel founders' sculpted portraits from the outer wall, and pettily covering the logo in the entrance floor with a huge carpet.

But the most emotional reactions came from Amstel's

production managers, those who believed until the last minute that the quality of the product would guarantee the brewery's survival. One Amstel adviser witnessed a poignant scene on the day of the takeover: 'With a heavy heart, Van Marwijk Kooij walked down to the cellar to talk to our master brewer. The two men sat there together for two hours, sharing memories and crying on each other's shoulders like scolded schoolboys.' Later that week, it took many soothing words to win the confidence of the production plant's manager. During the merged group's first production meeting, he stubbornly refused to share his most intimate secret, the recipe for Amstel.

Amstel's faithful employees feared that the brand would be withdrawn from the market completely. This idea was, in fact, floated by the merged board, but the discussion was short-lived. According to the brewery, it was Freddy Heineken who swept the proposal off the table, insisting that the Amstel brand should be revived.

Freddy's motives were entirely practical. He realised that a strengthened Amstel could be used as an effective buffer to protect Heineken from the price aggression of lesser brews. Still, it would be several years before Amstel really found its place in the Dutch market, and Heineken formulated a clear-cut, two-brand strategy.

By the time Heineken had gobbled it up in 1968, Amstel had turned into a flat, dried-out brew. In the three years that followed the takeover, it suffered a further battering in the Dutch market. The lager's image, which had been pretty weak before the alliance, became totally obsolete after the takeover. In fact, it was believed that many Amstel drinkers turned away from their favourite brew because they suspected it was coming out of the same kegs as Heineken.

The Amstel weapon was beginning to look uselessly blunt. More faceless than ever, it was stuck somewhere between Heineken and the private labels, the cheap beer produced at the request of supermarket chains. Even temporary price cuts could not halt the slide. So, in a last-ditch effort to preserve the brand, in 1972 the brewery's board abandoned one of the sacred principles that had guided its strategy since the launch of bottled beer in the retail segment: its control over the margins at which its products were sold. This arrangement had guaranteed that stores would not downgrade a product's image by playing around with its price. The abolition of this system meant that the retailers would be free to determine their own margins on the sales of Amstel beer.

The move was bound to stir up emotions among the country's beleaguered small shopkeepers, who were struggling to compete with the increasingly dominant supermarket chains. Free prices were a bonanza for mass retailers, who could afford lower selling prices to lure even more consumers away from the street-corner shops, because they could compensate for reduced margins with huge volumes and lower operating costs. As a result, Heineken attempted to break the news of its turnaround as discreetly as possible, but the small shopkeepers got the message loud and clear. They set up a protest committee, and furious milkmen blocked the entrance of Heineken's Amsterdam brewing plant.

Efforts to upgrade Amstel's packaging proved much more popular. At the insistence of Claessens, the graphic design agency, Heineken agreed to drop the only element that really served to distinguish the Amstel brand: its two-tone, red and white, circular logo. The symbol was well known, but it carried not the faintest emotional message – as Claessen's research uncovered, it was actually associated with a no-entry road sign.

Amstel's packaging was thus subjected to a drastic face-lift. On the bottles the circle was replaced with a wide oval sticker, embellished with Amsterdam's proud coat of arms and crowned by the Amstel brand name in straight, supposedly virile capitals. The new logo, which played on the beer's strength and Amstel's glorious brewing history, was greeted with loud cheers by the brand's sales representatives.

The new branding inspired a nationwide campaign that was arguably Amstel's most hard-hitting ever in the Netherlands, based on the slogan "s' Lands beste brouwers brouwen Amstel bier' ('the country's best brewers brew Amstel beer'), with a catchy tune to accompany the television ads, which would be picked up again in the '90s.

Freddy Heineken had already become a familiar face on Amsterdam's social scene, but with the acquisition of Amstel his public image acquired another dimension: not just an idle heir, Heineken had turned into a shrewd deal-maker, the hard-headed owner of a brewery that made up more than half of the Dutch beer market.

6

The Making of Freddy

With the acquisition of Amstel, Heineken became the undisputed leader of the Dutch beer market, but Freddy Heineken had yet to be formally installed at the helm of the breweries. Just as he had done with the buy-back of the company's shares, the forty-four-year-old was preparing to seize power at the right time. This strategy had added advantages: while he remained out of the chief executive's chair, Heineken could indulge in his many other interests.

The 1960s in Amsterdam were a particularly propitious time and place to enjoy creative experiments of all sorts. With its relaxed attitude to weed and mushrooms, the Dutch capital attracted free-thinking young people from Europe and beyond. The late '60s saw the rise of the Provo movement, a group of anarchists and beatniks in favour of squatting and shared parenting. Freddy Heineken held somewhat more conservative views, describing the creative protesters as 'long-haired riff-raff that should be taken off the streets'.

However, Heineken relished the company of all sorts of artist, cultivating such relationships by hanging around De Kring, a club on the Kleine Gartmansplantsoen in central Amsterdam which at this time was the meeting place for a clique of prominent artists, including the writer Harry Mulisch, the composer Peter Schat and the actor Ton Lutz, as well as scores of columnists and their groupies. Freddy Heineken seemed strikingly out of place in this circle of impecunious, left-leaning artists: he was wealthy and impeccably dressed, donning suits he bought from the royal supplier Spalton & Maas in The Hague.

Although the Heineken breweries owned the premises of the club and contributed to its survival by renting them out at well below market price, the club's ballot committee initially rejected Freddy's application for membership, which was formally reserved for 'artists and intellectuals'. 'It was an extremely tricky matter, considering that he more or less subsidised the place', said one long-time member, 'but many staunchly opposed his membership. They thought the only reason he wanted to join was to pick up girls, young models, actresses and ballerinas.'

Still, many came to regard Freddy Heineken as an entertaining companion. 'Freddy was really receptive to arts and his views were particularly sharp. The way he looked at people, it was always funny and spot-on', said Jan Blokker, a well-known Dutch columnist. 'On the other hand, he was very wary of all the empty-pocketed artists who were constantly clawing at his wallet.' In fact, those who clung to Freddy Heineken in the hope of getting free beer were invariably disappointed: the brewer refused to buy rounds, arguing that he had to earn a living from selling beer. 'Rumour has it that Freddy even fell out with Harry Mulisch because the writer asked him for ten guilders and never returned the note', said Blokker.

It was Fons Rademakers, an award-winning Dutch filmmaker, who finally persuaded Freddy to loosen his purse strings and invest in Dutch arts. Rademakers needed funds to produce a filmed version of *De Donkere Kamer van Damocles* ('The Darkroom of Damocles'), a famous wartime novel by Willem Frederik Hermans. Freddy set up Cineurope B.V., a film production company, and financed roughly half of the movie. The film, titled *Als twee druppels water* ('Like Two Drops of Water') cost about 800,000 guilders, and Freddy made a Hitchcock-style appearance at the end (he was very proud that he even had a line). When it came out, the investment brought huge publicity rewards, with Freddy hailed in Dutch newspapers as a generous financier who would revive the fortunes of the national film industry.

By Dutch standards, the film was very well received. Critics acclaimed the film as a masterly *film noir*. It was even dubbed into English (*The Spitting Image*) and French (*Comme deux gouttes d'eau*), and it was selected for the Cannes Film Festival in 1963. 'Heineken made a big splash in Cannes. He entertained people from the movie industry on his yacht and he inundated the resort with Heineken beer mats', said Bob Bertina, then film critic at *De Volkskrant*. The film was distributed in French cinemas. But then, all of a sudden, Freddy Heineken outraged the Dutch film industry by withdrawing it from the market and insisting that it never be shown publicly again.

It turned out that one of the actresses in the film, Nan Los, had been Freddy Heineken's long-time girlfriend. Freddy had got to know the smart brunette when she worked in Heineken's advertising department, and the relationship continued after she left to become a model and an airline stewardess with KLM. Nan had played the lead character's girlfriend in the movie. She had never acted before, but Rademakers insisted she was chosen on her own merits rather than as a favour to the film's financial backer. The director just spotted her at Freddy's side and picked her after convincing auditions.

In those days Freddy was often seen in town with pretty young women, even after the arrival of his daughter Charlene in 1954. But his relationship with Nan Los was more than a fleeting fancy. Los herself was quoted as saying that the affair lasted seven years. The couple were a regular fixture in Amsterdam's social life, and those around them said the brewer appeared to be infatuated with his companion.

It was Nan Los who put an end to the affair. 'Around the time when the film came out I started a relationship with Gerard van Lennep', she said much later. Van Lennep was a Dutch motor racing champion and another Amsterdam socialite. Friends have said that the split between Heineken and Los couldn't have been more abrupt. 'It was all extremely sudden', said one of the couple's friends. 'One day I was sharing a beer with the two of them, as usual, and a week later she was married to another guy.'

Heineken apparently no longer wanted others to watch his former girlfriend cavorting on screen. 'The aftermath of the production was extremely bizarre', said Rademakers, somewhat bitterly. 'The film had received a tremendous welcome in the United States and without Freddy's ridiculous intervention it could have turned into a huge success around the world.' Heineken's revenge was exacted with characteristic stubbornness: until his death, anybody who wanted to watch the film (still described as one of the best in Dutch film history) had to write to Heineken to request a private viewing.

Nan Los left Amsterdam shortly afterwards to become an English teacher in the Caribbean, but Freddy Heineken long continued to mull over the end of the relationship. When Van Lennep opened a store with motor racing paraphernalia on one of the most upmarket shopping streets in Amsterdam, Heineken regularly made a point of driving by. 'He was delighted when the store was empty', another friend recalled.

Under the circumstances, it could be surmised that the brewer's second investment in the Dutch film industry was another act of spite. The film, financed by Cineurope at a cost of an estimated 130,000 guilders, was *Een ochtend van zes weken* ('A Morning of Six Weeks'), by Nikolai van der Heyde. 'The whole story of this movie is about the tragic failure of a relationship between a small-time model and a car racer', said an industry source. 'Freddy immediately bought it.' This person further remembered Freddy for his crude comments during the editing of love-making scenes and his rewarding of the crew 'with half a dozen beers'.

Cineurope went out of business after the production of one last film, *Mixummerdaydream*, by Hattum Hoving, an arty documentary about the Amsterdam Danstheater, which made it to the San Sebastián Film Festival in 1968. Freddy said he pulled out of the cinema business because the earnings were too unpredictable. 'Look, when you order a glass of beer, I know that I've earned a few bob. Everything else is a waste of time', he told Blokker.

Profitable or not, Freddy Heineken appeared to spend almost as much time at the brewery as on his social and creative pursuits. 'My basic philosophy, which led to all those films and other nonsense, is that I find it enormously useful for people to have hobbies on top of their work', he said. 'I'm trying to be something of a *homo universalis*. Building houses is one of my hobbies. Paintings, music, Mingus, Herbie Mann, I love them. I would love to have a car factory, for the design aspect.' Such statements became even more cringe-worthy when he changed his ambition to being a *hetero universalis*.

Heineken incessantly came up with plans and products entirely unrelated to beer – from wheelchairs to aftershaves. Among his most unlikely brainwaves in those years was the

World Bottle (WoBo). Freddy said this idea sprung from a trip to Curaçao in 1960, when he saw the shabby timber huts of local shanty towns littered with empty Heineken bottles. He contracted the Amsterdam architect John Habraken to design square, ribbed bottles that could be fitted into one another to build glass bungalows in developing countries. About 100,000 such WoBos were manufactured in 1963, and Freddy Heineken used some 3,500 bottles to have a prototype house built in his property in Noordwijk, with a corrugated-iron roof.

Although colleagues repeatedly warned Heineken that an association with waste and squalor was not the most ingenious of marketing ploys, Freddy pushed ahead. He assigned five employees from Heineken's marketing department to study the project together with TNO, the technical research institute in Delft. After about two weeks of serious research, the marketing department came to the conclusion that the World Bottle would not work. They were too expensive, too heavy and the conditions inside the houses would be unbearable: the inhabitants would be roasted like chickens in a greenhouse.

For the marketing managers 'the fundamental problem was that it seemed completely lacking in taste to build houses for the poor in developing countries with the waste of rich white drinkers'. But Freddy later alleged that the project was aborted because his colleagues could not stand the thought of the young owner coming up with such a revolutionary bottle. 'It was a drama because it was my idea', said the brewer. 'Had it come from a middle layer in the brewery, it might have been accepted.'

Freddy's affinity for fast cars, artists and pretty women sometimes infuriated his superiors at the Heineken breweries, who felt he should refrain from tarnishing its serious reputation. Freddy was repeatedly summoned to cut down on the frolics. As he once told a visitor: 'I can't behave too wildly, otherwise the managers will be on my back again.'

The tycoon's relationship with the brewery's executive board in the '60s was still very awkward. Although the managers sometimes resented Freddy's bold actions and reckless behaviour, his effective control over the majority of the company's shares forced them to put on a diplomatic face. They had also come to realise that, for all his extravagance and shenanigans, Freddy was sharp, committed and had an instinctive business sense.

The organisation of the Heineken breweries at the time meant that majority ownership did not give Freddy Heineken the right to implement any changes he wanted. He would have wielded more influence as a delegate board member, which at least provided a veto for important decisions, but all appointments had to be approved by both the management board and the supervisory board, and he was twice turned down for this post.

Freddy had to manoeuvre carefully. He evidently aspired to Heineken's chairmanship, but the memories of some shareholders' suspected betrayal of his father were still fresh and the executive board contained managers of uncertain loyalty. Unlike most heirs in family-owned companies, he could not rely on the support of a ruling father. So Freddy Heineken only attended the board meetings as an 'observer', and he had to fight to get approval for any changes he wanted to implement.

It was only in 1958, four years after he had amassed the majority of the shares, that Freddy Heineken obtained his coveted appointment as a delegate member of the supervisory board. He then effectively had the power to veto some of the most important decisions taken at the breweries. He went on to push through an amendment to the company's articles of association. The revision gave more influence to the shareholders of the company – in other words, to Freddy himself.

But it was another trick, in 1962, that ultimately secured Freddy Heineken's ownership of the breweries for the decades to come. Heineken then decided to get his personal holding company, HBBM, floated on the Amsterdam stock exchange. That holding company still held a majority of the shares in Heineken, and Freddy Heineken himself retained just over half of the shares in HBBM. The remainder of the holding company's shares were sold – enabling Heineken to clean up the debts he had contracted to acquire his majority.

To make it all more tax-efficient, his controlling stake in HBBM was placed under a personal holding company established in Switzerland. Ten years later, in 1972, HBBM became Heineken Holding, while HBM was renamed Heineken N.V., but the three-tier ownership structure remained the same: it was a clever system that allowed Freddy Heineken to remain the majority shareholder of Heineken while holding only 25 per cent of its shares.

Freddy still refrained from barging into the chief executive's office, but he allowed himself a few more moves that raised eyebrows among the company's leaders. Many frowned when Freddy pushed one of his friends, Jan Ton, to the executive board in 1963. Ton's appointment appeared quite puzzling: he was Heineken's former general manager in Venezuela and at least partly responsible for the company's costly misadventure in that country, the only true disaster in Heineken's post-war years. Freddy esteemed him highly, however. Just like Freddy, the humorous, sparkling Ton was a pilot and also enjoyed the company of women. His interest in advertising led him to the chairmanship of the Genootschap voor Reclame, the Dutch advertising society. He was known as an erudite theatregoer, a connoisseur of classical music, a talented photographer and a well-read lover of Spanish literature. 'In his car, on the plane, anywhere and all the time, he was reading', said one former executive, and 'Bartok's fourth string quartet was more likely to feature in his conversation than Heineken beer.' The two men were often spotted together, both at social events and in the corridors of the breweries. 'Ton was Freddy's court jester', said a former Heineken director. 'Together, they walked from one office to the other to humiliate employees. It was awful for the victim but absolutely hilarious. It was like a game of ping-pong, with the two men batting jokes at each other.' Former Heineken staff said Freddy puckishly resisted several years of pressure from other board members who grew increasingly irritated at Ton's perceived inactivity. Still, this incident was not disgraceful enough to halt Freddy's rise. When one of the sitting board members suddenly passed away, in 1964, Freddy judged the time ripe for the move to the executive board – in charge of financial affairs.

Freddy concluded his ascent in the late '60s, when the company was officially led by Oscar Wittert van Hoogland. A former cavalry officer, the descendant of a long line of Dutch military officers, the tall, bleak chairman was known for his utterly stern and humourless leadership style. 'Oscar ran the breweries like an Army commander', said one former executive. 'He always looked sour and irritated, as if he was looking at a pile of steaming dung.' The pompous series of initials printed on his business card, reading 'O. A. E. E. L. Wittert van Hoogland Esquire', was the butt of many inside jokes. Employees recalled that a British business partner, to whom Wittert once gave his card, looked up and asked sarcastically: 'Is all of that you?'

Freddy Heineken himself painted a picture of Wittert van Hoogland as a half-witted, gullible manager, as illustrated by the story he told about Wittert based on a popular joke that was doing the rounds. When a paper-shredder was delivered to the management offices of Heineken, he said, several board members gathered to examine it. 'Press the top button, and the documents stacked on the holder will be swallowed and torn to shreds', Ton explained. 'And what happens if I press the other button?' Wittert asked. 'Then the paper will come out intact again', came the reply, and Wittert's mouth opened in amazement.

While Wittert was technically in charge, Freddy continuously challenged his authority, which caused much friction and unease among the staff. The rivalry only came to an end in the summer of 1970, when Wittert suffered a heart attack on a golf course. He recovered and joined the supervisory board but spent more of his time in his picturesque villa in the south of France, the former home of the archbishop of Grasse.

Freddy became the chairman of Heineken N.V. in February 1971, at the age of forty-seven. 'The others thought that I was the right person', he later said. But as the brewer often stated, 'you don't get power just like that, you have to grab it'. And by the accounts of those who watched him in those years, he did so with unflinching determination. 'It was truly stunning to observe how he grasped power within the brewery', said one former Heineken executive. 'He was regarded by the outside world as a playboy who toyed around with women, fast cars and movie projects. But when it came to the brewery, he played his cards with remarkable shrewdness.'

Traditionally, the company's executive board was run by a collegial team. Less than one year after his promotion to the chairmanship, however, Freddy more or less appointed himself as 'President'. 'This term may never have been recorded in the Heineken statutes but Freddy consistently presented himself as such, which gave him an additional air of authority. He always referred to his colleagues as "my board".'

Raymond Boon Falleur, the then chairman of the Stella Artois breweries in Belgium, had jealously watched Heineken's growth over the previous decades. He had come to the conclusion that 'the sun never goes down on the Heineken breweries'. Like many other European rivals, Boon Falleur observed Freddy's rise with a mixture of astonishment and *schadenfreude*. With this frivolous youngster at the helm he reckoned the brewery's lucky star would fade at last. 'For competitors like us, it seemed a good thing that Freddy should take the lead', he said.

The Belgian would revise his judgement over the next few years, as Freddy Heineken embarked on a crusade to spread his name around Europe, from France to Spain and from Ireland to Greece. But in the meantime Heineken was saddled with an embarrassing issue: there was at least one key European country where wayward drinkers had forced Heineken to deviate from its strategy, with very far-reaching consequences.

7

Refreshing the UK

For many years it wasn't safe to stand next to a discerning European drinker who ordered a bottle of Heineken in an English pub. It wasn't unlikely that he (or she) would spit it out and squint at the label in disbelief: the Heineken served in the United Kingdom was nothing like its European equivalent. Unbeknown to most British drinkers, the Heineken that came out of the beer taps in their local was much weaker than in other European countries. While the standard Heineken has an alcohol content of 5 per cent, in the UK it was just 3.4. If Freddy Heineken really regarded a weak Heineken as a personal insult, as he often stated, the thin beer served under his name in the UK must have been a slap in the face.

It was embarrassing for Heineken's marketing managers as well: 'We were selling Heineken as a class act, an international brand with great taste. We were telling consumers that they would get that same taste wherever they ordered their Heineken – except that it was almost unrecognisable in Britain', explained a former European marketing manager. 'And that's the second biggest market in Europe.'

The problem was that for many years the British did not care for lager at all. Insular in their drinking habits, they still mostly drank UK-brewed ales and bitters when Heineken resumed exports to the country after the Second World War. They could chatter endlessly about their bitter but treated lager with a degree of contempt that would have appalled even the least dogmatic of European master brewers: it was served like a hop-flavoured soup, lukewarm and often without a head. No wonder that lager made up only 3 per cent of all British beer sales.

Another obstacle was price. To make sure that workers turned up reasonably sober to the munitions factories during the First World War, the British government had jacked up beer levies. Then, in 1924, it started imposing levies indirectly based on the alcohol content of the beer. With some adjustments these regulations were broadly upheld well beyond the Second World War, and so publicans continued to serve bitter that was much weaker than European beers.

The issue triggered intense debate in Amsterdam. There were clearly drawbacks to customising beers for specific markets. People were travelling more often, and it was important to avoid them being unpleasantly surprised when they raised a Heineken to their lips in London. But the urge to build up sales in Britain rapidly after the war proved stronger than the patience recommended by the advocates of standard Heineken. In 1951, four years after its return, the company decided to start exporting a weaker beer.

This was a major concession, as the weaker beer not only had a lower alcohol content but also compromised Heineken's distinctive taste, which the company had made enormous efforts to keep consistent across the rest of its global empire. To make a lower-alcohol beer, Heineken had to reduce the amount of wort – the infusion of ground barley that is fermented with yeast to produce alcohol and produces a part of the flavour. For more than forty years Heineken then watched with a mixture of glee and dismay as a whimsical advertising slogan turned this weaker Heineken into one of the most avidly drunk lagers in the British market.

⊙

Heineken regularly sent young managers from its export department to study the British market in the 1950s. They had gone out of their way to accommodate the Brits with lagers of lower gravity (a brewers' measurement of the concentration of original wort, usually expressed in degrees), and yet their sales figures for the country were trivial. Heineken failed to grasp what was stopping the country's drinkers from enjoying their drink, despite all the explanations provided by the British sales team.

For starters, Heineken wasn't very refreshing. The imported lager was mostly sold to publicans in bottles. Most of the pubs had yet to be fitted with fridges, so the bottles nearly always sat on shelves behind the bar, languishing at room temperature. When they weren't gathering dust, the bottles were mostly served with a small glass to female customers. Women had started going to pubs in the war years and weren't prepared to retreat to their stoves thereafter, but they still didn't want to be seen swigging a pint of ale in their local. 'Women want a drink which is not too intoxicating, which is "lady-like" and does not put too much strain on their escorts' pockets. Lager meets these requirements', explained the marketing manager of Ind Coope Tetley Ansell, the brewery that went on to make Skol lager, as quoted in a market report drawn up by Heineken.

For Heineken, what was even more bewildering (and frankly appalling) was that many drank their lager with a shot of lime, which destroyed any remaining trace of the distinctive lager taste. It was estimated that about 60 per cent of drinkers had taken up the ghastly habit. 'For that reason, it is very difficult indeed to present the "fresh taste and well-brewed" angle,' one of the reports lamented, 'as most of the consumers do not care.'

Faced with such abhorrent behaviour, Heineken gave up all scruples towards British beer drinkers. They had already made what they regarded as a major concession in 1951, when they agreed to ship a Heineken beer with a gravity of 1040°, slightly less than the standard Heineken, at 1048°. Seven years later they went all the way and started selling an import beer with a gravity of 1030°, which amounted to an alcohol content of just 3 per cent. It could only be regarded as a distant relative of Heineken.

Cheaper than its rivals, this thin Heineken started to make an impact, yet the Dutch were encouraged to take even more decisive action. They were receiving increasingly bullish reports, highlighting appetising prospects for the lager market. The documents pointed out that the spread of refrigerators was likely to stimulate sales of lager, which was meant to be served chilled. Just 3 per cent of British households had a refrigerator in 1950, but the number was growing rapidly, and it would reach 21 per cent by the end of the decade. Lager had come to be regarded as a drink for the young, so the post-war baby boom would work to their advantage. Heineken stood to achieve huge sales increases – if it managed to reach the consumers.

As the export managers explained, most of the country's thousands of pubs were tied to breweries. That had already been the case for many decades, but the breweries invested even more in pubs after the war, to try and halt a sharp decline in consumption, down to just 18 gallons per head per year in 1960 (although that still amounted to more than 80 litres, far more than the continental average). Pubs were often either owned by the breweries outright or had some form of financial arrangement that curbed their independence. Either way, an estimated 86 per cent of the pubs in England and Wales were tied houses, with obligations to serve the brews made or sold by their financial backers. Heineken could reach only a few hundred independent pubs, the 'free houses', which were already being courted by many other import brews. The simple solution was to team up with British brewers, who could open up thousands of pubs for Heineken at a stroke.

Jop Cornelis, one of the young managers in Heineken's export department, produced an update on the British market in 1961 and urged the company to open talks with Whitbread. 'They are interested in a partnership in Africa. They approached us for this purpose', Cornelis wrote. 'Colonel Whitbread an influential person in the British brewing business. Director at countless breweries where he has a minority share.' In any case, Cornelis advised, Heineken should get in touch with Colonel Whitbread.

The colonel in question was Bill Whitbread, a distant relative of Samuel Whitbread, who had established the brewery in 1742. A devout Puritan from Bedford, Whitbread was widely regarded as the most gifted brewer of his generation. The huge brewing plant he opened in 1750 in Chiswell Street, in the centre of London, was the envy of the industry. About a century earlier than Gerard Heineken, Whitbread was already trying out all sorts of modern techniques for his plant, such as an impressive steam engine installed alongside horses in 1785.

The Second World War had caused only minor damage to the central London brewer, and after the war Whitbread was one of half a dozen or so companies that led the concentration in the British beer market by acquiring stakes in a raft of smaller outfits and forming what became known as the Whitbread umbrella. Whitbread itself had been listed since 1948, but the Whitbreads and partner families still owned part of the company.

By the time Heineken came along, Whitbread had five

breweries and exported to sixty countries, selling beers such as Whitbread Tankard and Mackeson's. But most importantly for the Dutch, the entire Whitbread umbrella encompassed an estimated 15,000 pubs around the country. The advice by Cornelis paved the way for a relationship of more than four decades, which was marked by triumphs as well as tantrums, and joy as well as bitterness.

◉

The start of Heineken's tie-up with Whitbread in the early '60s came just as several other lagers were starting to make an impact with large-scale advertising in Britain – mostly to impress on men that it was safe for them to drink lager. The first nationwide campaign for Carling did not beat about the bush: 'Men like Carling lager beer', proclaimed hundreds of billboards depicting four big jugs of cool lager. Just in case the public didn't get it, the word 'men' was underlined. The print ads were slightly more elaborate, but the message was the same. 'When a man has a thirst on him, a man thinks of tankards full of cool, invigorating Carling Lager Beer', it read.

Others were even less subtle. 'Gentlemen prefer Harp, Europe's finest lager', claimed the Irish brand, which was sold in Britain by a joint venture between Guinness, Courage, Bass and Scottish & Newcastle. A series of print ads showed a tankard of Harp next to a curvaceous blonde doll (literally): 'Meet the new blonde in your bar', went the slogan. The major continental competitor for Heineken was Carlsberg, the Danish brew. 'Call for a Carlsberg and enjoy the real flavour', said a series of posters, showing the face of a bearded man enjoying his lager in various outfits, from rugby kit to boating hat. Carlsberg was described as 'The glorious lager from Copenhagen'.

By comparison, the earliest ads bought by Whitbread for Heineken lager 'brewed in Holland' were unconventional. They featured a bottle next to a foamy glass and a large question mark. 'Whatsitsname – that splendid lager they all drank abroad? Here. Now. And going with a wow. Heineken! The world's most-imported lager beer.' Another campaign gave British consumers a little trick to remember the name of 'whatsitsname': 'All around the world, millions of hands are raising millions of glasses – and millions of palates are saying "Hi!" to Heineken. Nothing like it. Once you've had a Heineken, you'll never again simply ask for "lager". You'll remember the name. The world's most imported lager.'

Heineken was marketed by Heineken UK, a company based in Cheapside in London. Heineken and Whitbread had equal shares in the small firm. The manager dispatched by Heineken to watch over the business from 1962 was Gerard van Os van Delden, an expansive Dutchman with a handlebar moustache who had earned his stripes at the brewery with several years' service in Africa. He was picked for the job because of his affinity for the British, which led to productive partnerships with Unilever as well as smaller British importers in African countries.

The plan was to import Heineken with the reduced gravity of 1030° in a distinctive bottle: instead of the green-and-white label intended for import Heineken in the United States, consumers were to be alerted to the weaker Heineken through a distinctive red circle around the label. While Heineken supervised the management, Whitbread should provide support for distribution. Once they reached sufficient sales, in the range of 50,000 barrels, Heineken and Whitbread would open a brewing plant for the Dutch beer. And on the side they would work together on projects in Africa, starting with a brewery in Nigeria.

But Van Os van Delden wasn't particularly enthusiastic about the partnership because he felt that Whitbread was not doing its part to sell Heineken's bottled imports in its own pubs. The problem was that these pubs were already selling several other lagers, from Carlsberg to Stella Artois, Ekla and Skol. 'There is little or no pressure brought to bear to sell Heineken beer in preference to Carlsberg', grumbled Van Os van Delden. While Whitbread could discontinue Carlsberg, it was tied to both Stella and Skol: Stella Artois was selling Whitbread's beers in Belgium, and Whitbread had a wider trading agreement in England with Ind Coope (which became part of Allied Breweries), the makers of Skol.

For several years in a row Heineken UK dismally failed to reach what it had regarded as easily attainable targets. Both parties suffered considerable losses. Heineken UK had invested about £100,000 in advertising and expanded their organisation with the intention of reaching sales of at least 20,000 barrels in 1963, but they ended the year at just 11,000 barrels – far behind the joint sales achieved by Carlsberg and Tuborg, of 130,000 barrels. Two years later Heineken was still shipping fewer than 16,000 barrels, far from the target of 50,000 barrels. By now Van Os van Delden was 'bursting with indignation' at Heineken's partners, who he felt had 'led Heineken up the garden path'.

Whitbread managers could have been forgiven for being somewhat distracted because the British beer industry was in complete disarray. The agitator was a Canadian investor, Edward Plunket Taylor, who owned several breweries, including Carling. In 1953 he introduced Carling beer into Britain after striking a deal with the Hope & Anchor brewery in Sheffield. But rather than just letting his partner sell Carling in Britain, Taylor persuaded the Hope & Anchor brewery to go on a buying spree. He had worked out that many British breweries had become complacent and that their pubs were woefully undervalued. Just as he had done in Canada a few years earlier, Taylor acquired breweries, then rationalised their plants and their brands. For several years other brewers watched in dismay as the impudent Canadian ripped through their market, before retaliating with their own mergers and acquisitions.

Whitbread still had partnerships with several other breweries through its umbrella organisation, but the market pressures pushed the managers on Chiswell Street into bidding for ownership in at least some of their partnerships. When the dust settled by the late 1960s, about 70 per cent of beer production was in the hands of the Big Six: Bass Charrington, the company formed by Taylor after his acquisition of both Charrington and Bass; Allied Breweries; Courage; Scottish & Newcastle; Watney Mann & Truman; and Whitbread.

For Heineken, Whitbread's expansion was a compelling reason to reaffirm the two companies' partnership. Despite the frustrations of the previous years it started negotiating an agreement that would cause splitting headaches for decades to come: instead of just importing a weaker Heineken beer, it allowed Whitbread to start making its own version of Heineken in a brewing plant to be built in Luton. This time the gravity was set at 1032°, which corresponded to an alcohol content of around 3.4 per cent.

The deal was signed in January 1969, just as sales of Heineken and other lagers were finally starting to pick up. Just as the market analysis had predicted a few years earlier, the surge was driven by post-war youngsters who wanted to try something new, whether that was peace, rock music, pills – or simply a light beer. A crucial step forward was that British pubs started adopting draught lager. Unlike the bottles stacked behind the bar, lager pumped from the cellar was chilled, so that British drinkers could at last experience just how refreshing the European beers were. The launch of Heineken's draught lager was such a hit that Whitbread was 'faced with the embarrassment of having to ration it quite severely'. While Heineken UK had struggled to shift 16,000 barrels in 1965, a few months after the licensing agreement in 1969 Whitbread reported that it would need to produce 180,000 barrels to satisfy soaring demand.

'There's a Terrific Draught Blowing Your Way', Heineken's advertising announced, in print ads as well as television commercials. The number of households with TV sets soared to about 60 per cent in the late '50s – and the channels could be counted on one hand, so commercials were certain to draw millions of viewers. A print ad for the trade summarised the impact for the pub landlords, depicting a man on the beach with a beer glass in his hand and a cigar in his mouth, a pretty blonde woman in a bikini under a parasol behind him:

> A few years back, I'd never really heard of Heineken. And business was nice and peaceful. Then the advertising boys got hold of this Terrific Draught idea. You'd see it almost every night on TV. And pretty soon, the lads started asking for it, and drinking the stuff by the gallon. I'd never been so busy. Hardly ever had time to go and have a chat with any of my chums in the trade. The wife was run off her feet as well, bless her. So we had to get a new barhand. And another Heineken set.

It went on to list the things the couple had been able to buy with their Heineken windfall, and their certainty that business would grow further with more ads on their way: 'It had to be Bermuda this year, I can tell you. I need it, I really do.'

⊙

Instead of rejoicing together about the long-awaited surge in sales and profits, Whitbread and Heineken got embroiled in a vicious dispute. Less than a year after the start of their licensing agreement, it looked as though the two parties would split. What it boiled down to was that Alex Bennett, the Whitbread manager who handled the contacts with Heineken's executives in the early days, wanted more certainty in Whitbread's relationship with Heineken. He argued that Whitbread had already invested £2.5 million for the production, distribution and promotion of Heineken's draught lager. The huge demand for draught lager required yet more funds – a commitment Whitbread was unhappy to make, given the uncertainty of its licensing agreement. Bennett was referring to intense speculation about takeover bids in the European brewing business. There were rumours that Unilever would absorb Allied Breweries and then attempt to swallow Heineken. Such a deal would most likely lead to the termination of Whitbread's licence for Heineken lager.

However, Oscar Wittert van Hoogland, chairman of Heineken's executive board at that time, clearly felt that these supposed worries were merely a strategy by Bennett to negotiate improved terms with Heineken. 'Whitbread apparently has a hangover about its relationship with our company', he wrote. The spectacular take-off of Heineken sales underlined the growing demand for lager, and Whitbread did not want to be entirely dependent on Heineken in this frothy market: as Wittert found out, his British partners had been thinking about making their own Whitbread lager as well as beer from Stella Artois.

About 20 per cent of Whitbread's sales were taking place

in Belgium through Stella Artois, Bennett told Wittert, so Whitbread felt obliged to offer more support to the Belgian brewery in Britain. The British family's relationship with their Belgian counterparts went back a long way: Whitbread started importing Stella Artois back in 1938. Bennett impressed on Wittert that the De Spoelberch family, who owned Stella Artois, were 'such friendly people', with whom Whitbread cultivated an outstanding relationship.

Wittert returned from London in October 1969 with serious doubts about the tie-up with Whitbread. 'I do wonder if we wouldn't be better off ending the relationship with Whitbread altogether', he wrote. 'At the moment it looks very much like Whitbread thinks they have learned all we could teach them about brewing lager, and so we're as much use to them as a toothache.' Bennett was equally unsettled about the discussion. 'I want to follow up immediately because our conversation was not at all a happy one, in that you accused Whitbread's of consistently breaking our agreements, and we think that you are not helpful partners in South Africa', he wrote. 'You have no confidence in this project, in which we have staked millions of pounds.'

The complaint about South Africa related to another joint venture between Heineken and Whitbread. Heineken was providing technical advice to the brewery in Johannesburg, but, much to Whitbread's consternation, Heineken refused to let the joint venture use the Dutch brand's name. It was all the more awkward because, uncharacteristically, the major international lager on the South African market was Amstel. After it had gulped down Amstel in 1968, Heineken was therefore 'sitting on both sides of the fence', involved in a joint venture with Whitbread that competed directly with another company selling its own Amstel beer. Bennett sent Heineken an ultimatum: either fully support the South African venture – in other words, allow it to use the Heineken brand – or 'reconsider your position as shareholders' in Whitbread South Africa and on its board. The somewhat dramatic conclusion to his letter was that 'An unhappy partnership between two great companies can hardly survive, let alone succeed. I believe the time has now come, therefore, when we must decide once and for all whether we are to work really closely together in the future or go our own separate ways.'

The two agreed to iron things out at a meeting in Amsterdam in early December. At Whitbread's insistence, Freddy Heineken was to be involved in the talks. Bill Whitbread's nephew Charles also made the trip to the Netherlands so that the two family heirs could talk things out. The reason for the owners to be in attendance rapidly became clear: to tighten the relationship between the two companies, Charles Whitbread suggested that the two companies should acquire shares in each other. Predictably, Freddy Heineken had no interest, but he did reassure his British partner that he had no intention to sell to anybody else. The talks ended with weak promises to reconsider the exclusive aspect of the British licensing agreement and Heineken's participation in the South African joint venture.

However, this diplomatic achievement was apparently annihilated by an angry exchange between Wittert and Bennett after dinner. 'It is always dangerous to talk business after an excellent dinner, but I felt I had to make our position quite clear and frank between friends, and I must say I was rather astonished at the outburst that followed', Bennett wrote upon his return. 'It's hard to believe you want to break up the Heineken/ Whitbread relationship with so much promise of success ahead, but if allegations of dishonesty and ungentlemanly behaviour are continually hurled at your partners, who are contributing all the hard work and all the finance, friendship is bound to wear a bit thin and finally dissolve in bitterness and a look for more congenial partners.' The Dutch 'outburst' backfired badly. It could well be that Wittert felt personally cheated and that he regarded the relationship as untenable. But if that was the case, he was overruled: a few months after the encounter in Amsterdam, the Dutch backed down.

To begin with, Heineken agreed to pursue the licensing agreement with improved financial conditions for Whitbread. There was no doubt that Whitbread had achieved outstanding sales: while the two parties had estimated sales of less than 200,000 barrels of Heineken lager over three years, Whitbread projected that it would exceed that figure in 1970, the second year into the licensing deal. Whitbread claimed that it had already secured an 18 per cent share of the UK lager market for Heineken – and the British were quaffing more lager than ever. These impressive sales required more investment, because Whitbread said it had capacity to make only 240,000 barrels at its plant in Luton. So it started considering the construction of another brewing plant in Lancashire, which would enable Heineken to move further into the regional market.

Yet the most startling concession was that Heineken also gave up on the exclusive aspect of its deal with Whitbread: with their combination of feigned uncertainty and threats, the shrewd British managers got their Dutch counterparts to agree that they could start making a competing international lager brand in the UK, the Belgian Stella Artois. They assured the Dutch that Stella Artois would not compete directly with Heineken: Whitbread would continue to peddle the weaker Heineken as an affordable international lager, while they would market the stronger, more alcoholic Stella Artois with a price to match.

Stella made in Britain was ready to hit the market in 1972,

with an advertising campaign that clearly identified the targeted consumer: 'Stella's for the fellas who take their lager strong', it said. The picture showed a glass of Stella Artois and a telephone directory cleanly torn in half, supposedly by a Stella-swigging fella. Heineken's managers must have gulped even harder at the tagline for Stella: 'Europe's strongest-selling lager'.

The entire situation was less than satisfactory for Heineken. Then again, the figures shown by Whitbread indicated that Heineken could achieve a breakthrough in Britain at long last. The effortless revenues generated by the royalties would come in handy – all the more so since political agitation in Africa was endangering sales in one of Heineken's most important regional markets. The extra revenues amply made up for any ill-feeling in the next years, after far-reaching changes to Heineken's advertising tactics.

The offices in a tatty back street off London's Tottenham Court Road didn't have any carpet, and the desks were of plain steel. The former clothing warehouse's rooms were so cold in winter that employees often sat working in their overcoats, and so warm in summer that they turned up in shorts. Yet this unglamorous advertising agency was recurrently described as the best in the world, and it delivered the advertising line that turned Heineken into a best-selling lager in the UK.

Collett Dickenson Pearce (CDP) brought together a group of ultra-talented and often chaotic people who created some of the most iconic UK advertising campaigns in the 1970s and '80s. Awards piled up in the corridors, and the agency was a launch pad for such creative sparks as Alan Parker, Charles Saatchi, Ridley Scott and David Puttnam.

While the level of creativity in advertising in the early '70s was generally high, CDP valued and fostered this quality more than any other agency. The top floor of the building on Howland Street was reserved for the creative team, not the management, and they could organise their time any way they liked – provided they came up with outstanding campaigns. 'It was fairly anarchic and it was exhilarating, because we knew we were producing great work', as one of the former employees put it. 'In fact it was a bit like being one of the Beatles, with the women to match.'

Some of the creative people who thrived in this atmosphere were somewhat 'dysfunctional', taking little interest in schedules or in sobriety. Lunches regularly stretched until mid-afternoon, and sometimes the consumption of cheap Italian wine was part of the job interview. Other interviews were conducted by an account manager who spoke through a Sooty glove puppet. Wearing long hair and tight-fitting velvet suits, some of the people who authored award-winning campaigns at CDP had no formal education to speak of, but plenty of creative talent.

The advertising agency reaped praise for its humorous commercials for brands such as Birds Eye ('it can make a dishonest woman of you') and Hamlet ('Happiness is a cigar called Hamlet'). Among the most inspired commercials for these mild cigars was 'The Bunker': the golfer and sand are hidden from view because the shot is taken from the green, but the top of his sand wedge swinging furiously above the bunker allows us to guess at his desperate efforts to get his ball out – the frustrated groans only ending when a puff of smoke is seen emerging from the bunker accompanied by Jacques Loussier's rendering of Bach.

Creative teams in other agencies watched CDP with admiration and a hint of jealousy: 'In those days it was all about going places you'd never been before. There were two or three other agencies that emerged in these years but none was in CDP's league. They believed in creativity more than anyone else', said Dave Trott, who then worked for Boase Massimi Pollitt, probably CDP's most creative rival in London.

Among the characters who emerged at the time was Frank Lowe. He started his career at Lintas, the in-house advertising agency of what was then Lever Brothers, and switched to CDP as an account executive in 1969. As former colleagues recalled, Lowe fitted in neatly. For several weeks he walked around with a cricket sweater and a bat under his arm. On other occasions he would turn up in a scruffy T-shirt and socks. Much more importantly, Lowe was a fierce proponent of creativity: he had a remarkable ability to stretch people's talents and constantly drove them to produce outstanding work.

Lowe always instructed his creative teams to produce their best effort – just the one, no alternatives. 'It's just not nice to go to creative people and force them to do something they're not proud of. It's very unkind', he said. 'If you only have one campaign, they will try hard, because the responsibility is absolutely on them.' He did so well that he persuaded the agency's owners to resign accounts for important clients such as Ford and Nestlé, who did not want to abide by such rules. Lowe rarely agreed to take part in pitches that could sap the creative team's morale, preferring to 'present credentials' instead.

Copywriters and art directors recall that, under Lowe's leadership, they would be sent back time and again until their work hit Lowe's most exacting mark. 'I always figured the pub across the road was a place where they all could go after I had turned down a campaign', he said; 'they could curse and criticise'. At the same time, Lowe 'learned not to let the planners in', so that the campaigns would always be driven by the creative teams.

They were given plenty of time to retouch their work and rewrite their copy, until it was declared 'sublime' or 'sensational'. It would then get a stamp from Lowe and the art director, which was CDP's equivalent of quality control.

Lowe adhered fully to the CDP principle that the brilliance of the creative work should be rewarded with passionate sales-manship. So once he had approved a concept, the creative teams could be almost certain that he would sell it. This made working with him all the more gratifying for writers and art directors, especially as he always gave them credit for their work. And all the while, Lowe built intense personal relationships with clients – a consummate account manager.

The man to schmooze at Whitbread at the time was Anthony Simonds-Gooding, the company's marketing director. He and Frank Lowe had once shared an office at Lever Brothers, and they had stayed friends. The contact remained very personal when Simonds-Gooding was appointed as the marketing man for Birds Eye and CDP obtained the account – with Lowe as an account supervisor.

Investors had been grumbling about the old-fashioned management at Whitbread, which had failed to invest time and resources into building up a leading bitter brand. When asked what he was doing about marketing, Colonel Whitbread replied that 'two girls in the library' were taking care of that. He was eventually persuaded to hire Simonds-Gooding. The young man was unimpressed with the Heineken ads, which sold the brand almost like a bitter. Without even bothering to organise a pitch, he turned to his friend Lowe at CDP. 'I knew that if they did what they usually do, they would get it', he said. CDP were appointed not only for the Heineken brand but also for Stella Artois.

Stella Artois's significantly higher price, and the fact that it was full strength, meant the Belgian brand should be positioned at the top end of the lager market. The copy turned out by the creative team highlighted the ingredients used by the Belgian brewery. Somewhere in the middle of a long paragraph, as one of the team members recalled, Frank Lowe spotted the two words 'reassuringly expensive'. He immediately circled them and turned them into a lasting slogan for Stella Artois.

The sharpest pens at CDP exercised their talents on Stella print ads with clever writing. 'Every silver lining has a cloud', one of them started.

There you are in the midst of convivial company, laughing, joking, holding forth on the issues of the day and pausing only to savour your Stella Artois. And then the awful truth dawns. It will soon be your turn to stand a round. And not just any round, mark you, a round of Stella Artois, no less. The beer that is brewed with the most fragrant of female hops. The beer that is malted with the choicest of Europe's barley. The beer that is matured not in the usual meagre 21 days, but for six long weeks. The beer that, as a consequence, is eye-wateringly expensive. If we are to maintain Stella's reputation for quality there is, alas, nothing we can do to reduce the quantity of money you must part with. We can, however, offer you a sound piece of advice. When it is your turn in the chair, make sure you are sitting down.

Heineken was much harder to categorise. The taste of the Heineken brewed by Whitbread was not sufficiently distinctive for advertising purposes. Nor did the brand's Dutch identity seem particularly relevant – and any claims about that could backfire as the beer sold in Britain was actually made in Luton. Lowe and his team racked their brains thinking about what attributes they wanted to give the Heineken brand.

◉

Among all of those in CDP's creative teams at the time, Terry Lovelock was one of the most exuberant characters. A jazz drummer, he had taken up a job as a copywriter at the agency to round off his earnings when he started a family. He often arrived at the office 'at the crack of lunch', to search for a few companions and would then disappear with them into one of the nearby eateries until the middle of the afternoon. But Lovelock was entirely clear-headed when he sat down to write, and was the author of some of the most memorable lines in CDP campaigns.

The agency's way of working at this time was for the account manager to work out a basic strategy and to send a yellow card upstairs to the creative team, with just a few keywords. Lovelock's intense relationship with Heineken started some time in the second half of 1973, when one of these yellow cards landed on his desk. The strategists had worked out that they should not make any claims about the way Heineken tasted, or tell consumers that Heineken was cheap and that they could drink an entire barrel without getting excessively intoxicated. They hit on another attribute that was much more appealing: that it was refreshing.

The claim that Heineken was 'refreshing' had the advantage of being quite accurate. It was certainly more refreshing than the thicker and heavier ale and bitter that most drinkers were quaffing at the time, often served at barely chilled temperatures. The problem was that this was true of almost any lager. It was Lovelock's task to make sure that consumers would equate 'refreshing' with Heineken. Most importantly, for Lowe and for the customer, it would have to be creative. 'A brief was born to say we wanted a long-term strategic campaign for Heineken based on refreshment. But refreshment is such a boring idea that it would only be acceptable if it was backed by creative treatment that was utterly different and exciting and eye-catching and would have legs to last many years', as Simonds-Gooding recalled.

Lovelock endured 'three months of agony' over the assignment. Extra-long lunches did not suffice to spark the ebullient copywriter's inspiration. 'What a terrific state to get into', was one of the earlier submissions that didn't get past his own desk. Lovelock said some of the agency's executives came to 'threaten' him regularly. As deadlines came and went, even the indulgent Simonds-Gooding started to get irritated. Lowe summoned Lovelock to his office on a Monday morning.

When he failed to turn up, the director started a search. Lowe shared a mews house with Vernon Howe, the art director with whom Lovelock worked, so he knew that Howe was travelling to Marrakesh for a photo shoot that morning. He soon found out that Lovelock had decided to tag along. Although the copywriter's assistance was not required in Morocco, he had decided to escape the pressure by leaving his desk – and the Heineken assignment. Just as Lovelock was preparing to board his flight, the receptionist at the departure lounge handed him the phone, with an irate Lowe at the other end. The ultimatum was clear: either come back with a campaign or don't bother coming back at all.

Several days relaxing at La Mamounia with beers from a barman in a fez did not help Lovelock any more than his habitual tricks in London. As he recalled, it was during one of the nights that he got up to write two lines. One of them read: 'Heineken refreshes the parts other beers cannot reach.' The other was: 'Heineken is now refreshing all parts.' The copywriter could then write several scripts around this concept, showing the transformation before and after refreshment. Lovelock explained upon his return that the second option was an alternative, in case the advertising watchdog misunderstood the 'parts'. But Lowe had no such qualms. All he had to do was to convince his friend Simonds-Gooding.

As it happened, the two had scheduled a little outing to the Hermitage Museum in Leningrad (now St Petersburg) with their wives. Somewhere in the sky between the UK and what was then still the Soviet Union, Simonds-Gooding started grumbling about Heineken. 'This Heineken campaign is really bugging me. I think it has gone on long enough. Have you got anything at all, Frank?' asked the Whitbread manager, who had watched several deadlines expire. 'Sure, I've got it', the account director replied. 'And when are you going to pitch it to us?' Simonds-Gooding inquired. In lieu of a reply, Lowe just started scribbling. The Whitbread manager was a little bewildered, but he entirely trusted his friend. 'Well, if you think it will work, we had better go and do it', he said. A line and a drawing on an errant piece of paper ('it may have been a sick bag', Lowe said) marked the start of an iconic campaign that would last about two decades.

Once they had all returned to London, CDP started executing three commercials based on the 'refreshing' line. One of them showed a line of policemen, their trouser legs turned up to reveal bare and tired feet. In a mock scientific experiment, the policemen were to drink a pint of Heineken lager, to check if the beer did indeed refresh parts other beers could not reach. And yes, after a few seconds, the tired policemen's toes started to wriggle. The character in the second commercial was a piano tuner, unable to perform his job due to tired ears. This was fixed with a pint of Heineken, almost instantly refreshing the piano tuner's ears. The last one showed a dancing couple refreshed by

Heineken, but it wasn't deemed sufficiently creative to make the pitch. For the voice-overs, CDP managed to hire the Danish-American comedian and pianist Victor Borge. Borge initially turned down the assignment, protesting that a Dane could not possibly be heard praising Heineken beer. His reluctance disappeared when he heard that Carlsberg had hired Orson Welles for its own campaign.

CDP then went about 'researching' the ads, putting them in front of consumer panels. But instead of the praise it was hoping to garner for its creative approach, CDP faced a barrage of criticism. The reports compiled from the panel discussions in April 1973 indicated that consumers were unimpressed with the slogan as well as the entire commercials. One of the respondents complained that the commercials contained a 'blatant untruth' because the man described as the 'finest piano tuner in Europe' was in fact a character from the BBC TV series *Are You Being Served?* Another felt that the policemen commercial carried almost medical overtones and that it 'would be more effective as a Lucozade ad'. As for the pay-off, the respondents couldn't even remember it. 'On its own it doesn't stick. No rhythm about it', one of them said.

However, Lowe decided to ignore the findings. He was not very interested in research for such creative commercials anyway, declaring that it was 'like researching Elvis, or art deco'. Simonds-Gooding went along with him. While he did like the commercials, his endorsement was mostly based on trust. Unlike many other marketing directors, Simonds-Gooding never felt the urge to assert himself against an advertising agency. He didn't have much trouble getting it past the other Whitbread managers either. 'I could do what I wanted, because it was so small', he said. 'If I had been talking about bitter, I would have had the whole board around me. This was my little plaything.' As the youngest member of the board, Simonds-Gooding himself had come to be regarded at Whitbread as an intriguing novelty, 'to be indulged'.

The last hurdle was to get the campaign past the Dutch head office. Simonds-Gooding held regular meetings at the time with the Heineken managers in charge of European sales. But when it came to advertising, they admitted that they would have to run it past Freddy Heineken. Simonds-Gooding was a little intrigued by Heineken – 'pretty enigmatic, three cigarettes a minute' – and so nervous about his reaction that he decided to organise the presentation almost in private. As things turned out, Freddy immediately approved the campaign, and even asked for the advertising boards to be sent to him. He apparently bought it on trust and instinct, even though there was little to like from his standpoint: 'It was the wrong gravity, an unsatisfactory royalty, a marketing campaign that was totally off-message', Simonds-Gooding admitted.

Once it was aired, the campaign took some more flak. Heineken received various letters of complaint, including one about how the claims were outrageously misleading, because beer could in fact not refresh policemen's feet. (The regulators hadn't seen that one coming – they had probably allowed the campaign because the claims were so ludicrous that nobody could take them seriously.) More worryingly, some viewers were concerned that the adverts reflected the white-collar humour at CDP and would not appeal to working-class drinkers. But in fact, the Heineken campaign proved an almost instant hit. 'With its whimsical, metaphorical approach, it flattered the consumer's intelligence', another advertising manager explained.

One of the advantages of the 'refreshing' line was that it

could apply to an almost endless variety of quirky situations. The executions included many popular posters with two or three pictures showing a character before and after a pint of Heineken. A sip was all it took for J. R., the wicked brother in *Dallas*, suddenly to grow a saintly halo. Tanked up with the Dutch beer, the sharp nose of the Concorde airplane straightened up again. The posters often had very British cultural references, and sometimes tied in with current affairs.

Frank Lowe was particularly enamoured with the Mr Spock ad, a triptych featuring a cartoon version of the pointy-eared character from *Star Trek*. Spock looked piteous in the first image, the tips of his ears wilting. After a sip of Heineken, in the second image, they started jittering back up. And in the third image his pointy ears were fully restored. 'Illogical', Spock mused in a bubble.

It was a little too offbeat for Anthony Simonds-Gooding. As Whitbread's marketing manager criticised the visual, Lowe started to sulk. He was certain that the tone was just right and couldn't accept the criticism. His anger reached such theatrical proportions that he smashed the concept board over his knee and dragged his chair to a corner to sulk some more, facing the wall. He then stormed off, back to the agency. The customer was apparently so startled that he gave in. 'All right, Frank, I'll buy it', Simonds-Gooding said.

The concept and many of the executions were resolutely British. Back in Amsterdam, the Heineken managers often failed to grasp the humour, and they were still annoyed that the British were drinking a non-standard variety of their beer. Yet even the least Anglophile of Dutch managers could not fail to acknowledge that CDP had managed to reach parts of the British market that other agencies couldn't reach. Fresh instalments of the campaign were eagerly awaited, and Heineken did become known for its refreshing qualities, just as the strategists had instructed. As if on cue, the launch of the campaign was followed by the two scorching hot summers of 1975 and '76, calling for plenty of refreshment.

Ever the consummate account manager, Lowe never failed to praise Freddy for his vision for the brand. 'Unlike many clients today he had a real understanding of the importance of brands and how you build them over a very long period of time', the Englishman said much later. The two sometimes socialised together. They even arranged for Charlene, Heineken's daughter, to spend some time at the agency's TV department.

Over the years the slogan would become part of the English language. It was constantly used in newspapers, by politicians and even by royalty: Prince Charles wrote that painting transported him to another dimension, refreshing parts of his soul that other activities could not reach. When he heard about this, Lovelock wrote to the prince, seeking permission to be distinguished as a purveyor of slogans for His Royal Highness.

However, Heineken's popular advertising was only the most eye-catching factor contributing to its success in the British market. More far-reaching were the reforms instigated by Simonds-Gooding at Whitbread for the distribution of the company's beer. As consumers increasingly shopped at supermarkets and made fewer visits to their local, the take-home market was expanding much faster than the number of pints drunk in pubs. None of the British brewers was fully equipped to deal with this shift, as until the '70s canned beer was brought to retailers by draymen who often had little interest in pushing retail sales.

Not unlike Pieter Feith in Amsterdam, Simonds-Gooding figured out that Whitbread could swiftly conquer shelf space if it targeted the retailers with a dedicated sales force. 'We delivered to supermarkets in our huge big drays, full of barrels and a few tins at the back', he said. 'So I had very scary negotiations with the unions to remove that part of the business from them.' Instead he wanted to give it to Speedy Prompt Delivery (SPD), an arm of Unilever, which delivered to retailers everything from margarine to frozen foods. They were to drop off Whitbread's beers at supermarkets and off-licences.

The Whitbread manager's plans were met with stiff resistance, from the trade union as well as his own regional managers. 'You're taking business away from my draymen', they protested. The marketing manager pressed ahead regardless, setting up a take-home division. Whitbread's board watched him much more closely than they had done with advertising because the plan could put its entire distribution in jeopardy. 'It was really tough and crucial', said Simonds-Gooding, but the result was rewarding: 'we immediately became by far the market leader in the take-home market.' Whitbread was the first brewery to address the retail sector with custom-made deliveries and a dedicated sales force.

Another fundamental change came a few years later, when Simonds-Gooding decided to tackle the brewery's regional organisation. Unlike any of the country's other conglomerates, Whitbread still had regional managers (some of them members of the Whitbread family), who all ran their own teams for production, wholesaling and catering. Simonds-Gooding wanted to replace this system with centralised national management and teams that covered each of these activities across the entire country.

Again it was a tough battle: he was not only fighting against some of the people in his own organisation but also breaking with Whitbread's long tradition. Simonds-Gooding, who became managing director of the entire brewing business, said that 'slow-moving warfare' wore him out. But at last Whitbread had an infrastructure that enabled it and Heineken to compete more directly with the more astute brewers who had gained market share in the previous years – even more efficiently in the take-home market.

With all that in place, Heineken could play a central role in the spectacular transformation of the British beer market, known as the Lager Revolution, which took place over the next years. During the 1970s lager's share of British beer consumption jumped from about 5 per cent to 32 per cent, and by the end of the '80s it had reached over 50 per cent. Few at Heineken's head office in the Netherlands appreciated the popularity of their brand's watery brew in Britain. But it earned the company millions in royalties – money that helped to finance Freddy Heineken's most ambitious project.

8

Fortress Europe

Freddy Heineken launched his public bid on the Brasserie de l'Espérance in Strasbourg on 2 August 1972. This date had been picked very deliberately. Freddy knew full well that the entire country comes to a virtual standstill from the beginning of that month, as the holidaying French trek to the beaches. Some local companies even close their gates in August, and only a small core of civil servants stay behind their desks. 'Small wonder the management offices of the brewery were deserted', smiled one Heineken executive close to the deal.

At any other time of year it was a safe bet that Heineken's bid would have been met with roars of incredulous protest from the proud Alsatians. It was the first takeover raid in local history, and its object was the jewel in the brewing crown of the Alsace, the cradle of France's beer industry. The Brasserie de l'Espérance, established in Schiltigheim and run by the Hatt family, boasted a capacity of some 1.4 million hectolitres. It also held a majority stake in the Alsacienne de Brasserie (Albra), a group of local breweries that jointly formed the third-largest French brewing consortium, with the breweries of La Perle, Colmar and Mützig as minority stakeholders.

Freddy Heineken had studied his targets closely. Undercover visits paid by his underlings to Colmar and Strasbourg revealed ultra-modern facilities: for instance, the completely automated brewing room at Mützig was the biggest in Europe. They estimated that, although Albra made up only about 7 per cent of French beer sales, the operation was remarkably profitable because production had been rationalised in previous years. About 80 per cent of it consisted of quality beers, chiefly with the Ancre and Mützig brands. 'With a Ffr 100 million market capitalisation, l'Alsacienne de Brasserie seems to be particularly undervalued', they concluded.

The takeover was set in motion in the summer of 1972, when Freddy Heineken was relaxing at his house in Cap d'Antibes. He was advised to interrupt his holiday to attend a dinner in Strasbourg with René and his son Michel, the managers of L'Espérance and Albra's largest shareholders. As things turned out, it was the younger 'Mickey' Hatt who joined up for talks at the restaurant Au Crocodile, a three-star eatery in Strasbourg. Just before the two settled down at their table, in the first-floor eating-room, Freddy said, 'Listen, before we order our food, I must warn you that I intend to launch a bid on Albra.' Turning white, Michel ran to the phone to call his father.

In the Alsatian brewing scene René Hatt was known as a quick-tempered entrepreneur. 'On his desk René had a small bronze statue that he sometimes hurled at visitors', said Michel Debus of the Fischer breweries, a former competitor and friend. Hatt told colleagues that he regarded Heineken's bid as a personal assault, but he was unable to rally the other leading Albra shareholders behind him. Two days after Freddy Heineken filed his bid, the Hatts declared that they would not oppose it, 'due to the convergence in the industrial and commercial interests of the two firms'.

Roland Wagner, the most influential man in the family that controlled Mützig, was another large stakeholder.

Through Mützig and shared ownership of the Colmar brewery the Wagners held roughly 20 per cent of Albra. 'I felt that I was stuck. All I could do was to strengthen my position by acquiring a blocking minority through the stock market. With this enlarged stake under my belt, I went to meet Freddy in the offices of my bankers in Paris and settled the deal with him', Wagner recalled matter-of-factly. He was later appointed to the board of Heineken's French operating company.

Freddy Heineken was apparently not overly nervous about the deal. The only revision he requested in the press release was that he 'would rather be called Alfred than Freddy in official papers'. Once he returned from the Alsace to Cap d'Antibes, he was updated most informally by his assistant. In their telex exchanges, brief instructions about the deal were punctuated with personal messages.

The Strasbourg municipal council was so piqued by the Dutch intrusion in Alsatian brewing land that it refused to surrender its 77 shares in Brasserie de l'Espérance. But Heineken's offer proved irresistible for the other small stockholders: he offered Ffr 600 for the shares, which had been quoted at about Ffr 420 in the regional Nancy bourse over the previous months. So by 25 September, when the offer closed, Heineken had acquired a majority of the Albra group. For several years René Hatt continued to drive to his office every day in his Citroën 2CV – 'just to piss Heineken off', he told friends.

It would have been short-sighted for the Alsatians to prevent the deal, because at the time Albra looked condemned to a slow and painful death. Although the breweries were still in relatively good shape, they didn't have a hope of surviving independently in the long term. As rapacious as they might be, the Dutch would at least keep some of the group's breweries alive. Other French brewers had let Albra down: 'The market leaders just sat back and waited for Albra to exhale its last breath', said Jean-Claude Colin, an Alsatian beer writer. 'Had they been able to predict what Heineken's entry meant for the French beer market, and ultimately the whole European market, they would never have left the door even half-open.'

The brutal Albra takeover can be seen as the overture to Freddy's grand strategic scheme. What was at stake here was the leadership of the European beer market, a patchwork of nations that roughly matched the United States in beer consumption. Freddy wanted to turn this into an American-size home market for Heineken, an impregnable bastion that he pompously referred to as Fortress Europe.

When Freddy became chairman of the executive board in the early '70s, beer drinkers around the world, from New York to Lagos and Hong Kong, were already swigging his brew. Yet Heineken refreshed under 3 per cent of Europeans. While the company's beer vessels cruised the seven seas, there was an enormous chunk of almost completely Heineken-barren territory lying at the company's doorstep.

Fortress Europe would help compensate for Heineken's troubles in other continents, where the company was increasingly frustrated by protectionist hurdles. But at the same time the changing face of Europe made the attack even more compelling. Although the European Union was still a long way off, the six founding members had already pledged to tear down their internal borders. Much earlier than some of his closest rivals, Freddy became convinced that this would eventually make it easier for wealthy and expansionist companies to operate Europe-wide.

In the early '70s the game was still entirely open. The four largest brewing companies in Europe were British. One of them, Allied Breweries, had revived the Skol brand and formed a network of foreign partners to storm the European market. Carlsberg and Tuborg, the Danish breweries that merged in 1970, also intended to spread their wings in Europe. The same was true of Boussois Souchon Neuvesel (BSN), the owners of Kronenbourg. And then there was the Belgian Stella Artois, which also had the potential to scupper Heineken's plans.

There were still so many contenders in the European market that these companies could easily grab market share without stepping on each other's toes. But to take the most interesting pieces, Heineken had to hit faster than the rest. Some of Freddy's most astute managers were assigned to supervise these efforts in the 'Group Europe' of Heineken's international division. Ultimately, he wanted to be first or second in every single European country.

Freddy's personal affinity with France was one reason for starting the construction of Fortress Europe in that country. More pragmatically, the decision was aligned with one of his favourite sayings: that 'beer travels from north to south'. Wine drinkers by birth, southern Europeans still gulped down far less beer than their northern neighbours: in 1973 Heineken estimated that consumption in France was about 44 litres per capita annually, drunk mostly in the Alsace and in the north of the country; in Spain the number was lower – about 37 litres – and in Italy it was just 17 litres. Yet sooner or later, Heineken reasoned, southern Europeans would learn to appreciate the virtues of a refreshing lager.

Furthermore, Freddy recognised the influence that the growing tourist industry was having on beer consumption. The millions of miserable northerners who flocked to the Mediterranean in pursuit of sunshine created demand for lager in the bistros and tapas bars there. And sunny memories of Heineken-soaked afternoons reminded northern tourists how nice it could be to have a refreshing beer.

The Dutch moved their green bottles across the European chessboard with characteristic shrewdness. Instead of going on a spending spree that they could ill afford, they adjusted their approach in each of the markets. In some cases, such as France, where they spotted an opportunity at an unbeatable price, they went ahead. In other cases, they were willing to accept a minority stake and then wait patiently for several years until the situation was such that they could make a bid for a majority share.

Freddy regarded the construction of Heineken's European fortress as the finest feather in his cap. It was his pet project, a long-term venture that would earn him a place in corporate history as the man behind Heineken's decisive international expansion in the 1970s and '80s. But also, more than any other grand scheme, it gave Freddy the opportunity to shine as a clever strategist, a slick deal-maker and a remarkable brand-builder.

Freddy Heineken relished cruising around the streets of Paris in his cabriolet. There he could enjoy himself as he couldn't in Amsterdam, where he would often be subjected to envious remarks. His drives must have become even more delightful when his car glided down the Champs-Elysées. In Heineken's shoes even the most uninterested of tycoons would have struggled to repress a self-satisfied smile: half-way down the avenue, clear for all to read, Heineken's name was emblazoned on the balconies above Fouquet's restaurant.

Freddy owed this delight to Moët & Chandon, the illustrious

champagne house in Epernay. Heineken had contracted them in the early '60s to distribute Heineken in France. The market for imported beers in France was at that point dominated by Carlsberg and Tuborg. Moët & Chandon held the keys to the country's most select establishments, and the champagne's exclusive image rubbed off on the Dutch beer. But by the early '70s Heineken was keen to expand its position in France beyond a few prestigious exports. The brewery wanted volume, which meant local beers and national distribution – and that's precisely where the Alsatian Albra fitted in.

Soon after Heineken took over the reins in the Alsace, they trimmed Albra's operations down to two breweries, in Schiltigheim and Mutzig. The closure of the Colmar plant, in January 1975, prompted emotional reactions. A virulent editorial in *Les Dernières Nouvelles d'Alsace* even called for a halt to the 'massacre' of the regional beer industry by 'les étrangers', but Freddy coolly pressed ahead. After these closures, some Alsatians started to refer to Heineken as 'Le Grand Méchant Loup' ('The Big Bad Wolf'). The Albra takeover was completed in 1976, when Heineken acquired the rest of the shares. The Dutch then ended their contract with Moët & Chandon, and four years later started brewing Heineken in Schiltigheim.

Back in the '70s, when the French still largely rejected beer as a blue-collar product, Heineken's association with champagne made the proposition of selling an international beer to inveterate wine drinkers even more absurd. Publicis, the Paris advertising agency, argued that Heineken should start from scratch, by initiating the French to the delights of the frothy stuff. 'The message was that drinking beer should not be regarded as some sort of a bestial urge, but more like a ritual', said Grégoire Champetier, former Heineken account manager at Publicis. In the resultant commercials a middle-aged man humorously shared sophisticated thoughts while longing to make a start on the fresh and sparkling beer in front of him. For millions of French people Heineken would long remain 'la bière qui fait aimer la bière' ('the beer that makes you like beer'), as the slogan went.

With a 9 per cent slice of the market, Heineken France was still only a dwarf in the French beer business. About half of the market was in the hands of BSN, France's largest bottle-maker. With its ownership of the Kronenbourg breweries and a large stake in the Société Européenne de Brasserie (SEB, the makers of Kanterbräu), this group eclipsed all other French brewers – and was one of Heineken's leading rivals in the European market.

The stories of Kronenbourg and Heineken and their founding fathers are remarkably similar. Kronenbourg's begins in June 1664, when Jérôme Hatt sealed his first beer barrel in the Brasserie du Canon, on the banks of the River Ill in Strasbourg. But like Heineken, the Kronenbourg brand only became a European heavyweight under the leadership of a youthful Hatt descendant with a knack for marketing. After the liberation, at the same time as Freddy Heineken worked on Heineken's brand identity, Jérôme Hatt junior (a cousin of René Hatt from L'Espérance) was reinventing Kronenbourg.

Since Alsace-Lorraine had fallen into French hands, the Strasbourg district of Kronenburg, where the brewery was located, had been renamed Cronenbourg. Jérôme Hatt smartly reinstated the K in Kronenbourg, to give it an authentic, Germanic touch. He then launched the stubby bottle with a crown cap and other forms of packaging hitherto unknown to the French, such as the cardboard pack. He designed distinctive branding for Kronenbourg with gothic characters and the red-and-white rectangles. Promoted by heavy-hitting advertising, Kronenbourg was selling about 2 million hectolitres by

1968. Unlike Heineken, however, Hatt was unable to keep his independence. Heavily in debt after the construction of a mega-plant in Obernai (known locally as 'The Refinery'), Kronenbourg was swallowed up in 1970 by BSN, which would later become Danone.

Freddy Heineken and Antoine Riboud, BSN's chairman, cultivated a respectful entente. Although compliments didn't come easy to Freddy, he described his French counterpart as one of Europe's finest tycoons, another full-blooded family entrepreneur. The BSN chairman had turned to the food and drinks industry after a failed raid on Saint-Gobain, another French glassmaker, in 1969. Although he came from a wealthy banking family, Riboud liked to tell reporters he had known since childhood that he was destined for the food business: aged ten, Antoine sold vegetables from the family garden to his grandfather, charging him twice the price of the local grocer.

In the Alsace, Riboud was often ridiculed as an 'anti-alcohol' chairman, who would happily sell off Kronenbourg to concentrate on his other projects, such as Evian mineral water and Danone's dairy products. 'Heineken's looking more Alsatian than Kronenbourg ever did now that Riboud's taken the top spot', said beer writer Jean-Claude Colin. Riboud did, however, fiercely protect his beer territory, which led to a relentless duel between 'Les Rouges' (Kronenbourg) and 'Les Verts' (Heineken).

This battle came to a head in the mid-'80s, when Freddy and his lot pulled governmental strings to consolidate Heineken's position as second biggest brewery in the French market. This time the target was the tie-up between Union des Brasseries (UdB) and Pelforth, the second-largest French brewing group, behind BSN's Kronenbourg.

In 1980 the three Bonduel brothers, who managed the

northern French Pelforth brewery and owned about one third of its shares, had been forced to sell out to Brasseries et Glacières Internationales (BGI). This group operated in former French colonies and counted among its partners Alain Gaston-Dreyfus, the son of Heineken's former Cobra partner. 'It was just one year before the Socialists swept to power. The other shareholders were scared, because they knew there would be Communist ministers in the government and that many private companies would be nationalised. We couldn't afford to buy out the other families, so we settled for a deal with Gaston-Dreyfus', said Patrick Bonduel, the youngest of the brothers.

At the time BGI was itself in the hands of the Compagnie du Midi, a French financial conglomerate. Once it became known that the Compagnie du Midi intended to sell its beer interests in order to focus on insurance, UdB-Pelforth entered talks with Stella Artois, said Patrick Bonduel. However, Freddy Heineken was also circling, and in 1983 he discreetly arranged talks with Bernard Pagezy, the influential president of the Compagnie du Midi.

The two men met in Freddy's plush apartment in Paris. As Pagezy later admitted, he was highly impressed by Freddy and his lieutenant, Gerard van Schaik. The board member in charge of European subsidiaries, Van Schaik was often described as Heineken's 'cunning man'. Although he was a business veteran himself, Pagezy confessed that he had never before encountered such endurance and precision in negotiations. Having started before dinnertime, the talks sometimes dragged on until the early hours of the morning.

To ease tensions as the night progressed, the two men would joke about the ugly faces on a Brueghel-style painting by a Yugoslav artist that was hung in the apartment. (In a typically 'Freddy' move, the Heineken tycoon arranged for a similar tableau to be delivered to Pagezy about two years later, without any warning.) Even after the two had worked out the terms of the UdB-Pelforth transaction, however, there were still many hurdles in the way.

Understandably, Kronenbourg's Riboud was hell-bent on thwarting the deal, and he called on friends in the highest places to intervene. In theory, the acquisition of UdB-Pelforth by another European company should not have required the French government's approval, but protectionism was at its height in Paris at this time. Riboud was mighty enough to cause agitation in the corridors of French ministries. 'The deal may never have been formally recorded on the agenda of cabinet meetings, but it sure caused a hell of a stir', said one of Riboud's opponents at the time. 'Riboud even spread the ludicrous rumour that Freddy Heineken was not actually a European Community citizen because he had secretly acquired Swiss nationality for tax purposes.'

But Freddy Heineken had connections too. Conveniently, the right-wing liberal brewer who became a Chevalier de la Légion d'Honneur in 1983, counted himself among the coterie of François Mitterrand, the Socialist president. The magnate's Paris apartment was only a stone's throw from the Elysée Palace. Nevertheless, to justify further Dutch intrusion into the French beer market, Freddy had to combine diplomatic massaging with thinly veiled threats. He remarked aloud that Heineken's French operations were still making a loss, despite cost-cutting and investments of about Ffr 700 million since 1975. So unless it solidified its French base, the company might have to start importing Heineken from the Netherlands again. *Le Nouvel Economiste* estimated that this would cost the French economy an annual Ffr 200 million in currency income, as well as about 200 Alsatian jobs. Heineken further pledged that

BGI's African activities (the 7 million hectolitres of the famous "33" brand sold annually in several French-speaking countries) would be excluded from the deal.

The UdB-Pelforth takeover was eventually cleared just before Mitterand paid a state visit to the Netherlands in March 1984. With a 51 per cent share, Heineken owned the merged company, which was renamed Société Générale de Brasserie (Sogebra). The acquisition extended Heineken's range of French 'blondes' (Pelican and "33") and also added the Pelforth ale and the amber lager George Killian's to their range. Heineken still lagged behind Riboud's Kronenbourg, which held roughly half of the market, but with its slice of about 25 per cent it had inched much closer.

While Heineken was pursuing this deal, it was also cleaning up its local brewing operations. It unleashed even more Alsatian fury by unveiling a second round of cut-backs, which included the closure of the Mutzig brewery, the last one left in the Lower Rhine region. Shopkeepers in the picturesque village closed their stores in a gesture of solidarity when the old brewery's workers took to the streets in a silent protest march in October 1987. In a last-ditch effort to reverse the decision radical trade unionists even called for divine intervention. They asked Monseigneur Brandt, the archbishop of Strasbourg, to get Freddy on side, as it was known that the two sometimes played cards together in the south of France with Prince Rainier of Monaco. But those prayers fell on deaf ears. The historic Mützig plant was eventually closed down in January 1990.

The Dutch deemed the pruning unavoidable, as they needed to draw more than a decade of losses to an end. The Mützig shutdown was part of a restructuring package in which Heineken said it invested about Ffr 1.6 billion. By the end of the decade the operation was complete and Heineken had full control of its French activities. It had cleaned up its large brands portfolio and reduced its operations to three modernised breweries in Schiltigheim, Marseille and Mons-en-Baroeul, in the north of France. Once this restructuring was complete, the French group was regarded as one of Heineken's most profitable, mostly owing to the structure of the market. According to one of the beer industry's adages, you can only start making interesting profits in a market when 60 per cent of it is dominated by no more than three players: Kronenbourg, Heineken and Stella Artois in this case.

It had taken Heineken more than two decades to reach this position in France. Heineken's advance towards the Mediterranean would be even more complicated in Spain, which in the 1980s was one of Europe's most effervescent markets. It was there that Freddy Heineken refined his branding strategy with a daring marketing trick.

Alberto Comenge was already in his seventies when he shook hands with Freddy Heineken in Madrid in 1984, having signed an agreement that allowed the Dutch to take a stake in El Águila ('The Eagle'). A former captain in Franco's troops, Comenge had been at the helm of the Madrid-based brewery ever since the end of the Spanish Civil War. Originally a chemist, he was more or less parachuted into the role by the Franco regime. It helped that he was married to the daughter of one of the brewery's founders.

Situated in the south of the capital, in the '80s the brewery's head offices still bore the pockmarks of Civil War bullets. Yet under Comenge's leadership El Águila had emerged as the most powerful player in the Spanish beer industry. Its sales had grown from about 200,000 hectolitres per year upon Comenge's arrival in the 1940s to some 7.5 million in the early '80s. El Águila was not only the best-selling Spanish brewery, with a market share of more than 20 per cent, but it also had the country's one and only truly national beer brand – a frothy version of Franco's ambition.

According to his eldest son, Alberto Comenge Jr, 'El Jefe' commanded enormous respect at El Águila. 'My father was so charismatic that he could easily ask employees to work longer hours for less money', claimed Alberto Jr. The late Comenge made a fortune in the process, which he invested in the brewery and property. In the mid-'70s, however, he took out a loan with two banks to finance the construction of another brewing plant in Valencia. Interest rates then soared to such heights that El Águila sank into a deep financial quagmire. El Águila was therefore unable to invest in the upgrading of its brewing plants, which was clear for all to taste. Pressed by the two banks, which also held stakes in the brewery, and crippled by its debt of about 11 billion pesetas, the brewery threw itself on the market.

Heineken had already tried its luck in the Spanish market several decades earlier, when it teamed up with Unilever to build a brewery in Burgos. The project had been initiated in the mid-'60s, when Heineken was looking for alternative markets to compensate for the difficulties it was facing in Africa. Both Heineken and Unilever regarded Spain as a 'semi-African' country: with its hot climate and booming economy, it seemed the perfect location for a repeat of the two companies' successful joint venture in Nigeria. So they set up the Compañía Hispano-Holandesa de Cervezas, together with a local bank.

After several trials it was decided to test the market with a standard brand called Gulder. But only two years later

Heineken and Unilever were forced into a humiliating retreat. 'The entire plan was torpedoed by a hostile campaign from Spanish brewers and wholesalers who resented the interference of foreign players', said a source at Heineken's international department. At the same time, he admitted that Heineken and Unilever shot themselves in the foot with their short-sighted approach. 'The site for the brewery, in the north of Spain, was chosen largely on the back of favourable fiscal arrangements, rather than commercial arguments', he said. 'This in itself was a recipe for disaster.'

This flop was still fresh in Heineken's memory when a London merchant bank invited the Dutch to take a look at El Águila in the early days of 1983. By that time, annual beer consumption in Spain had rocketed from a paltry 3 litres per head in the early '50s to over 50 litres in the late '70s, and it looked likely to increase for several decades to come. Spain was also preparing to join the European Union in 1986. Heineken, which had set its sights on becoming the market leader in Europe, could hardly afford to stay away.

A complete team of Dutch technicians and marketers scoured the country to examine El Águila's position and the prospects for Spain's beer market. These investigations turned up a string of decrepit brewing plants – in Cartagena, El Águila even had vessels that dated from the '20s. But they also confirmed that El Águila was the only Spanish beer brand with national distribution. Provided Heineken poured significant investment into production, El Águila could form a solid basis for the company's Spanish expansion, the advisers concluded. In May 1984 the Dutch announced that they would acquire a 'significant minority interest' in the group.

Unlike the Alsatians, the Spanish community kept a cool head. Family shareholders and the two lending banks supported the transaction, which was valued at some 100 million guilders, during a shareholders' meeting in September 1984. The deal left Heineken with a 32 per cent share in the Spanish group. With this interest Heineken trumped Carlsberg, which was already linked with El Águila through a licensing agreement. 'Heineken came across as a much more persuasive partner than Carlsberg. It was not money. The Dutch always seemed just that little bit more eager and determined', said Alberto Comenge Jr.

Beyond the figures, El Águila's bankers and Freddy Heineken, described by Spanish newspapers as 'El Rey de la Cerveza', had come to another very firm agreement. Although it was still a minority shareholder, Heineken should be allowed to take immediate control of El Águila's management. This was in urgent need of rejuvenation: El Águila's *consejo*, a Spanish-style combination of an executive and supervisory board, was even more timeworn than the company's brewing plants. One of Heineken's envoys used the term 'gerontocracy' to describe it – a fitting term, considering that most members were well into their sixties and a number were in their eighties.

By far the most urgent task for Heineken was to redress El Águila's balance sheet and to upgrade its breweries. Although Heineken's investigators had been unequivocal in their warnings, things turned out to be even more horrifying by Heineken's standards. Each of the seven breweries was producing a different El Águila beer; the master brewers more or less dictated the company's commercial policies; and the general managers marketed the beer as they pleased in their own region. 'The set-up was completely alien to us', sighed Kees van Es, a Spanish-speaking employee of Heineken's legal department who acted as an intermediary between the Spaniards and the Dutch. Heineken went on to sack a string of brewery directors and close down three of the company's seven brewing plants, in Mérida, Cartagena and Alicante.

They provoked the rage of many other El Águila veterans when they replaced the company's three speciality brands with another beer, called Adlerbrau. Local managers howled that this was an absurdity: the name could never roll off a Spaniard's tongue. Javier Posada, the mastermind behind Águila Imperial, one of the three sacrificed specialties, was particularly bitter about the switch. 'Heineken basically killed a premium brand that was selling well to replace it with something monstrous. It didn't have a chance', he said. 'Coming from Heineken, whom we trusted as superior marketing people, this seemed an incredible blunder.' For all the emotional background of Posada's anger, he was right: although Heineken supported Adlerbrau with very costly commercials, the brew did so badly that it had to be withdrawn from the market. El Águila also gradually lost market share in the mid-'80s, especially in the regions where Heineken had closed down breweries.

In the meantime the Spanish beer market had turned into a prime European battleground for international brewers, drawing large-scale investments from Guinness and BSN, among others. Throughout the 1980s, annual beer consumption grew by an average of 4 per cent year on year, peaking at 72 litres in 1990. By then Spain had become Europe's third-largest beer market, after Germany and the United Kingdom, with a production that year of more than 27.3 million hectolitres.

To try to stem increasing losses, Heineken got rid of another two brewing plants. Simultaneously, they mooted yet another marketing offensive, known as Operación Camaleón. In 1994 they pumped billions of pesetas into the market to transform the El Águila brand. The result must have looked rather odd to Dutch tourists: the beer, renamed 'Águila estilo Amstel', bore almost precisely the same label as Amstel bottles back in the Netherlands, complete with Amsterdam's coat of arms and the red-and-white semicircle.

In the early 1970s, after it swallowed Amstel, Heineken used the brand in its home market as a buffer between Heineken and lower-priced beers. But in the '90s, since Heineken regarded more or less the entire continent as its domestic market, it started to apply the same strategy in Europe: while selling the Heineken brand at the top of the market, the company could use Amstel as a Europe-wide contender in the segment for standard lagers. The effort was backed by marketing investments meant to have a Europe-wide impact, such as the sponsorship of the UEFA Champions League.

By the end of the 1980s Heineken had planted its sunshades in most European countries, and Freddy Heineken declared the company ready for the abolition of Europe's internal borders. As Freddy had planned, Heineken was strongest in the south of Europe. Alongside its interests in France and Spain, Heineken had patiently built up its business in Italy, taking more than two decades to achieve market leadership.

Heineken's investments in Italy, even more than those in France, are illustrative of its long-term approach and brand-building tactics. As a ruling proprietor, Freddy Heineken could afford to take a long-term view: he ploughed hundreds of millions of guilders into turning around and restructuring breweries and consolidations, where other breweries caved in under the pressure of shareholders' demands for immediate returns. This is exactly what occurred in Italy: when it turned out that the investment would require some nerve and improvisation, other investors got jittery, but Heineken stayed the course.

Heineken started in 1960 by acquiring a small stake in Cisalpina. Owned by the Luciani family, this company's assets included the Dreher brand and five brewing plants around the country. At the end of the decade the company was in dire need of capital to spruce up the brewing plants, and the Lucianis were eager to divest. Heineken brought Whitbread on board, and in August 1974 the two of them paid 8.4 billion Italian lire each for a 42 per cent share in Cisalpina. Although Cisalpina's finances were in a 'deplorable' state and the brewery had failed to integrate production or marketing, it still made about 2 million hectolitres that year.

When they bought their shares in Cisalpina, the Dutch made several assumptions. First, the company predicted that southern Europeans would come to appreciate beer, which turned out to be right. Italian consumption soared from about 11 litres per capita in 1968 to nearly 30 litres a decade later, owing to the increase in purchasing power and many of the societal changes that pushed lager in other parts of Europe, such as fridges and television advertising.

Second, Heineken assumed that they could improve the price structure of the market by holding talks with their competitors, as they had in other countries: in the absence of European Union officials, who went into a frenzy at the suggestion of price agreements, brewers regularly met to discuss their business. (It was even Heineken's suggestion to form the informal Opio Group, which was made up of several European brewers, and would meet at a restaurant in Hamburg or beside a swimming pool in Provence to discuss issues ranging from packaging to pricing.) A few months after the takeover Heineken reported that this had worked in Italy: the country's brewers had jointly agreed to lift their prices by no less than 35 per cent, as a means of absorbing galloping inflation. But the next year Peroni, the market leader, rejected further agreements and launched a fully fledged price war.

Peroni's aggressive approach badly upset Heineken and Whitbread's plans rapidly to restore Cisalpina. Added to this, there were unfavourable government regulations, recurrent management issues and the devaluation of the lira. Whitbread quickly decided to throw in the towel. The British brewer's shareholders were more interested in building up Whitbread's business in their own country's soaring lager market. Heineken held firm, seeing through several rounds of closures and brand adjustments, until their Italian business was exactly as they wanted, with a couple of strong Italian brands, Dreher and McFarland, and then Heineken brewed in Italy from 1976. About a decade later Heineken was the second-largest brewing group in Italy behind Peroni (and in 1996, with the acquisition of Moretti, it pulled ahead).

The French, Spanish and Italian investments thus formed the tallest towers in Fortress Europe. There were a number of other attractive assets, such as the near-monopoly held by Amstel in Greece and the Murphy breweries from Cork, which were acquired in 1983 and added another shade to the company's international offering with Murphy's stout. However, next to the bastion constructed by Anheuser-Busch in the United States, Freddy's fortress was a small and unstable edifice with an unsightly variety of architectural styles. The abundance of regional brands and brewing plants meant Heineken was far less efficient, with some estimating that the Dutch group's workers yielded about four times lower profits than their American counterparts. And there were still some wide-open breaches in Heineken's construction.

Tellingly, some of the European countries where the Heineken brand failed to make an impression were those with the most deeply rooted beer traditions. What made Heineken so strong in many international markets was a weakness in these countries: the Heineken brand appealed to many because it was crisp and easy to drink, but to discerning drinkers from countries with a plentiful range of succulent beers on offer, the Dutch brew was a pretty weak alternative. Asked about Heineken's failure to break through in his country's beer market, one Belgian brewer quipped: 'We already have water running from the taps.'

The same could be said for Germany. Since they had invented lager, the Germans continued to take their beers so seriously that they upheld the extra protection of medieval purity laws: the famous *Reinheitsgebot* that dictated that all beers sold in Germany should contain only barley, hops, yeast and water. Some competitors, such as Carlsberg and Stella Artois, had already made inroads by brewing special beers that matched the German requirements, but Heineken refrained from doing so. The hurdle of the purity laws was removed only in 1987, when the European Court of Justice ruled that they could not justify a ban on beer imports. The Dutch remained hesitant, arguing that the market was still too fragmented. In the early '90s, the Germans downed an average of 140 litres per capita per year, but there were over 1,200 breweries in the country, nearly all of which were regional if not local outfits (and the others were not for sale).

Yet by the end of the 1980s Freddy Heineken had beaten the pants off all his international rivals in the European beer market. When Freddy laid the foundation stone of his Fortress Europe in the Alsace, Heineken was the sixth-largest player in Europe, behind the four British leaders and Kronenbourg. Less than two decades later, the European market looked completely different, and the Heineken group controlled about 10 per cent. It was selling some 27.7 million hectolitres throughout the continent annually, compared to Kronenbourg's 18.8 million and Carlsberg's 14.6 million.

This European business would become less appealing when beer consumption started to stagnate in several large European countries, often undermined by regulatory changes designed to tackle alcohol abuse or boost the treasury's revenue. The group's market share also came under pressure in several European markets due to a growing thirst for special beers and the proliferation of craft breweries. But leadership of the European market still gave Heineken a steady stream of income for many years, supporting its expansion into faster-growing markets. By the end of the '80s Heineken had become a household name across Europe, which meant all the more headlines for the man behind the beer during the most dramatic days of his turbulent life.

9

The Kidnapping

As he did most other nights, Freddy Heineken switched off the lights on the second floor of his office and pied-à-terre, around the corner from the Heineken head offices just before seven o'clock. His personal assistant had already left, pulling the heavy door of 'The Pentagon' closed behind her, and now the thick-set tycoon emerged from the brightly lit foyer. It was nearly freezing in Amsterdam as Freddy stood in front of the building that evening, on Wednesday, 9 November 1983.

As the sixty-year-old brewer paused to locate his black Cadillac Fleetwood, four armed men rushed forward. One of them, wearing a balaclava, grabbed Heineken by the lapels of his suit jacket. 'Hey, what's going on, let go of me!' Freddy shouted, startled. The two women who had left the building with him ran away in panic after the attackers slapped them and sprayed gas into their faces. 'Ab, help me, damn it', Freddy screamed at his chauffeur.

The heavy brewer struggled, but two of the thugs had him firmly under the armpits and pushed a motorcycle helmet over his head, slightly scratching him because the gangsters had under-estimated the size of his head. Then they hauled him across the street, his knees dragging on the pavement, and into the back of an orange Renault van which had been parked outside the office about an hour earlier.

Ab Doderer, the tycoon's fifty-seven-year-old chauffeur, was smoking a cigar near the car when he heard the screams. But as he sprang to rescue his boss, Doderer himself was assaulted by two bulky men, wearing weird wigs and false moustaches. They pulled the chauffeur into the van as well. 'Mitkommen, schnell', one of the gangsters commanded in German, threatening the driver with a pistol. Doderer was hit on the head as he struggled against his assailants. With the back doors still open and the two victims lying face down on the floor, the van screeched off.

One of the kidnappers later said that, as the Renault veered towards the Frederiksplein, Freddy Heineken offered to buy his freedom with a cheque. This time, however, the power of the brewer's chequebook was not only useless – it was the very cause of the gruelling ordeal towards which he was heading. Heineken and his chauffeur would spend the next three weeks chained to the walls of two damp, concrete cells, in constant fear for their lives.

For once, Freddy Heineken, the man who had built the world's best-known brewing empire on the strength of his shrewdness and wit, was utterly defenceless. 'The powerlessness, you know. That was so awful, that I could not do anything about it', he said, in the evasive, laconic style that characterised his response to the abduction in later years.

Although the Dutch public had been shocked by two other kidnappings in the late 1970s and early '80s, the abduction of the popular Freddy Heineken aroused unprecedented disgust at the cowardly crime, and heartfelt sympathy for its victims. It appeared that the entire country held its breath as police struggled to outwit the kidnappers, five ingenious Amsterdam criminals.

●

Over the years he worked at Heineken, Willem Holleeder senior's devotion to his employer, Freddy Heineken, developed pathological traits. According to one former corporate source, Holleeder was 'at Freddy's feet'. In *De Ontvoering van Alfred Heineken*, the best-selling story of the kidnapping written by the Dutch crime reporter Peter R. de Vries, the kidnapper Cornelis van Hout said of Holleeder Sr: 'He was permanently occupied with Heineken. He could not talk about anything else, except for his doves. You could really drive him mad, for example, by walking into his home wearing a Grolsch cap.'

Holleeder had joined Hoppe, the distilled drinks company, after a successful cycling career. When Hoppe was bought by Heineken in the early '70s, he moved to the brewery's 'publicity service' as a driver of promotional vehicles. As a result, the employee's son, Willem Holleeder Jr, was allowed to hang around the garage of the breweries on the Ruysdaelkade with his young friend Cornelis van Hout. The two teenagers often went into raptures over Freddy's car, a green Mercedes 350 SE.

When Heineken swallowed up Amstel in 1968, Holleeder Sr staunchly refused to drive promotional vehicles bearing the Amstel logo. On the eve of the start of the Amstel Gold race, a well-known Dutch cycling event, he drove around the Rembrandt Square in Amsterdam in the early hours of the morning in a Heineken truck, destroying the Amstel banner that hung above the departure line. It was said that Freddy Heineken twice bailed Holleeder Sr out of police custody, when he was caught destroying advertising material belonging to competing breweries. This sort of behaviour didn't stop Heineken from using Holleeder Sr for security purposes.

According to Van Hout, Holleeder Sr gradually became 'unruly, physically violent and out of touch with reality'. His son observed how his father's latent alcoholism broke up the home, and resolved never to touch a drop of alcohol. He made few efforts to hide his resentment towards the Heineken breweries. 'To make matters worse, his father, who had become difficult to deal with due to his heavy drinking, was suddenly sacked by Heineken after forty years of loyal services', Van Hout told the reporter De Vries. So when Van Hout came up with a plan to kidnap a leading Dutch industrialist and presented a selection of four potential victims (Wisse Dekker, Philips chairman; Piet van Doorne, DAF chairman; Alfred Heineken; and an unnamed banker), Holleeder responded without hesitation. He wanted to catch the brewer.

As the police soon discovered in November 1983, the abduction was not an impulsive act of revenge; it had been meticulously prepared. The kidnappers had been working on it for nearly two years, pouring countless evenings and many thousands of guilders into the planning. Cornelis van Hout, later described as the 'brains' behind the kidnapping, said the plan stemmed from a New Year's resolution made in the early hours of 1 January 1982, when a group of former schoolfriends gathered in Amsterdam. The meeting was a tradition the young men had cultivated for several years: it was a celebration of their friendship, a mafia-style, secret get-together to evaluate the events of the previous year and talk of plans for the next twelve months.

The leader of the gang said that the idea of abducting Heineken was inspired partly by the kidnapping of Maurits 'Maup' Caransa, a wealthy Amsterdam property dealer who was freed in October 1977 after his family paid a ransom of 10 million guilders to his Italian kidnappers. For Van Hout the Caransa case was proof that such a crime could be carried out in the Netherlands – only Van Hout and his friends wanted to do it much better, and much bigger.

Those present at the New Year's meeting had grown up together, playing truant and refining their punching skills at the gym. The gang was composed of: Van Hout, who went by the name of 'Flipper'; Frans Meijer, a somewhat erratic, dark-haired man known as 'Stekel' ('Spikes') because of his crew-cut; Jan Boellaard, a pot-bellied, married man known as 'De Poes' ('The Cat'), because he always tilted his head sideways when he was listening carefully; and Willem Holleeder Jr, the brother of Van Hout's girlfriend Sonja, known as 'De Neus' ('The Nose').

In his conversations with the reporter De Vries, Van Hout painted a picture of four gutsy, fun-loving lads who hadn't always resisted the temptation to break the law, but who had built up a profitable business in construction and property. The money started streaming in when they set up Epan B.V., which became a successful Amsterdam building firm. In the early '80s Van Hout and his mates owned several apartment blocks in Amsterdam. They drove around in flashy cars and even acquired racehorses, one of which, the mare Varinsja, won some prestigious races.

Van Hout, the apparent gang leader, had only had one run-in with the law. Together with three partners, he had tried to evict squatters from one of his properties in the centre of Amsterdam, on the Leidsegracht. He was locked up for four days. Holleeder had run into trouble with the police too. He was arrested for providing illegal employment services in the building industry.

Several police officers who were closely involved, however, believe that the construction and property companies were nothing more than a cover for activities of an even more brutal nature. They alleged the gang was responsible for a string of ten hitherto unsolved armed hold-ups in Amsterdam in the late

'70s and early '80s, which together brought in about 7 million guilders.

One former Amsterdam policeman, Paul van Hove, battled for many years to charge the kidnappers in relation to a frantic shooting incident that took place in October 1977. During a wild chase through the streets of Amsterdam 146 shots had been fired at Van Hove and his partner, some of them at close range. It was a miracle that Van Hove escaped alive, and many years later the shoot-out still caused him sleepless nights. When he saw the pictures of the Heineken kidnappers, he immediately identified them as his attackers.

The kidnappers said they had a budget of about 150,000 Dutch guilders for 'Operatie Heintje', as they called the scheme to abduct Heineken. They had decided that they would detain Heineken in the warehouse of a construction company run by Jan Boellaard, called Jadu BV. It was a 42-metre-long, almost empty storage space attached to the offices of Boellaard's building company in De Heining, an industrial site in the western port district of the capital.

In November 1982 the gang's preparations were seriously disturbed by the kidnapping of Toos van der Valk, the wife of a Dutch motel tycoon. It concluded relatively happily, with the payment of 12.5 million guilders to the Italian kidnappers and the release of Mrs Van der Valk, but the four decided to lie low, suspecting that police would be especially vigilant.

They continued to observe Freddy Heineken through the spring of 1983. Almost daily, Meijer watched the road leading to the entrance of Heineken's villa in Noordwijk. Meanwhile, Van Hout recruited his half-brother Martin Erkamps to steal cars for the abduction. The twenty-year-old was not an equal partner with the others. On the whole, he carried out the 'menial' tasks, for which he said he was offered 1 million guilders.

'Operatie Heintje' really started taking shape in the summer of 1983, when Van Hout and his three partners built two concrete cells at the back of De Heining. By September the kidnappers had all they needed: six stolen cars, one revolver Colt Python 357 Magnum calibre, two 9 mm FN pistols, one 9 mm Walther pistol and two Uzi machine guns, as well as an entire arsenal of communications equipment, wigs, paper, a typewriter and other items they had purchased in Germany to confuse the police. To practise with the guns, they often went to the Osdorp Shooting Club. Of course, Uzis were strictly forbidden at the club, but it was easy to smuggle them into the practice grounds, because Jan Boellaard was a sort of honorary member. An extremely sharp shooter, he sometimes turned up there in full cowboy gear.

With the help of young Erkamps, the four meant to capture Heineken one morning, as he drove from Noordwijk to his Amsterdam office. One car would force the Cadillac to a halt by suddenly veering into the road, while another was meant to sandwich the vehicle by bumping into its rear. Heineken and Doderer would then be bundled into one of the abductors' cars and driven to De Heining.

For four mornings in September, De Vries wrote, all of them got up in the early hours and drove to Noordwijk. Freezing for hours in their cars, or hiding behind bushes, they waited for Freddy's Cadillac. Four times Freddy escaped – he apparently spent those nights away from home. But the brewer's luck ran out on 9 November.

Superintendent Gert van Beek says he already knows the last words he will utter on his death-bed. 'The meadow is green for the hare', the coded message placed in the classified ads pages of Dutch newspapers, at the request of Freddy Heineken's kidnappers, is engraved deep into the officer's conscience. It came to symbolise the exhausting battle of wits waged over three weeks by the four shrewd gangsters and the fifty-strong team of the Amsterdam police force, led by superintendents Van Beek anad Kees Sietsma.

In this message, which was meant to indicate that the ransom was ready, the police were 'The Hare', while the kidnappers called themselves 'The Eagle'. The choice of code names was an extra psychological pique. 'The most nerve-racking aspect of such a cowardly crime is that you never know where or when the opponent will move', said Van Beek. 'It was like a long game of chess with two human lives at stake.'

The code names 'The Hare' and 'The Eagle' were communicated in a letter addressed to 'the Heineken family' that was delivered to a small police station in The Hague about an hour and a half after the kidnapping. Lucille Heineken and her daughter Charlene, who had just married the banker Michel de Carvalho in a discreet ceremony in Switzerland, immediately entrusted the negotiations to the Amsterdam police. They designated Rob van de Vijver, the legal expert of Heineken's executive board and Freddy's former private lawyer, to represent the family's interests in police meetings.

The envelope contained two proofs of authenticity: Freddy's wrist-watch and Doderer's passport, as well as the letter in which the abductors demanded the equivalent of 34.6 million guilders (about €15.7 million), to be paid in four currencies. It was a ransom of unprecedented proportions in the Netherlands, yet the criminals thought the amount, which they estimated at about 2 per cent of Freddy Heineken's total wealth, was 'reasonable'.

Two thousand bundles of Dutch guilders, French francs,

German Deutschmarks and American dollars were to be stuffed into five Dutch postal sacks – weighing about 400 kilograms in total. Then, the kidnappers wrote, the sacks should be taken to De Ark, Freddy Heineken's villa in Noordwijk, and loaded into a white Volkswagen van with two red crosses painted on the sides. And then, within three days of the preparations being completed, the negotiators would warn the kidnappers with the 'meadow' message in the 'Congratulations' column of *De Telegraaf*'s classified ads.

In one sense, the letter was reassuring for the police and Freddy's friends, as it indicated that the kidnapping was motivated by money, rather than politics. They realised it would be easier to deal with greedy gangsters than with extreme left-wing groups such as the German Red Army Faction, which was believed to have listed Heineken as one of its potential targets. Freddy himself pondered this possibility. 'The scary uncertainty at a moment like that is: am I dealing with reasonable men who just want money, or is it – bang bang – the Red Army Faction? It was somewhere in between', he told *NRC Handelsblad*.

The Amsterdam police had a full investigation team set up in its headquarters on the Elandsgracht just a few hours after the abduction. A group of detectives knocked on every door near the brewer's office. They questioned the two women who had left The Pentagon with Freddy, as well as Freddie Wuyts, the taxi driver who had alerted the police.

With a passenger in the back, Wuyts had briefly chased the kidnappers in their orange Renault van, following it over the River Amstel. To his surprise, the kidnappers then turned right, into a tunnel normally reserved for cyclists. Planning ahead, the kidnappers had removed the bollards that blocked access for cars. At this point the taxi driver went into reverse and dived under his dashboard as one of the kidnappers jumped out of the van and pointed a gun at him. Still, he was close enough to testify that, at the other end of the tunnel, both Doderer and Heineken had been bundled into a white Citroën GS. They left the Renault van behind, with bloodstains where the injured Doderer had been, a bag with the Uzis, to suggest that the kidnappers were heavily armed, and a pair of broken glasses.

As the kidnappers had made known that they would get in touch via Heineken's personal phone line at De Ark, it was guarded permanently. Freddy's secretary, Elly van Gaans, was to pick up the phone and keep the kidnappers talking as long as possible. Four months earlier, she had pluckily dealt with a blackmailer who had poisoned cans of Heineken with digoxine, a medicine for heart patients. This time Van Gaans was coached by Hans Kazemier, a police officer trained in psychology, as well as the Briton Peter Cheney, from the specialist firm Control Risks Group. A tap was swiftly installed in the Noordwijk telephone exchange so that the conversations could be heard live in the police headquarters.

As for the kidnappers, they were having a ball. Everything had gone according to plan, so less than two hours after the kidnapping they were buying rounds in well-known Amsterdam bars. Both hostages had been stripped and left behind at the warehouse in De Heining in their socks and underpants. 'A pity, because it was a fine suit', Heineken later told police. He had been wearing a grey suit, with Cartier cufflinks and a blue Hermès tie. Doderer's shirt was ripped off his chest so violently that he later found the buttons on the floor. It was only the next morning, on Thursday, 10 November, that the kidnappers returned to De Heining with beige pyjamas for their captives, and to tell them their fate.

In a little note the kidnappers asked Freddy whether he would prefer the ransom to be paid from his personal account or the brewery's (he opted for the company), and they gave him the stalk of a biro so that he could write a letter himself. Freddy bemused the kidnappers by requesting a whole list of items: 'A dressing gown, slippers, shaving equipment, a comb, a mirror, another pair of glasses, a simple clock, a desk and a decent chair.' According to De Vries's book, Freddy also wrote a short and rather cryptic letter to his wife, which the kidnappers burned: 'Dear Lucille, this is Fred Emmer. Everything's fine. It's only about money. No politics. I'll be home very soon.'

If Freddy really wrote that he was fine, he was slightly overstating the case. After he had been thrown into his cell on Wednesday evening, the brewer briefly passed out. His left wrist was tied with a pair of handcuffs, cemented into the wall of the bunker with a heavy, 40-centimetre chain which was so tight he could only sleep on one side. 'I thought it was a shipping chain, I licked it to check whether there was any salt on it', he said afterwards. Twice he succeeded in freeing his wrist from the handcuff, using fatty juice from meals. And ingeniously, he placed a piece of cardboard from a toilet roll on the inside of the handcuffs to stop them digging into his wrists.

Each cell was equipped with a chemical toilet, which was placed next to the pillow, and a bare mattress. 'I could talk about that dirty mattress for hours on end. Degrading', Freddy told police after his release. At first he only had one thin blanket. 'Later I asked for another blanket and I obtained a good one. It saved my life.' The cell was so humid that condensation trickled down the walls, making the brewer's socks wet.

Heineken had to wear those soaked, smelly socks for three weeks. He used a broken plastic fork to comb his hair. Sometimes he was given a bucket of fresh, warm water to wash his face, and he persuaded the kidnappers to let him brush his teeth after meals. Both detainees were fed twice a day, with four sandwiches early in the morning and a warm meal around seven o'clock in the evening, but they attempted to spread this food through the day and night. 'I kept one of the sandwiches that I got in the evening to eat at night', said Freddy. 'I hid it under my wet mattress and then at night I ate the disgusting, soaked piece of bread.'

Perhaps the most torturous element of the detention in the early days was the auto-reverse tape which the kidnappers played in the cells through loudspeakers. The tunes echoed in the bunkers from morning until evening. Heineken compared this to Chinese water torture, which involves a leaking tap that drips on to the victim's forehead. In response to the brewer's pleas, the kidnappers later switched to Radio Caroline, which broadcast little news but at least helped Heineken to keep better track of time during the day.

The kidnappers left a few second-hand books in the cell, and Doderer was given a pack of cards to play patience with, but the cell was so damp that, after a few days, the cards became too sodden to shuffle. One of Freddy's worst fears, he later told police, was that the thin pipe which let air into the cell would get blocked. He tried to make a small conduit for himself by sticking together the straws he got from the kidnappers with his drinks. Doderer's nightmares were equally chilling: he feared that the small hole in the ceiling would be used to gas him, and that the door might be booby-trapped, because he spotted two wires that led to square black boxes on the ceiling.

The two victims were not guarded continually. The kidnappers only turned up at De Heining for meetings, messages and meals, but they could hear what was happening in the cells through a baby monitor: the transmitter was placed in the cells and the receiver in a caravan, stationed somewhere else in the warehouse. It was Martin Erkamps, Van Hout's half-brother, who attended to the two detainees, wearing blue overalls, socks and a balaclava. He was sometimes aided by Frans Meijer, who hopped around like a frog to conceal his tall stature.

Erkamps was instructed not to speak to the victims. He communicated with them only through written messages and sign language. Still, especially in the first days, Heineken often attempted to make contact with Erkamps in German and English. Van Hout said Heineken once even tried to bribe the young man. 'Listen, if you free me or tell the police where we are, we'll share the ransom. Then I'll hire you to work at my house in Switzerland', he was quoted as saying. But Freddy's appeals fell on deaf ears. 'I tried to joke with them, but those silly buggers didn't even understand', he said long afterwards. Erkamps's response was so mute that Freddy suspected his guard was a foreigner, perhaps a German or a Yugoslav.

Freddy was most annoyed when the kidnappers came to take his picture on Saturday, 12 November, holding that day's edition of *De Telegraaf*. Publicity-conscious even during his captivity, the tycoon protested: he feared that the pictures showing him dirty and unshaven would be printed in the newspapers.

Ab Doderer was forced to read a message on a tape recorder, and in the evening the tape was phoned through to Noordwijk, telling the police to pick up the pictures and further instructions in locker 2150 at Utrecht Central Station. Even though Doderer's family were staying in Heineken's villa, after their flat had been besieged by the press, the negotiators failed to identify Doderer's voice. It was only on Sunday, 13 November, four days after their abduction, that Freddy Heineken and Ab Doderer found out they were being detained side by side. The kidnappers would open the doors to the cells for brief periods to allow the two to converse. Freddy joked at first, asking his chauffeur: 'Ab, what are you doing here? How can it be? You don't have any money at all!' and 'Well, never mind, Ab, I'll still pay your wages for these lost days.'

During those conversations, which usually lasted about five minutes, Heineken clearly appeared the more composed of the two. Even the kidnappers were impressed by Freddy's coolness, and the dignity and good humour he displayed in the face of his ordeal. 'He really had personality this chap, the skills of a psychologist', Van Hout was quoted as saying in *De ontvoering van Alfred Heineken*. When the kidnappers asked him what he wanted to eat, he wrote down a whole menu, with many courses and delicacies. Then at the bottom of the little sheet, he noted dryly: 'And if that is not possible, a boiled egg will do just fine.'

Doderer later told police that he suffered a nervous breakdown during his captivity. Twice he collapsed and cried on Erkamps's shoulder. 'Doderer always played a subservient role, so we thought he might be able to cope with the situation better than his boss', said Superintendent Van Beek. 'But this theory was entirely contradicted in Heineken's case. He was tremendously composed and level-headed.' Then again, perhaps Doderer feared he would be killed first if the negotiations went wrong in the kidnappers' eyes – as they did.

The money was never an issue. Although Rob van de Vijver knew first-hand of Freddy's aversion to needless expense, he never attempted to negotiate the price of his boss's freedom. The problem for the police was that an enormous press corps had set up base in front of Heineken's villa, and the kidnappers had demanded that Heineken's envoy should use a white van with two red crosses painted on the side to hand over the ransom. There was no chance it could leave Noordwijk without a pack of journalists trailing behind it.

So when the kidnappers phoned Noordwijk on Tuesday 15th, instructing the car to depart, the police were unable to comply. Elly van Gaans tried desperately to make contact with 'The Eagle'. She shouted throughout the taped message, to make it clear to the kidnappers that, for practical reasons, their demands could not be met. As recorded by police, it ran: 'Hello. This is The Eagle … Hello, listen to me … a message for The Hare …, this is very important, for heaven's sake listen to me …, with the white van in the …, we want to pay the ransom …, with the ransom … Listen to me. This is important …'

But the kidnappers hung up as soon as the tape ended and returned to Willem Holleeder's flat, on the fifteenth floor of an apartment block overlooking the motorway from Amsterdam to North Holland. If the van left Noordwijk immediately and followed the instructed route, they would be able to spot it on the road with binoculars. For the next few hours the kidnappers thought they could relax. To confuse the police and to tire out the driver of the white van, they had prepared an intricate route that would take the driver on a five-hour tour of the Netherlands, with instructions hidden in plastic beakers they had buried by the roadside.

Although the kidnappers did not see the van, they drove to the spot under a flyover on the motorway near Utrecht where the ransom was to be handed over in the early hours of the morning. As the police admitted, the plan was very cleverly thought out. As instructed in one of the kidnappers' last messages, the driver would have switched cars. He would be seated in a conspicuous blue Citroën GS, with a wheelbarrow on the roof and a walkie-talkie on the passenger's seat, heading towards Arnhem.

Long before he reached this destination, however, he would hear a message on the walkie-talkie. The kidnappers would instruct him to pull over on top of a flyover, in a spot that had been marked in advance by red traffic cones. Then the driver would let the sacks of banknotes glide down a water conduit from where they would fall into the boot of the kidnappers' Mercedes Hanomag pick-up, allowing the criminals to drive away fast, unseen and a lot richer.

The kidnappers had expected the driver to arrive at around seven o'clock, but they returned to De Heining that morning at around nine, empty-handed. Nothing had happened. They were incensed and puzzled: it seemed incredible that the police would gamble with the detainees' lives by ignoring the instructions. Van Hout said that, informed about the delay, Freddy Heineken lost his composure at last. 'Well damn it', he was quoted as saying. 'I'm the boss. Me and nobody else. Give me a pen and a piece of paper! They're all fired. All of them. I'm giving them the boot. What do they think they're doing? ... Have they gone completely mad?'

In a written message Heineken was asked what could possibly have messed up the negotiations – such as a special insurance policy. 'I'm a businessman, not a hero. There is no scenario. No notary', Freddy told the kidnappers. And he instructed them to get in touch with Gé van Schaik, vice-president of the management board, at his home in Wassenaar.

Perhaps the pressure was highest for the police negotiators in this second week. For six days the kidnappers showed not the faintest sign of life. Suspecting that the police had driven the first route, to end up in Arnhem, they prepared another, even more complicated, treasure hunt.

The negotiators on the other side placed several small ads in *De Telegraaf*, urging the kidnappers to get in touch. To dodge the press, they wanted another point of departure. They also wanted to make sure the ransom would guarantee the freedom of both detainees. And, perhaps to put pressure on their opponents, they insisted that the van carrying the ransom should be driven by two chauffeurs.

All they got, however, was a couple of gruesome pictures. Both Freddy Heineken and Ab Doderer were photographed with a bandaged arm, to suggest that some of their fingers had been cut off, and a noose around their neck. 'Collaborate and look pitiful. Your hand is wounded, it must look that way', Heineken was told. 'If you refuse to collaborate, we'll make sure you're really wounded.' Freddy counted himself lucky that the bandage was fake, but he complained that he wanted to comb his hair and angrily snapped at Meijer, the impatient photographer.

Freddy was unshaven again, and his eyes looked frighteningly hollow. Yet those morbid pictures did not have the intended effect. 'We made it clear to Mrs Heineken that it was pure intimidation', said Kees Sietsma, head of the police team. 'In fact the picture stimulated us. Heineken was definitely all there, lucid and combative. You could see that he could have eaten these boys alive.'

Over these tense days, the team in De Ark did commit one amateurish mistake. Notes scribbled by Peter Cheney, the British expert from Control Risks, were inadvertently thrown in a waste paper basket. The bin bags were then put out on the pavement as usual. But when the waste disposal truck arrived in front of De Ark the next morning, the papers had gone: Peter R. de Vries, the crime reporter, had got hold of them and was patiently gluing the bits back together. The police had been struggling to keep the abduction out of the news, which was one of the kidnappers' demands, and De Vries's interference was, as Van Beek pointed out, 'rather disturbing'. De Vries had evidence that negotiations were taking place. To keep the story from being published, the police had to promise him an exclusive interview with the team leaders after the case had been resolved.

The news that did emerge about the kidnapping as it unfolded was extremely thin, because unusually the Amsterdam police had imposed a blackout. This state of affairs was captured accurately by a headline printed in the Dutch daily *De Waarheid*, which read: 'Heineken kidnapping: no news.' Few Heineken employees apart from Van de Vijver and Van Schaik knew about the negotiations. The breweries continued to operate as normal, although many office employees suddenly started bringing radios to work.

At last on Sunday, 27 November, about two and a half weeks after the abduction, the practical problems of paying the ransom were cleared up. Heineken's negotiators placed a small ad in the Amsterdam daily *Het Parool*, as instructed, to indicate that they were ready. The kidnappers' final taped message to the police was read by Freddy Heineken (Doderer had become too nervous at this stage) and played to Van Schaik over the telephone. This time it had been agreed that the 34.6 million would cover both detainees, and that the driver (one single person) would set off from the vice-president's home. 'Yes, I understand the instructions and we are ready to go', Van Schaik said. This time, the kidnappers thought, nothing could go wrong.

For several years Ed van Kerkhof, a detective with the

Amsterdam serious crime squad, had been racking his brains over a series of unsolved armed raids in Amsterdam. Van Kerkhof and his men were so preoccupied with solving these hold-ups that they had come to call the clever, violent criminals behind them 'our robbers'. When he heard a description of the kidnappers, the detective immediately thought they could be the people he was looking for.

For the next two weeks Van Kerkhof and about fifteen other detectives set to work in a systematic manner, ploughing through hundreds of files and shadowing scores of criminal groups known to the police. 'My team virtually drew a map of the Dutch criminal world', he said. They followed up the most bizarre tips, including one from 'a sheriff in the American Far West who reported that somebody had seen Freddy Heineken in his dreams'.

As the kidnappers had intended, the detectives wasted days investigating false leads, such as the broken glasses they found in the Renault van. Traces of skin and hair stuck to the frame were examined at the police laboratory, while detectives visited scores of opticians. To no effect, of course: the glasses belonged to the owner of one of the cars the kidnappers had stolen. The German make of most of the accessories, from the paper to the ribbon in the typewriter, effectively threw the police off the scent. And what the detectives really wanted – fingerprints – they could not find.

Still, tips kept flowing in. Number 547 reached the Elandsgracht on Wednesday, 16 November, exactly a week after the kidnapping. It consisted of a simple typed letter, which hinted that a group of criminals unknown to the police might be the kidnappers. 'Number 547' was registered only two days after its receipt and was checked out a week later. Three days later, all other running investigations were dropped.

Following this lead, undercover agents found themselves trailing the kidnappers as they prepared the second run. Messages in the beakers buried along the route contained new passwords, which made the criminals' identity as the kidnappers incontrovertible: 'The Owl' for the kidnappers, and 'The Mouse' for the driver. The whole operation was carried out with extreme caution, as the smallest mistake would endanger Heineken and Doderer's lives. Patiently, however, they built up a solid case.

Permanent surveillance led them to the kidnappers' addresses, and they came close enough to the warehouse to ascertain that human beings were detained there. Sietsma and Van Beek were ultimately convinced that 547 was the golden tip when, on the evening of Sunday, 27 November, detectives saw the kidnappers enter De Heining with two portions of takeaway Chinese food.

That Sunday, as planned, the kidnappers took another set of photographs. Both Heineken and Doderer were pictured holding up an edition of the German *Sport am Sonntag*. Judging by the light in their eyes, a police expert established that the two victims were still alive. So when the kidnappers phoned Van Schaik at home late that evening, to order the departure of the van, their instructions were followed.

In the early hours of Monday morning, after a five-hour drive, the police officer selected to hand over the money was heading towards Arnhem. Undercover police cars followed from a safe distance, picking up the written messages he was throwing out of the window in empty soft drinks cans. As the kidnappers' voice crackled through the walkie-talkie, ordering the driver to stop on a flyover near Utrecht, a helicopter hovered above the scene. The sacks of banknotes glided smoothly down the water conduit. Incredibly, however, as the kidnappers fled with the money, and the gyroscope that was meant to stabilise the infra-red camera in the helicopter collapsed, so that it lost track of the kidnappers at this crucial time.

First the kidnappers buried some of the money in the forest near Zeist, in four waterproof plastic barrels; then they returned to De Heining separately and informed the two detainees that the ransom had been paid. Heineken and Doderer were told that they would be picked up at three o'clock in the morning and left in the car park of a hospital in Delft.

At that stage the kidnappers had realised they were being followed, as Van Hout told De Vries. Angry and dispirited, they met in an Amsterdam café on Tuesday morning, decided to split some of the money and to go separate ways: Jan Boellaard wanted to free Heineken himself, at any cost; Martin Erkamps stayed in Amsterdam, judging that his relatively small part in the kidnapping would not be punished too harshly; Frans Meijer went into hiding in the Netherlands; and Holleeder and Van Hout fled together, to Paris.

The negotiators had pleaded with the kidnappers to release Heineken and Doderer 'as quickly as possible'. To them, that meant about twenty-four hours after payment of the ransom. But by late Tuesday afternoon there was still no trace of the two victims. The only signs of activity at De Heining were the flashy cars parked at the front and the smoke billowing out of the warehouse's chimney as the kidnappers probably burned evidence.

The police deliberated for hours. Storming the building was an extremely hazardous operation: the detainees might not be there after all, and if they were, there might be a shoot-out. An expert examination proved the pictures of Heineken and Doderer had been taken by two different cameras, so perhaps they were held separately (this had been done deliberately). On the other hand, a specialist had warned that those last hours of uncertainty could cause immense psychological damage to the victims.

The ransom had been paid, and Heineken probably knew it, so he realised his life had become worthless, even a potential threat to the kidnappers. The psychologist was right: 'I was thinking to myself, let's pay and get out of here', Heineken later told police, 'but when I heard that the ransom had been paid and I was still there, I thought that I had become worthless and that I wouldn't make it out alive [...] That uncertainty was terrible. Once the ransom is paid, they can let you kick the bucket. I was terrified of that.'

The decision to storm De Heining was taken late on Tuesday evening, with the approval of the Dutch Justice Minister, Frits Korthals Altes. At about five o'clock the next morning, some fifteen police officers moved into position around De Heining. Two helicopters circled above the warehouse, communicating by radio with some of the team leaders. The police officers were instructed to sneak in very carefully, in the dark.

They used a vacuum cleaner to break the window of the office building attached to the warehouse, and progressed silently towards the warehouse itself. Once they reached the partition that split the warehouse, the rescuers paused briefly. If they were lucky, they would find Heineken and Doderer alone and alive behind it. But if they weren't, and the kidnappers were there too, Freddy and his driver might end up being held at gunpoint, or worse.

As it turned out, they found nothing at all. For a few dreadful seconds the police line transmitted only swearing, and cries of horror and disbelief. 'Damn it, how could that be?' Van Beek screamed, sinking desperately into his car seat. 'That's impossible, they must be there', cried an incredulous Sietsma, and scores of others bit their lips in stunned silence. 'It seemed so unreal', said Sietsma many years later, 'as if the whole world was suddenly falling apart.' The police officers had reached the end of the building. Except for a van, some loose bits of timber and scaffolding, it seemed definitely, hopelessly empty.

Until, suddenly, one of the police officers pushed gently against the timber of the wall. 'Damn it, there's another panel here', he cried. It gave way. Behind it was a small corridor, with one door on each side. The kidnappers had concealed the two cells behind a false timber wall at the back of the warehouse. As Van Beek admitted, 'it was pure luck that our officers discovered the hiding place', although it was staring them in the face. Behind the left-hand door, at 5.17 a.m., they found Ab Doderer. And behind the right-hand door, an exhausted and bewildered, but impressively alert, Freddy Heineken.

Jan Baas and Rob Neve, two detectives from the Afdeling Overvallen (Assaults Section), rushed inside. It was their task to comfort Heineken and record his statement. Despite the absence of natural light in the cells, the tycoon had noticed that the kidnappers were late. One of his worst fears had been that the thugs would be shot dead during the payment of the ransom and that police would be unable to find him and Doderer. So when the officers burst into his cell, he greeted them almost sourly. 'Could you not have come a bit earlier?' he asked. 'Heineken had a short emotional outburst but regained his composure within minutes', said Neve. 'He was unbelievably sharp and together.'

To reassure the victims that they were safe at last, Baas and Neve had brought Freddy's lucky suit and cigarettes, as well as Ab Doderer's favourite sweets. Freddy was angry to hear that three of the five leading suspects had escaped, but he never lost his cool. According to Baas, he felt well enough to tease the detectives when they drove through a red light. Ab Doderer, on the other hand, erupted in violent fits of tears when he read a short, sweet letter from his wife.

After a quick cognac and a bath in Wassenaar, in Gé van Schaik's home, Freddy was reunited with his wife and daughter in Noordwijk. Police had to smuggle him back to his own home in a van. Heineken employees, who found a green memo about the boss's release on their desk in the morning, broke off their work to watch special news bulletins. The Dutch tricolour was flying all around Noordwijk, and a small aircraft criss-crossed the skies above the resort with 'welcome home' messages. But Freddy's proudest memory of the release was a telegram from Frank Sinatra. A copy of it was pinned inside a cupboard in his office suite. 'Why didn't you call me?' The Voice asked.

Police struggled to convince Doderer that he should contribute to the investigation, because the kidnappers had made him sign a declaration that he would remain silent. 'If a man breaks his word of honour, his entire family (including his son-in-law) will be taken out by us', they warned, and Doderer was scared. Heineken, who had signed the declaration as well, deemed it worthless.

Baas and Neve, who stayed at De Ark for two days to record the brewer's fourteen-page statement, were again impressed by his energy. Only hours after his release he interrupted the interview to sort out business at the breweries and cheerfully answer royal telephone calls. In the afternoons he only stopped briefly for a light meal on a tray, which he shared with the detectives in front of the television.

Frank Lowe was another friend who called. 'I'm free, but it was pretty bad. They tortured me', Freddy Heineken said. 'That sounds awful. What did they do to you, Freddy?' Lowe inquired anxiously. 'They made me drink Carlsberg', came the reply.

FOUR GENERATIONS

Gerard Adriaan Heineken, an impassioned brewer, gave his name to a crisp lager.

Alexander de Carvalho drank in the marketing lessons from Freddy Heineken, his grandfather.

Henry Pierre Heineken (middle) would have preferred the life of a musician. He gave away the family's control of the brewery. His son Freddy (right) gutsily regained control and turned Heineken into the most desirable international beer brand. On the left is Leo van Munching, the theatrical Dutchman who flooded the United States with Heineken's green bottles.

Mother and daughter: Lucille Heineken (right) came from a family of Kentucky distillers. Freddy and Lucille's only child, Charlene Heineken (left), inherited the family's majority shares in the brewing group, becoming one of Britain's wealthiest residents.

Charlene's husband, Michel de Carvalho, is a prominent British banker. A former child actor, he also competed three times in the Winter Olympics and is pictured here on his way to Sapporo, Japan, in 1972.

The former Heineken brewery in the centre of Amsterdam that turned out the first Heineken lager. In the 1970s production gradually moved to a huge beer factory in Zoeterwoude, the largest in Europe. The historic Heineken plant in Amsterdam is now a tourist attraction.

Freddy Heineken on the opening night of a movie he produced in 1963. He
tried his hand at several other arts, from music to architecture, and
enjoyed the company of women.

A popular personality, Freddy (second from right) is surrounded by other
famous Dutchmen, such as the football player Johan Cruyff (far left) and the
banker Wim Duisenberg (right).

ROYAL CONNECTIONS

Photo: Photo De Telegraaf

Freddy Heineken (middle) said Princess Grace of Monaco (right) would just water down the soup when he turned up without notice for dinner at her residence.

Photo: Photo De Telegraaf

Sylvia Tóth (middle) spent holidays on Freddy's yacht and at his home in Cap d'Antibes. King Willem-Alexander (right), dubbed 'Prince Pils' in his student years, described Freddy as a family friend.

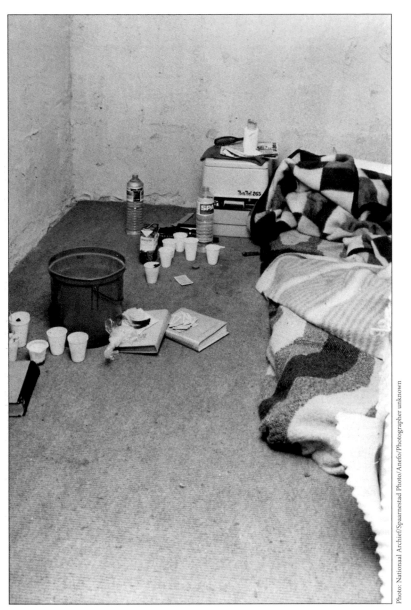

The cell in an abandoned warehouse in Amsterdam where Freddy Heineken was held for three weeks in 1983. His five captors obtained what was at the time the largest ransom ever paid for a kidnapping in Europe.

Freddy Heineken and his driver, Ab Doderer, after their release, in front of the Heinekens' villa in the beach resort of Noordwijk aan Zee. From that day Heineken was almost always accompanied by bodyguards.

Photo: Nationaal Archief/Spaarnestad Photo/Anefo

Before global advertising: Heineken was marketed in the United States (top) as an imported product with class, while an iconic advertising campaign (bottom) created a thirst for an embarrassingly weak version of Heineken in Britain.

Police eventually managed to get a statement out of Doderer, and then, two days after the happy ending of the drama, he left De Ark. Doderer would never drive for Freddy Heineken again. Police and other sources suspected he was paid generously by the Heineken breweries – partly to compensate for the trauma of the kidnapping, and partly to make sure he would not sell the sensational story to the press.

Although the 'Heineken' police team was disbanded little by little, Ab Doderer sent them a Christmas card for many years. Less discreet, Freddy Heineken treated the families of about a hundred officers to a comedy show in the Carré Theatre in Amsterdam, and he outraged many by donating half a million guilders to the capital's police force. Although the beneficiaries insisted that the gift would be used to buy the special detection equipment they had been forced to borrow during the kidnapping, the police union criticised Heineken's tactless reward. By that time, however, Freddy had already decided not to rely on police for his protection.

Els de Laat, one of the witnesses to Freddy's abduction, had reportedly known him for about ten years when he was kidnapped. As the German magazine *Stern* wrote tactfully in the aftermath of the ordeal: 'Everybody knows Els. Even Mrs Heineken knows about her.' In her statement to Amsterdam police, Els recounted a strange incident. 'About three to four weeks ago,' she said, 'Mr Heineken told me he had a dream in which he was kidnapped and held in a bare room at Schiphol airport. He knew because he could hear aeroplanes flying above. He urged me to remember this dream.'

In fact, Freddy said he had been aware of the risk posed by

kidnappers, and had conscientiously tried to protect his wife and daughter from it. On the other hand, he always refused to have his fun spoiled by an army of bodyguards. He exposed himself to risks that would have unsettled the most easy-going life insurers: he was often seen in crowded Amsterdam cafés, elbowing his way to the bar like any other punter, apparently without any protection. And on the day he was kidnapped, he had stood on the pavement unguarded, unarmed and apparently unaware. But three weeks later, on Wednesday, 30 November 1983, Freddy swore it would never happen to him again.

Immediately after his release, Heineken pleaded for clemency for the kidnappers, and especially for his carer, Martin Erkamps. 'I think that mitigating circumstances should apply to him', he told police. 'I know that all the books describe the relationship between carer and victim. But at some stage he just becomes your mother [...] It could really have been worse [...] It would have been very easy to kick me in the side, right?' But those feelings rapidly faded away. The brewer recruited around forty agents to form Proseco, a private security firm based in Katwijk. The company, a fully owned subsidiary of Heineken Holding, lured several former police officers from the Amsterdam West team that had taken part in the dawn raid on the warehouse. Proseco was set up officially in August 1984 with Arjo de Jong, a former employee of the Dutch royal family's security service, at its helm. Although the company had been created to guard the brewer and his family, it also spent a significant amount of time and considerable resources making sure that the kidnappers would not get away unpunished.

'Bingo in Amsterdam West!', the joyful cry let out by the police officers who found the hidden door to the cells, was the signal for the other teams to join in the action. They rounded up twenty-four suspects, including Martin Erkamps, Jan Boellaard and his wife, Van Hout's girlfriend, Holleeder's girlfriend, Frans Meijer's ex-wife and his girlfriend, and the accountant of the construction company based in De Heining.

Most of the money was recovered on 5 December 1983, when a (very honest) couple spotted a bundle of dollar bills while walking in the forest. The plastic barrels unearthed about seventy metres further on contained roughly 21 million guilders. The rest, about 13 million guilders, had apparently been shared among the kidnappers before they fled.

Nearly three months later, on 28 February 1984, Cor van Hout and Willem Holleeder were arrested in a cosy apartment on the rue de Penthièvre in Paris. That night, to celebrate, Freddy Heineken invited Van Beek for dinner in Sama Sebo, his favourite Indonesian restaurant in Amsterdam, along with half a dozen other policemen and Els de Laat. Van Kerkhof, one of the party, remembered the evening with a mixture of pity and contempt. When someone inquired about Freddy's 'boys', who had been waiting outside for several hours while their boss dined, the tycoon shrugged: 'They're fine, they've got their own sandwiches.' And when the owner of the restaurant said the meal was on him, on account of the good news, Freddy rubbed his hands as if he'd just concluded a million-dollar deal.

The legal battle for the extradition of Van Hout and Holleeder to the Netherlands, which lasted more than two and a half years, caused a lot of political strain. They were detained in the infamous Santé prison in Paris and in three different hotels outside the capital, under permanent surveillance from French police as well as Heineken's private agents. To get rid of the costly prisoners, the French authorities flew them off to French-controlled Caribbean islands, but this only caused more embarrassment.

The two kidnappers were chased off St Barthélémy, St Martin and Guadeloupe, narrowly escaping the wrath of hordes of residents who refused to see their islands turned into a dumping ground for France's outlaws. Even there, the kidnappers were escorted by a Proseco team, and the private surveillance turned into such a routine that Van Hout and Holleeder sometimes shared a beer with the Heineken agents. They were eventually extradited to the Netherlands in October 1986, and four months later both were sentenced to eleven years in prison (minus the time in pre-detention in France).

Arjo de Jong, the man in charge of Heineken's security, said that Van Hout wrote a letter to Freddy from his cell in the Netherlands, proposing a meeting to offer his apologies and shake the brewer's hand. De Jong said that, at Heineken's request, he went to talk to Van Hout.

Jan Boellaard had received twelve years. 'The Cat', as he was known, was released in December 1991, but just over two years later, on 2 January 1994, he was arrested again for the murder of an Amsterdam customs officer. He was released in 2007. Martin Erkamps got off more lightly, with eight years, because he helped police to construct the criminal proceedings, giving detailed accounts of his role in this process. Like Boellard, however, Van Hout's half-brother was caught again. In January 1996 he was arrested by Spanish police while transporting 300 kilograms of marijuana. Then aged thirty-two, Erkamps was caught with two other Dutchmen after a road check near Baza in Andalucía, in a convoy of three vehicles.

Robbie Grifhorst, an Amsterdam property dealer with connections to Van Hout and Holleeder, was long suspected of being involved in the kidnapping. It was even thought that Grifhorst, who was known as 'The Builder', might have masterminded the operation, and merely recruited the other four for its execution, which he steadfastly denied. Shortly after the raid on the warehouse, police arrested Grifhorst at Schiphol airport, as he returned from his Spanish residence to declare his innocence. Van Kerkhof spent about a week on the Costa del Sol, looking for evidence of Grifhorst's suspected part in the kidnapping. Although the detective said he came across 'half of the Amsterdam underworld', he found nothing directly linking Grifhorst to the abduction.

Still, Grifhorst threw a massive party at the Marriott Hotel in Amsterdam to celebrate Van Hout's release. Adding insult to injury, the band reportedly played the tune of 'Heerlijk, helder Heineken'. The breweries ended their contract to supply Casa Rosso, a famous sex club in Amsterdam's red light district, when Grifhorst took over the management.

According to police sources, Van Hout and Holleeder later engaged in much the same activities as before the kidnapping. Loud and cheerful as ever, they were often seen supporting Ajax, Amsterdam's leading football team, attending horse races in Duindigt and Hilversum, and driving around Amsterdam in hired sports cars. Together with their friend Grifhorst, Van Hout and Holleeder were thought to rule over the red light district of Alkmaar, controlling an entire street of 'windows' on the Achterdam.

In March 1996 Van Hout disappeared from the Amsterdam scene, after an unknown hit man attempted to liquidate him in front of his home. The would-be killer shot Van Hout seven times at very close range as the kidnapper prepared to start his car. With bullets in his head and chest, Van Hout staggered out of his Mercedes and collapsed on the bonnet, while his attacker cycled away. The kidnapper survived, but was disfigured by a bullet that hit him in the jaw. After another four-year jail sentence for drug smuggling, in 2000 he was shot at again, but this time he wasn't hit. Van Hout was finally assassinated by a hit man on a motorcycle in 2003. The funeral procession in Amsterdam, featuring a white hearse pulled by eight Friesian horses and fifteen white limousines, was described as 'reminiscent of a Mafia funeral'.

The most painful thorn in Heineken and Proseco's side was the fifth kidnapper, the runaway Frans Meijer. On 28 December 1983, though, Meijer stunned the other kidnappers and Amsterdam police by giving himself up. Apparently distraught and regretful, he claimed that he had burned his share of the ransom on a beach. His share, as well as most of Van Hout and Holleeder's (some 8 million guilders in total), was never recovered. Martin Erkamps thought Meijer was 'a genius' but also 'somewhat mentally disturbed'. He told police on 7 December 1983 that Meijer always lit candles in a Catholic church before plotting his criminal projects, and 'he spoke of Heineken as a demon [...] because he drove so many people to alcohol abuse'.

Almost exactly a year after Meijer had walked into a police station, he escaped. On 1 January 1985 he was reported to have thrown a washing machine through a window of the Pieter Baan Centre in Utrecht, the psychiatric clinic where he was held. Although Heineken denied it, his security firm, Proseco, allegedly spent several years searching for Meijer.

Ed van Kerkhof was one of the few detectives who stubbornly continued searching for the runaway kidnapper long after it had ceased to be an official priority. 'Heineken put a lot of effort into the search for Meijer', said Van Kerkhof. 'We were happy to collaborate with Proseco because, obviously, they had a lot more money than us to get on with the case.' Together, Proseco and the police team investigated scores of tips: one day Meijer was spotted strolling down the Albert Cuyp market, the next day he was drinking at Short's of London in Amsterdam; then he was seen in a wheelchair, or had undergone plastic surgery, or had died.

Ten years later, in the summer of 1994, Meijer was finally tracked down. Not by Proseco or the Amsterdam police, but by Peter R. de Vries, the crime reporter who built his career on the Heineken kidnapping and had followed the story with great persistence. He said he finally got the scoop he had been longing for when an unknown source tipped him off about Meijer's whereabouts.

The kidnapper was living near Asunción, Paraguay, with his Paraguayan wife and their three children, and he had apparently become a devout Catholic. Meijer was arrested by local police in April 1995, after De Vries published his story. But just one month later 'Spikes' was freed again, officially on the back of a procedural mistake. Meijer was arrested again in 1998, after a long judicial fight. He was extradited from Paraguay four years later, but released in January 2005. Only a few weeks later he returned to Paraguay.

The kidnapper who attracted the most media and police attention was Holleeder. After various run-ins with the law, Holleeder was arrested in January 2006 on suspicion of extortion and in connection with a number of assaults on property investors.

Held in 2007 in an ultra-secure court room in Amsterdam with reinforced walls and few windows, Holleeder's trial was described in Dutch newspapers as 'the trial of the century'. It was interrupted for several months so that Holleeder could have a heart operation. He was sentenced to nine years in prison but was freed again in January 2012.

Since then, in spite of his notorious criminal history, Holleeder has strangely come to be regarded by many as a famous bad boy. When a Dutch film was made about the kidnapping of Heineken in 2011, Holleeder filed an injunction to try and ban it, on the grounds that it would damage his reputation. The injunction was rejected. Boellaard and Meijer also protested, claiming that the film made out that they were more brutal than they actually were and contained too many guns.

In public, Freddy Heineken would feign indifference when questioned about his kidnappers. 'If I feel anything at all towards them, it must be pity. Look, I might feel admiration for someone who digs a six-metre tunnel and then empties a safe in a bank. But boys who commit the easiest of easy crimes, and snatch a man – or even worse, a child – off the street […] I find them pathetic', he told *NRC Handelsblad*. 'They're the real victims in a way, victims of themselves. Here's the long and the short of it: I was bitten by a dog. The stupid dog can't do anything about it, because biting is what stupid dogs do.'

But understandably, this horrendous episode affected Freddy Heineken much more deeply than he cared to admit. When he heard about the killing of Gerrit Jan Heijn, the former chairman of the retail distribution giant Ahold, who was kidnapped and shot dead in 1986, someone close to Heineken said, 'Heineken completely freaked out'. As Freddy told police, 'The nasty aspect of this experience is that it stays with you for ever. You know what I mean. For example, I never sleep or go anywhere without armed people around me any more. That fear never lets go.'

After the kidnapping, Freddy's armoured car was always escorted by two other vehicles, one driving in front, the other behind. Barbed-wire fences and security cameras were erected at his home in Noordwijk. Strangers who ventured near the entrance of the villa were deterred by armed guards. Most of the Pentagon's ground floor was occupied by Proseco. When Freddy entertained guests in quiet cafés, 'the boys' sat patiently at the bar, from where they would rush to his assistance, seemingly out of the blue, when he reached the end of yet another box of ultra-light cigarettes. When he stood up, three other anonymous guests suddenly rose to their feet. The luckiest accompanied the brewer while he stayed in his house in the south of France, where they swapped their suits and ties for shorts, polo shirts and sunglasses.

Talking to me the day after Meijer's release, in a café on the Beethovenstraat, Heineken smiled coyly. He brushed his index finger against his thumb to imply that Meijer owed his freedom to money. While two bodyguards shared a soda behind him, he said the fate of his kidnappers had ceased to interest him, and that he had long overcome the trauma of the abduction. Only minutes later, though, the tycoon was unable to repress a nervous twitch when a stranger walked decidedly in his direction, only to then order drinks at the bar. 'The nice thing about being rich is you can fly off to the Caribbean whenever you feel like it. Then again,' he sighed, 'I can't even go to the movies in Amsterdam.'

10

Losing Its Fizz

Pete Brown was a young planner at Lowe Howard-Spink, the British advertising agency, when he was asked to rethink Heineken's advertising in the United Kingdom. In the late '90s, the agency was no longer consistently using the strapline that made the brand famous in the UK. Heineken was going through a process of intense soul-searching, and the agency figured out that it had to make a statement: either bring the strapline back or ditch it completely to embark on another ground-breaking campaign for the Dutch brand.

It took Brown and his research team four months to go through thirty years of beer advertising, read the consumer reports and examine current trends in the beer business. Their conclusion: the 'refreshes the parts' strapline was exhausted, made no sense in the increasingly global lager market and ought to be replaced. On the back of this brief, a few months later, a new campaign hit the market, with a strapline that still echoed the success of the previous years: 'How Refreshing. How Heineken.'

Unfortunately, that same week, an updated version of the *Oxford Dictionary of Quotations* came out, as Brown recalled. Among the new entries was 'Heineken refreshes the parts other beers cannot reach', described as one of the most successful advertising lines of all time. Later that week Brown said he received a phone call from Frank Lowe, the agency's chairman.

'I'm going to play golf all day tomorrow with the chairman of Heineken. He's going to ask me a couple of questions, so I just need your help,' Lowe said in a suave voice, in Brown's version. 'I am pretty sure he is going to ask me why we've ditched the most successful strapline of all time […] Can you go over that tonight and think about it over your fish and chips?'

The awkward exchange was indicative of the brand's disarray in the United Kingdom. Lowe and a few other advertising people felt that their campaign hadn't got tired, but there was no denying that, around the middle of the 1980s, the Heineken brand was losing its impetus in Britain, barely keeping pace with the unfaltering rise of the market. The brand that had fuelled the Lager Revolution in the '70s suddenly appeared to be losing its fizz.

The managers at Whitbread could identify quite a few reasons for the pressure on the brand's market share, and one of them was clear for all to see. Heineken commercials, which had broken the mould of beer advertising in the '70s, were no longer so unique. A flurry of other beer brands had taken a leaf from Heineken's book and were grabbing market share in the ever-growing British beer market with their own witty advertising.

In the 1980s commercial breaks between television programmes were described as 'sponsored entertainment' or 'subsidised jokes'. Rather than using these breaks to make a cup of tea, viewers deliberately stayed in front of their sets to watch the latest beer ads. Some of the lagers almost filled the breaks with a sequence of sometimes hilarious and thirst-inducing commercials.

The most popular beer commercials in the '80s were probably

those for Carling Black Label, by the WCRS agency. A classic in advertising circles is the 'Dambusters' clip, in which a low-flying Lancaster bomber drops its bouncing load on a German dam, only for the German sentry to lunge at the oncoming bombs like a goalkeeper. 'I bet he drinks Carling Black Label', the bemused British pilot says to his assistant. Other duos went on to witness many other similarly unlikely feats, invariably causing them to turn to each other and marvel about the other person's favourite beer brand.

As had been the case with Heineken a decade earlier, thousands eagerly awaited the next instalments of the Carling campaign, and they would trot out the line whenever one of their mates in the pub did something out of the ordinary. The Canadian beer was helped too by Edward Taylor's aggressive investments in football sponsorship and its early moves in the market for canned beer, but it was largely due to advertising that the Canadian brand became Britain's most popular lager.

Meanwhile, Heineken had refreshed neither its advertising nor its recipe. It was still being brewed in Britain by Whitbread, with a lower alcohol content, and Frank Lowe was still in charge of delivering snappy advertising. Lowe himself had moved away from Collett Dickenson Pearce (CDP) in 1981 to establish his own company together with planner Geoff Howard-Spink. A group of former CDP employees moved with them, as did Whitbread, with both the Heineken and Stella Artois accounts.

While the 'parts' strapline was still very fresh in consumers' ears, Lowe Howard-Spink had used it for Heineken commercials throughout the 1980s – albeit often with a linguistic twist. A group of dustmen who had a few sips of Heineken suddenly put on an impromptu drum performance in a dark courtyard using bin lids. 'Heineken refreshes the parts where other beers haven't bin' was the slogan. A partridge that was shot out of the sky escaped with a Heineken parachute. This was evidence that Heineken 'refreshes the partridges other beers cannot reach'.

Some of the most memorable Heineken 'refreshes the parts' commercials were made in the '80s, including 'Water in Majorca', an amusing take on *My Fair Lady*, in which a buttoned-up young lady learns to speak Cockney with a little help from a refreshing Heineken. However, even the advertising executives struggled to recall other Heineken commercials from the second half of the '80s that had made an impact. Although consumers remembered the 'refreshing' strapline, the adverts were no longer as ground-breaking as they had been a few years earlier.

In the UK Heineken was losing market share not only to Carling Black Label but also to its familiar foe Carlsberg. Despite voice-overs from Orson Welles, 'Probably the best lager in the world' never became as popular as the commercials for Heineken or Carling Black Label, yet Carlsberg still seduced many British lager drinkers. Since they had started their own British production from a plant in Northampton in 1974, Carlsberg's growing sales in the UK were particularly profitable: it was estimated in the '80s that more than half of Carlsberg's profits came from the UK.

Beck's, Löwenbräu and several other German brands entered the sweepstakes in British brewing with UK-based partners. Holsten Pils made a notable impression for a few years with its advertising campaigns starring Griff Rhys Jones. Another series for Holsten Export featured a man and his dog, playing the piano in all sorts of settings that 'call for a Holsten', including a tropical forest and an Egyptian desert. 'I don't know if we could have done it without Frank Lowe before us. Heineken freed it up. We didn't have to do it in a pub any more', explained Dave Trott from Gold Greenlees Trott (GGT), which handled the account.

But at the same time the country's beer market was suddenly swamped with even more outlandish lagers that grabbed the viewer's imagination with striking, witty advertising. Foster's Draught Lager led the way in 1984 with Paul 'Crocodile Dundee' Hogan. He played the part of Hoges, a former painter on the Sydney Harbour Bridge, who shared his experience of savouring Foster's with cocky Australian humour. 'G'day. They've asked me from Oz to introduce youse all to Foster's Draught, here it is ... Ahhh, ripper! Tastes like an angel cryin' on your tongue', he told Britain's growing hordes of lager drinkers.

Castlemaine XXXX even took British lager drinkers right into the Australian outback. Their commercials were mostly set in dry, gritty landscapes, where muscular farmers and mineworkers went to ludicrous lengths to save their beer. In one, two men are driving along in a pick-up truck, with a woman and a huge load of Castlemaine beers in the back. When they attempt to cross a canyon on a wooden bridge, the old planks crack, leaving the back of the pick-up truck dangling precariously over the canyon. After a shocked pause, the woman at the back calmly advises that they will all be all right if they get rid of some of the load. But the two men in the cabin clearly have no doubt about which load should be dropped. 'Australians wouldn't give a XXXX for any other beer', they claim.

Amid this burst of creativity, snappy slogans and foreign accents Heineken advertising no longer led the way. In 1985 Carling Black Label became the leading lager brand in the United Kingdom, and many others steadily gnawed at Heineken's market share. The Dutch response was to call in the lawyers.

◉

While lager consumption soared in the 1970s, Whitbread and Heineken had both enjoyed the spoils. Heineken was the brand that generated by far the most abundant sales for the British brewer, reaffirming its position among the six largest in the country. And the UK turned into an almost effortless source of income for Heineken: it was estimated that, in the most successful years, the Dutch company received royalties of more than £5 million per year, in cash, without any meaningful investment.

While the cash poured in, the Dutch could suppress their uneasiness about the weaker Heineken sold in the UK, but it quickly resurfaced when Heineken sales came under pressure. Whitbread managers argued that about 80 per cent of the group's advertising budget was spent on Heineken, to try and halt the decline in its market share. They were still startled when Heineken decided to take action, by threatening to serve notice on their licensing agreement.

Heineken had no serious intention of breaking up its relationship with Whitbread. 'It was continuing to disgorge cash, and Heineken needed that for their acquisitions in Europe', explained one of the managers involved in the negotiations. 'Anyway, they didn't have any distribution over here. They couldn't just turn their back on us and give up on sales in England. They may have been under pressure, but it was still a lot of barrels.' Instead of walking away from the deal, Heineken apparently wanted to take advantage of the market situation to tighten their grip on the brand's management in Britain, and to demand improved terms.

As one of the protagonists explained, the long-term agreement sealed in the early seventies included a sliding scale for royalties: the higher the volume of sales, the lower the royalties per barrel for Heineken. Owing to the rapid take-off of sales after the agreement, Whitbread had rapidly reached the higher end of the volume scale – meaning low royalties per barrel for Heineken. 'It was about half the level of the royalties in other countries', one of Heineken's managers said. Whitbread explained that this could be justified by the particular structure of the British market: they not only had to invest in advertising, but their own margins were also impacted by the financial support given to the thousands of pubs where Heineken was sold.

The same manager said that the contract contained several termination clauses: Heineken could call it off if the Dutch brand ended up making less than 75 per cent of Whitbread's lager sales in volume, or if the sales declined for two successive years and Heineken made up less than 80 per cent of Whitbread's lager sales in barrels. It was the second clause that applied. While Heineken sales had been slowing down, Whitbread had capitalised on the growing lager market with several other brands. It acquired the British trademark rights for Kaltenberg Diät Pils. Then it started making cheap lager for home consumption, with its own Heldenbrau brand. It still had Stella Artois as well, even though the Belgian beer's sales only amounted to a trickle in the '80s.

The above protagonist said that Heineken's opening gambit in the talks was to request that a separate entity should be established for Heineken in the UK, in which the Dutch company itself would own a share of 20 per cent. The request was met with incredulity at Whitbread – and flatly rejected. The next best thing for Heineken was to upgrade the financial terms of the new deal, which was meant to expire at the end of the decade. As well as much improved royalties, Heineken obtained an extra payment in Whitbread shares.

The adjusted licensing agreement anchored the relationship

between Whitbread and Heineken just as the British brewing industry was going through unprecedented upheavals. The many mergers and acquisitions of the 1960s had left the industry in the hands of six major British brewers, which between them made up about 70 per cent of the market. The insular aspect of the market had kept predators at bay. But in the mid-'80s these brewers suddenly came under attack from a pack of foreign investors, who regarded the frothy British market as a springboard for Europe. Whitbread, then the third largest UK brewer, was protected by a predator-proof construction. The others were bite-size targets for some of the larger foreign food and drinks groups.

Much of the agitation was triggered by the irrepressible John Elliott. He was among the mega-raiders who wreaked havoc in Australian business during the '80s, together with Alan Bond and Robert Holmes à Court. Starting from a run-down Tasmanian jam-making business, he built an Australian empire in beer and agricultural products. The brewing arm of this business, Elders IXL, consisted primarily of the Melbourne-based Carlton & United Breweries, the makers of Foster's lager, which Elliott gobbled up in 1984. Together with the Bond Corporation (owner of the Swan and Castlemaine XXXX brands), Elders IXL controlled about 85 per cent of the Australian beer market. But Elliott wanted to become one of the leading international players with the aggressive tactics that had made his fortune in Australia, based on spectacular takeovers and massive borrowing.

In September 1986 Elliott rocked the British establishment with a hostile bid of £1.8 billion on Allied-Lyons, the country's second-largest brewer behind Bass Charrington. Sir Derrick Holden-Brown, Allied-Lyons's chairman, was outraged: 'For this company, which is small and heavily borrowed, to think it can tilt at Allied-Lyons is impudence', he told the press.

Indeed, the offer for Allied-Lyons was four times the size of Elders IXL.

The bid was eventually rejected, but Elliott pounced again and again. The industry went up in arms as Elliott attempted to swallow Grand Met. The Australian raider's hostile bid to grab a hold of Scottish & Newcastle in 1988 unleashed yet more political unrest and even demonstrations in the streets of London. The disquiet came to an end only after an intervention from the Monopolies and Mergers Commission, which allowed Elliott only a reduced stake in Scottish & Newcastle. But in the meantime the Australian managed to net Courage, which gave him a 10 per cent share of the British beer market.

The unrest stirred by the takeover bids attracted the attention of Britain's regulatory authorities, and they started to grumble about concentration of the vertical sort (whereby the largest brewers still owned or held a financial grip on thousands of pubs). It was suggested to them that consumer choice and pricing were affected by the tied-house system, whereby these same six breweries more or less controlled what was to be served in thousands of pubs. The increasingly narrow range of beer on offer in British pubs was lamented with particular verve by the Campaign for Real Ale, which was upset about the decline of cask ale sales. Publicans argued that they were too much hassle – it was much easier for them to keep the plastic taps flowing with the lager supplied by the big brewers.

The investigation touched on such an important part of Britain's public life that it triggered heated parliamentary debates. The verdict was contained in the Beer Orders, published in 1989, which partly dismantled the tied-house structure in the British beer market. The Beer Orders had far-reaching consequences for most of the larger brewers: they recommended that breweries should be allowed to tie only 2,000 pubs, plus half the number they owned or financed above this limit by November 1992.

For Whitbread the Beer Orders initially meant they had to free from tie just over 2,300 of their roughly 6,600 outlets. But the company still had to deal with thousands of other pubs under its 'umbrella' – because the pubs tied to the breweries in which Whitbread held at least 15 per cent were to be added to its own count. Whitbread therefore reduced some of these stakes and restructured its business yet again, with separate divisions for pubs and 'retail activities'. The retail division contained restaurant and off-licence chains, such as Beefeater, Pizza Hut, TGI Friday's and Threshers. Whitbread went on to dismantle its bid-proof construction.

The Beers Orders radically changed the face of the beer business in Britain. They led to the rise of the pubcos but did not prevent a reduction in the number of pubs, which would shrink inexorably in the next two decades owing to the smoking ban and rising beer prices. Ironically, this bold piece of anti-cartel legislation probably contributed to even more concentration in the British brewing business: the number of big brewers dwindled to four, and less than twenty years later none of them remained in British hands.

At the same time British consumers apparently started to reject the uniformity and blandness of the beers served in their locals. They weren't quite prepared to ditch their lagers and return to their assortment of bitters. But many did enjoy the beers they tried on their European holidays and were no longer content to throw back watered-down lager.

If one culprit had to be singled out, it would be Jean de Florette, the character created by the French writer Marcel Pagnol. Released in 1986, with Gérard Depardieu as Jean de Florette, the eponymous film triggered a sudden enthusiasm for all things Provençal. The craze was quickly seized on by advertising firms. But unfortunately, the beer campaign, produced by Lowe Howard-Spink, that most enduringly captured the appeal of Provence was for Stella Artois, not Heineken.

Until then, Stella Artois had been consistently marketed as a 'reassuringly expensive' beer, and Whitbread made sure that the product fitted with the slogan. 'I had a rule that I wanted the Stella price to be raised every six months', said Anthony Simonds-Gooding, the former marketing director at Whitbread, who became managing director of the company's entire beer business. He insisted that the Stella Artois brewed in Britain should be made with the very best hops and barley around, so it could justify its top-shelf price and reputation. Only a few discerning drinkers were prepared to pay the premium.

The *Jean de Florette* commercials undoubtedly helped. Replicating the landscape, costumes, music and accents of the French film, one of them showed a farmer pulling a cart full of red carnations in front of a rural inn. When the *aubergiste* brings him a sandwich, the farmer fumbles in his pockets, only to find out that he does not have any change to pay for it. The owner signals that he would be happy to be compensated with a bunch of carnations. The deal done, the farmer sits down to eat his sandwich, but then he hears the sound of beer being poured into a glass. The commercial ends with the farmer savouring his fresh Stella Artois in front of the *auberge*. The façade is decorated all over with red carnations, while his cart stands empty. The story tied in neatly with the unchanged strapline for Stella Artois: 'reassuringly expensive'.

It did not appear to matter that Stella Artois is not in the least bit French. It comes from Belgium, which has a much more distinguished brewing tradition (in fact, picky Belgian drinkers do not care much for Stella Artois). The advertising managers argued that the exact provenance was irrelevant: all that mattered was that British consumers would come to regard Stella Artois as a 'continental' beer. France was unequivocally 'continental', evoking culinary delights and justifying the price tag.

Just in case some viewers did not get it, the dialogue was conducted entirely in French. As one of the planners put it, this had the added advantage of flattering the consumer. 'The commercial was shot in such a way that you would understand what is going on anyway', he explained. 'The French just made the consumer feel a little smarter. They would think, "Hey, I got that, my French is better than I thought".'

Lowe Howard-Spink went on to produce an entire series of Stella Artois commercials set in Provence, which hugely increased consumer awareness of the Stella Artois brand. But a radical shift in consumer tastes also contributed to the stellar rise in the Belgian brand's sales. Many of the country's drinkers no longer gagged at the somewhat heavier flavour of such supposedly 'premium' lagers. They no longer baulked at the extra expense, either.

The British consumption patterns that had made it so compelling for Heineken to move into the market with a weak brew had suddenly changed. As they neared the '90s, the Heineken managers watched in dismay as sales of their beer in Britain stagnated, while the lager market as a whole expanded massively. It was all the more irritating for Heineken that one of the main beneficiaries of the new trend was Stella Artois. 'The growth of the 5 per cent market crept up on us', admitted one of the Whitbread managers. 'We didn't promote Stella much, we had several failed campaigns, and then it all came together.'

The Dutch attempted to retaliate by introducing a proper European beer into the market alongside the weaker Heineken. An advertising campaign was aired to market Heineken Export in 1992, just at the time when the European Community turned into a single market. The commercial made by Lowe Howard-Spink humorously explained the changes brought about by 'Europe': bureaucrats would see to it that cricketers played with French 'boules', and runners would have to finish a race by cutting through Brussels 'red tape'. But there was one import the Brits would find easier to swallow: 'Heineken Export, matured a little longer, to taste a little stronger.' The latest Heineken brew was 'a great 0.57 of a litre', with a purple stripe on the packaging and beer taps to distinguish it from the weaker brew.

Another series sold Heineken Export 'as recommended by your smooth-talking bar steward'. The steward in question, played by Stephen Fry, worked at an establishment 'deep in the throbbing heart of Paris, a slick, chic haven where the dapper denizens of the city by the Seine come to unwind'. There they could find 'the globally renowned antidote to all roughness: Heineken Export, the strong silken lager that is smoother than a cashmere codpiece'.

The regulations made it compulsory for the adverts to mention that this 'Heineken Export' was not exactly the real thing – although it was the standard 5 per cent version, it was still brewed under licence in Britain, by Whitbread.

Despite the inspired advertising, sales of Heineken Export failed to make a dent in the market or to halt the rise of Stella Artois. Neither could the new beer compensate for the sagging market share of the weaker Heineken. Lowe Howard-Spink came up with several advertising concepts that won the company awards. One such campaign was the 'Blues Singer': sitting on a porch playing the guitar, the singer's uninspiring melodies turn into a gripping blues tune when the bailiffs confiscate his car, his wife leaves and he has a sip of Heineken. However, the efforts apparently weren't brilliant enough to tear consumers away from their pint of Stella.

That was when many felt that the 'refreshes' campaign was no longer adequate. 'The advertising had run out of steam', said Miles Templeman, who replaced Anthony Simonds-Gooding as managing director of the brewing business at Whitbread. 'We tried lots of different things, but we never found another great campaign.'

As Heineken's market share shrank with alarming consistency through the '90s, the relationship between Whitbread and the Dutch managers became increasingly acrimonious. Some managers recall unpleasant gatherings where Heineken executives expressed their frustration with complete frankness. 'It was the most uncomfortable meeting I have ever witnessed. It felt absolutely excruciating. We just decided to leave', said a seasoned manager from Lowe Howard-Spink, recalling one such discussion in Amsterdam.

The unease was partly due to divergences between the Dutch and the British in their business manners – the Dutch tended to be far more abrupt. But what really irked Heineken was that the brand had suddenly fallen behind another brand marketed by Whitbread – and of all brands it had to be Stella Artois, which was a particularly close rival for the Dutch. They watched the numbers in disbelief: at the start of the nineties Stella Artois' UK sales were said to reach less than 0.5 million hectolitres but by the end of the decade the Belgian brand had easily overtaken Heineken, with sales astonishingly soaring to more than 3 million hectolitres in 1999.

Whitbread representatives made repeated efforts to convince their Dutch partners that the shift in sales between Heineken and Stella Artois was a result of changing beer tastes – not part of a grand plan to substitute the weak Heineken with Stella and its higher-margin brew. They tried to assuage Heineken by pushing sales of Murphy's, the Irish stout bought by the Dutch in 1983 (alongside Boddingtons Bitter, which Whitbread bought in 1989).

At least once in the mid-'90s, Heineken reportedly threatened to terminate the agreement, due to the potential takeover by Whitbread of a competing lager brand. But Templeman and others acknowledged that Heineken did display an understanding of the market. Most importantly, the Dutch did not yet have the resources and infrastructure required to walk away from Whitbread and take the British market into their own hands. Towards the end of the '90s they already had their hands full with an even trickier and weightier changeover.

11

*Taking Over
New York*

Whenever their business looked a little unsteady elsewhere, Heineken's managers could always rely on the income of their exports to the United States. Before they had even reached their office at the start of the year, they could rest assured that they would receive a huge order from Leo van Munching for his American customers – enough to keep the breweries going for several months.

Since Van Munching had secured his improved contract as Heineken's importer, the Dutch beer's sales had soared. In 1960, when the deal was sealed, Van Munching sold about one million cases. By 1975 the volume had inflated to 7 million cases (more than half of Heineken's exports from the Netherlands). With a share of roughly 35 per cent of the foreign brands, Heineken could then rightly promote itself as 'America's number one imported brand'.

Van Munching had forged ties with more than 300 agents around the American market. Heineken's lager was exported to eleven American ports, which was tangible proof of its nationwide clout but also caused enormous technical problems, as each state had its own regulations about alcohol beverages and packaging. Getting enough crown caps, which each state had delivered separately, was a constant struggle.

The capricious importer was often at loggerheads with Heineken's managers in Amsterdam. Most of the disputes were about the margins that Van Munching should be allowed to make, and how costs for advertising in the United States should be divided. Yet Van Munching argued most vehemently when it was suggested that Heineken might start brewing in the USA.

The idea had first been floated after the Liberation at the end of the Second World War, when the Dutch brewery was beginning to find its feet again. Van Munching had travelled to the Netherlands to meet Dirk Stikker, and the brewery's chairman had informed the young importer that he was thinking of building a brewing plant in the United States. The plan was in line with Heineken's decision to hit fast in the most promising export markets before the Germans recovered. But fortunately, by the time the breweries had mustered sufficient strength to go ahead with the plan, Van Munching had talked them out of it.

Local production looked tempting in the face of soaring demand and astronomic shipping bills, and it was discussed regularly through the '50s and '60s. Still, Leo van Munching convinced Freddy Heineken that local brewing would destroy Heineken's most precious selling point in the USA: the three-inch piece of sticky paper with the word 'imported' on the neck of the bottle. And, ironically enough, it was Van Munching's best-selling competitor who proved him right.

Whenever he heard the word 'Löwenbräu', Freddy Heineken could not quite manage to suppress a gleeful smile. It was a sweet reminder of a glaring blunder by Heineken's former arch-enemy in the United States: the decision by Löwenbräu, the Bavarian brewery, to have its lager brewed on American soil. 'I mean, can you believe anybody could be so damn stupid?' Freddy sneered.

Back in the early '70s Löwenbräu wasn't much of a laughing matter for Heineken. Ever since European beer imports had been resumed after Repeal, the majestic lion on Lowenbräu's bottles had been clawing ferociously at Heineken's market share. The battle was largely fought in New York, the largest market for both brewers, in the shape of a knives-out duel between Leo van Munching and Hans Holterbosch, a former German restaurateur who imported and sold Löwenbräu. Although the German beer was affected by a Jewish boycott and the severe grain shortage after the war, Holterbosch steadfastly expanded his distribution network, focusing on bar and restaurant owners of German descent in New York.

Like Van Munching, the hard-working Holterbosch greased publicans with the promise of whopping returns and a prestige brew. He recruited the brightest Harvard graduates and taught them the art of selling Bavarian beer. He pushed Löwenbräu with full-colour adverts depicting a beer glass and a flute, with the slogan 'If you run out of Löwenbräu, order champagne'. And he continuously tormented Van Munching by publishing figures that arguably placed Löwenbräu ahead of Heineken in terms of volume sold. By the early '70s Löwenbräu imports had reached at least 200,000 hectolitres per year, and Holterbosch Inc. sold about 70 per cent of this in New York.

Back in Munich, however, the 'blue-and-white' brewery doubted that Holterbosch could ever come out on top of the Dutch. One of Löwenbräu's crippling weaknesses against Heineken and other German brands was the location of its brewing plant, hundreds of miles away from the north German harbours of Hamburg and Bremen. 'The competition forced us to sell at the same price as Heineken, while the inland freight cost us about one dollar extra per case', said Dieter Holterbosch, the importer's son. While Van Munching reported double-digit growth in the early '70s, Holterbosch Inc. was hard pushed to expand.

But it was the fall of the dollar against the Deutschmark in the early '70s that prompted Löwenbräu to rethink its American business. German newspapers reported that Löwenbräu's exports to the USA, which made up about 60 per cent of the brewery's foreign turnover, had plummeted. So in 1973 the Bavarians started negotiating a contract with the fifth-largest American brewer, the Miller breweries, to import and later produce Löwenbräu in Milwaukee, Wisconsin.

When the deal was concluded in 1974, Löwenbräu triumphantly predicted the end of Heineken's supremacy in the import market. The plan entailed Miller starting to market imported Löwenbräu in the Midwest, a region that had previously been supplied by a Löwenbräu subsidiary. The 'Cream City' brewers would then take over national distribution in April 1975 and perhaps brew locally in 1977, depending on the dollar rate.

Since its full takeover by Philip Morris in 1970, Miller Brewing had emerged as the fastest-growing and quickest player in the US beer industry. In eight years it had expanded from 5 million barrels to 31 million, with high-voltage marketing and by introducing the best-selling Lite brand, which opened up a gigantic market for low-calorie beers. So the Bavarians estimated that, once their rich partners started pushing the Löwenbräu brand with their aggressive marketing, sales might triple over three years.

Although Miller's efforts did indeed trigger an increase in

Löwenbräu's US exports in 1975, from about 110,000 hectolitres to 160,000, Löwenbräu's plans to expand its collaboration with the Milwaukee brewers were soon thwarted. Holterbosch took legal action and obtained a settlement. He was eventually bought out.

Things really turned nasty, however, when Anheuser-Busch of St Louis, Missouri, the maker of America's self-proclaimed King of Beers, Budweiser, started kicking up a fuss about Löwenbräu. Unfortunately for the Bavarians, their deal with Miller came in the middle of a decade-long battle of marketing skirmishes and backbiting between Miller and Anheuser-Busch.

In the 1970s the conflict between the two aggressive breweries escalated sharply. The roguish, red-haired Miller chairman, John Murphy, was reported to have a rug embossed with the Anheuser-Busch eagle under his desk to wipe his feet on – and a voodoo doll named August, after the Anheuser-Busch chairman. Every bit as abrasive, Murphy's counterpart in St Louis apparently didn't go out of his way to reprimand employees who turned up in red T-shirts with the words 'Miller Killers'.

At this time, Anheuser-Busch was the leader in the American beer market. It was August 'Gussie' Busch, the grandson of the brewery founder, a hard-drinking, loud-mouthed colourful character, who had established Budweiser as the most widely sold American lager in 1957. Budweiser's arch-rival was Schlitz, which had held the top slot for five years in the early '50s. In pursuit of the Milwaukee brewer, Gussie opened brewing plants around the country and bought his own railroad car so that he could shake hands with wholesalers and bar owners. He was such an aggressive salesman that legislators intervened – prohibiting any financial ties between brewers and bar owners. Gussie still managed to get wholesalers on his side by giving them exclusive contracts.

The ageing Busch began to lose his grip in the early 1970s, when Anheuser-Busch was facing rising costs for its beer production and shareholders complained about the lack of returns. Gussie responded by cutting costs, slashing advertising spend and sacking executives. These unproductive steps caused frequent clashes with his son August Busch III, who started grabbing power from Gussie – eventually ousting his own father in 1975.

While Gussie could be gruff, August Busch III inspired both fear and awe. 'I know I'm curt at times', he acknowledged, but that was a major understatement to those who aspired to 'stay the hell out of his way'. Short and impatient, the younger Busch sometimes came across like a Prussian general, and he was apparently humourless too: as the story went in St Louis, his idea of a great laugh was to call an executive by his middle name.

Still, even Busch's toughest critics were invariably impressed by his sharpness and his gruelling schedule. A college dropout, young Busch had given up his wild ways to work an eighty-hour week. He'd arrive at Anheuser's headquarters by helicopter at 5.30 in the morning, and each day ended with the same evening ritual – tasting a sample of the day's beer production. He terrified business partners with his razor-sharp eye for anything that was not exactly right – such as a chewing gum wrapper in a brewing plant or an out-of-date can of Budweiser at the back of a supermarket shelf. He could recall production and sales figures and rattle them off at any time. And he was utterly determined to keep anybody from dethroning the King of Beers.

Philip Morris's acquisition of Miller in 1970 triggered the battle between Anheuser-Busch and the Milwaukee brewer. Just before the ban on television advertising for cigarettes, Philip Morris, the company behind Marlboro, was prepared to pump millions of marketing dollars into Miller to grab share in the American beer market. So it did for the nationwide launch of Miller Lite beer in 1975, and again to reinvigorate Miller High Life, the company's flagship lager brand, with the 'Miller Time' slogan. In just a few years Miller rose from seventh position to competing directly with Anheuser-Busch.

For several years, the ensuing rivalry was played out in the market as well as in newspaper columns and the offices of the regulators. One of Miller's weapons in this conflict, Löwenbräu landed in Anheuser-Busch's firing line. Murphy had contracted Löwenbräu partly to hit back at Michelob, the premium brand marketed by Anheuser-Busch. But when Miller started testing their American-style Löwenbräu in 1976, the St Louis brewer complained to the Federal Trade Commission (FTC) that the competition was flawed: Miller was misleading the punters, Busch argued, because the labels implied the American Löwenbräu was the real thing – which it clearly wasn't.

'Anheuser-Busch started raising holy hell about Löwenbräu', said Dieter Holterbosch. 'While the Germans used high-quality hops, Miller's just made a cheaper beer. Anheuser-Busch made sure everybody would find out.' Even Löwenbräu admitted that the two beers could hardly be compared: 'There is no need to be ashamed of the beer that we will brew in the United States. Whether we actually like it or not, that is another question', Löwenbräu's export manager, Johann Daniel Gerstein, told German reporters.

'But wait, this is the best bit', chuckled Freddy Heineken. After the FTC agreed with Anheuser-Busch's complaint, Miller was forced to point out in its adverts that Löwenbräu was brewed in America. 'They could have picked this straight from a "how-to-kill-your-beer-brand" guide', Freddy laughed, and he was right: Löwenbräu lost its 'imported' appeal almost overnight.

Beck's eagerly filled the leading German import slot, but it was Van Munching who profited most handsomely from Löwenbräu's demise. While Heineken's sales had risen steadily from about 3 million cases in 1972 to 7 million in 1975, it recorded a massive jump in 1976, nearly doubling its sales to 12 million cases. 'Miller's completely blew it', said Holterbosch. 'They destroyed the trademark within a matter of months.'

Astonishingly, even after the Löwenbräu débâcle, Heineken considered producing their beer in the United States several times. But this suggestion was swept aside on the basis of market research. In the 1980s, for example, Heineken conducted a survey in which drinkers were given one bottle of 'imported' Heineken and one bottle of beer that they were told was 'brewed in the United States'. They both came from exactly the same batch brewed in Zoeterwoude, a huge plant built south of Amsterdam in the early '70s, but the members of the American panel invariably thought the 'imported' bottle tasted better.

As VMCO's turnover rocketed in the '70s, Leo van Munching got a taste of the American Dream. The Dutchman from small-town Harderwijk owned a holiday villa in Fort Lauderdale, Florida, and a mansion in Greenwich, Connecticut, decorated in true Dutch-American style with scores of Delft ceramics and

'Brabants bont', a traditional red-and-white checked pattern, in the kitchen. There was a joking rivalry between Van Munching and Freddy Heineken, who had once been a VMCO trainee. His protégé was now a billionaire, while Van Munching was 'only' a multi-millionaire. 'His yacht is even bigger than mine', Van Munching noted sourly.

The Heineken brewery went out of its way to flatter Van Munching with insipid pieces in the company's former international magazine, the *Heineken Bulletin*, and other tokens of gratitude. Yet Van Munching was permanently quarrelling with the Heineken management. 'He always felt that the brewery was fleecing him', said Jan Burger, Heineken's transport manager in Rotterdam. 'He'd phone at night and whinge for a whole hour. "Jan, they're at it again", he'd say. But perhaps that was all part of his game.'

Much of the aggravation focused on Van Munching's advertising budget. Despite the official cost-splitting arrangement, Van Munching insisted that he propelled the brand to prestige status all around the United States by generously topping his share of the costs with VMCO dollars. 'And I can always remind them of that', he said. 'I'd say, "Look, if you guys had looked after the market yourselves, Heineken would never have taken off here."'

As a self-made man, Van Munching particularly despised the assertive young managers of the export department. He regarded them as ignorant and snotty know-it-alls who needlessly interfered with the business he had so brilliantly built up all by himself. 'A degree from Nijenrode [a Dutch business school] was sufficient to disgrace any newcomer in the eyes of Van Munching', said Burger. 'He was unbelievably brilliant and engaging, but there was a darker side to his character. Nobody was ever good enough for him.'

This acrimony between Van Munching and his Amsterdam contacts took a most unpleasant turn in June 1975, when the importer gave a lengthy interview to *Het Financieele Dagblad*. He told the reporter about a 'terrible fight' he'd had with Heineken's head of exports, Jop Cornelis, and how their relationship was one of 'hate and envy'. 'Every evening, he calculated how much I'd earned again that day. He thought that I was earning too much', Van Munching was quoted as saying. The importer was in the Netherlands because Heineken was dedicating to him the 'Barremolen', a windmill outside its new brewing plant in Zoeterwoude: 'I believe that they offered me this windmill today partly to make up for what I've had to endure from that so-called export manager over the last two years.'

Rob van Duursen, a colleague and long-time friend, said that Cornelis committed suicide shortly after the publication of the article. Van Munching's attack came at a time when Cornelis was vulnerable, grappling with several personal issues. Burger said that Van Munching made a jubilant phone call to the Netherlands the next day : '"D-e-a-d! He is dead! No more Cornelis!" Van Munching yelled.'

At VMCO's New York headquarters on the 36th floor of the Sperry Rand skyscraper Leo van Munching didn't allow anybody to overshadow his authority. He drove his representatives relentlessly, requiring them to visit at least twenty outlets per working day. And he erupted in fits of rage about the most ludicrous of incidents, such as a letter slipped into a US-bound beer case by a Rotterdam bottler looking for an American pen pal. 'It was as though Van Munching's office had been hit by an atomic bomb', said one Heineken employee.

But, at the same time, Van Munching Sr commanded such clout in the US beer importing business that he could easily make his partners sweat. Van Duursen said that once, sitting in Van Munching's office in New York, he had received a distraught telephone call from Jan Burger. The Dutch export-transport manager complained about a new manager at US Lines, a shipping company that counted Heineken among its most prestigious clients. As Van Duursen recalled: 'Van Munching immediately fetched his secretary. "Gracie", he yelled, "get US on the line." "Like to do business with us, pal?" he asked the chairman, "then get rid of that new manager." Just minutes later Burger called back to tell us that, to his amazement, the manager had been sacked.'

When his car rolled off the sloping driveway that led to his garage and he broke one of his legs, Van Munching even pulled strings from his hospital bed. Burger said a young Roman Catholic curate then turned up at Van Munching's bedside and lectured him about his lack of enthusiasm for saintly affairs. 'Fair enough, Van Munching was not a fanatical church-goer,' said Burger, 'but he replied curtly that he had contributed $250 to the local parish. He thought the young priest was well out of line, so he went on the phone to his bishop. One week later, the poor chap was moved to Boston.'

VMCO's management became more restrained after Leo Jr returned from Los Angeles in 1972, after six years running the regional office in California ('as far away as possible from New York and his father', said a friend). He was far less loud and hard-headed than his father but equally hard-working, and he brought back with him a few suggestions to update the business. Among other reforms, Leo Jr overhauled Heineken's distribution in the '70s so that VMCO dealt mostly with beer distributors, instead of the larger drinks specialists contracted by his father. The reasoning was that, when beer distributors turned up, the bar owner would be focused on buying his entire beer assortment – so he would be more inclined to buy an import with a lucrative margin at the higher end of the range.

Leo Van Munching Jr persuaded his father to inject a little zest into Heineken's advertising as well. The older Van Munching had a very personal take on advertising: from time to time he would call a friend from an agency to get print ads inserted in magazines such as *The New Yorker*, his favourite read. They were nearly always sober shots of the green bottle, meant to convey the superior class of Heineken. The younger Van Munching came up with some more lively shots, and he even put Heineken on television. VMCO said it was spending more on advertising in the '80s than all the other imports combined, using slightly superior lines such as 'Come to think of it, I'll have a Heineken'.

Sometimes Leo Jr used his own contacts in Amsterdam to implement changes that he knew were abhorrent to his father. Heineken cans for the American market were designed in the Netherlands at his request – quietly, because his father had declared this packaging too tacky for the American market. Leo Jr obtained regulatory approval and had the canned beer shipped in. His father only learned about it when he spotted a Heineken can on the traffic manager's filing cabinet. Philip van Munching recounted Leo Sr's reaction in *Beer Blast*: 'Mistaking it for a foreign version, he said, "We'll never have these here." The manager let slip that cans were available. In fact, he told his boss, we're moving quite a lot of them. Exasperated, Leo Sr. threw the can across the room and stormed out.'

In the second half of the '70s Van Munching Sr's behaviour became increasingly erratic, and it transpired that he was suffering from Alzheimer's. Although his father continued to turn up at the office, Leo Jr started assuming more responsibilities at the company.

Since Löwenbräu's dramatic fall from its position as a premium German brand, Heineken had ruled alone as the most popular imported beer. The Dutch said they controlled up to 42.8 per cent of this lucrative category, which itself had grown from about 1 per cent of total US beer sales in 1975 to almost 9 per cent twenty years later. The closest competitors, Germany's Beck's and Canada's Molson and Moosehead, were well out of sight.

Leo Jr ran a tight ship. VMCO had just 135 employees, who supervised distribution across the entire country. Between them they dealt with up to 450 active wholesalers in the '80s, peddling about 40 million cases of imported Heineken. Leo van Munching Jr knew all the wholesalers by name, and he set himself apart with his impeccable business practices. 'It's a very dirty business, and he's a clean guy', as George Kahl, one of Van Munching's closest aides, put it. 'He was just a very reputable person that people related to.' It helped that Heineken provided attractive margins to the wholesalers, and Van Munching made a point of offering the same to all of them. He had a rule that Heineken was a class item: from the beer itself to packaging, advertising and the behaviour of Van Munching staff, anything that had to do with Heineken was meant to convey its distinctive quality.

Leo van Munching Jr reinforced the company's leadership by persuading Heineken to take part in the market for light beers. By then, all of the largest American brewers had latched on to the trend, producing lighter versions of their lagers, such as Bud Light and Coors Light. It was out of the question that Heineken would launch a light beer under its flagship brand, so instead he suggested to his contacts in Amsterdam that they start brewing Amstel Light. Van Munching apparently designed the label for Amstel Light himself, while the Dutch developed a light beer from scratch for the American market.

Freddy Heineken approved both the brand and the packaging, a brown bottle that clearly set Amstel Light apart from imported Heineken. The Dutch signalled that they were ready in the second half of 1979, but Leo van Munching Jr could not bring himself to start importing Amstel Light as his father's medical situation was becoming increasingly uncertain. As his son knew all too well, Leo Sr had always fiercely opposed product diversification. Just as Amstel Light got the go-ahead, Leo Sr was suffering bouts of disorientation and other medical complications. The man who made Heineken in the United States was finally advised to stay away from the office. His son formally moved into the captain's chair at VMCO in 1980.

Amstel Light hit the shelves in 1981, as one of the lowest-calorie beers in the American market. '95 calories never tasted so imported', Heineken told consumers. It was a smart way of telling consumers that they would be imbibing fewer calories without compromising on the snob appeal of the imported tag. The Amstel brand was entirely unknown to American consumers: it had not been sold in the United States for several decades. Even so, Amstel Light took on quickly, and after a few years, it made up an estimated 25 per cent of Heineken's total sales in the United States. It was the only low-calories brand among the ten leading imports.

But around the same time an unruly pack of more than 400 other imported brands, a gaggle of exotic brews, started shaking furiously at Heineken's pedestal. While those beers appealed to style-conscious consumers with colourful images of sea, sun and crocodiles, it seemed that Heineken's green bottles were suddenly fading to grey.

The offensive billboards started popping up in southern Texas in the early '80s. They showed a poster with scuffled, dirty bottles of Heineken peeling from a wall to reveal squeaky-clean, transparent, long-necked bottles of Corona. 'The secret's out', the slogan proclaimed, yet many were still puzzling over the phenomenon behind the sudden rise of Corona, the Mexican beer turned out by the Modelo breweries.

The swell was supposedly triggered by surfers in Orange County, who turned the Mexican workers' drink into a Californian beer craze. They took the habit of adding an 'authentic' touch to the beer by stuffing a slice of lime down the bottle's neck. The thirst for this Mexican version of 'lager and lime' spread so rapidly that Barton Beers, its largest US importer, could hardly keep up with the demand.

In the earliest days of his leadership Leo van Munching Jr had already faced a head-on campaign by Kronenbourg, produced by the French food conglomerate BSN-Gervais Danone. The cheeky Strasbourg brewers had spent about $3 million a year on ads proclaiming that 'Europeans like Heineken but they love Kronenbourg'. After Freddy Heineken had an informal chat with BSN chief Antoine Riboud, the French dropped the line. The British comedian John Cleese then urged Americans to 'Have a Kroney with your crony', but most of them declined. Launched in the United States in 1980, four years later Kronenbourg was selling only 700,000 cases per year. 'Kronenbourg is the reason why the French drink wine', Van Munching gloated.

Other Dutch brands, such as Bavaria, Grolsch and Brand, were taking their first timid steps into the American market as well. More formidable was the competition from Beck's, the German brew, which had moved up to second place after

Löwenbräu's disastrous deal with Miller's and which promoted itself as the largest-selling German import beer in the USA. Australian brews were also burgeoning on the back of young America's sudden infatuation with the land Down Under. As they had in the UK, Foster's marketers hired the star of *Crocodile Dundee*, Paul Hogan, to promote their nectar: 'It's Australian for beer, mate.'

When Corona came into the picture, Van Munching believed Heineken was so well established that it would easily be able to brush off the competition from this bold newcomer as well. He predicted that the 'Mexican soda pop' would fizzle out as quickly as it had crossed the California border. 'The lime kills the taste', Van Munching smiled, and he complained haughtily about the Mexicans' billboards. 'Look, they purposely made our labels look a bit shabby', he told a Dutch reporter. 'But the size is really outrageous. When you see this, it seems that the Heineken bottles are smaller than Corona's. They are simply suggesting that Heineken drinkers get less for their money.'

Still, Van Munching was powerless to halt Corona's spread. The see-through bottles with the blue-and-white, spray-painted logo appealed to America's drinkers, and they liked its light taste. By the mid-'80s the Californian surfers' fad had turned into a tidal wave. Corona's turnover soared from 300,000 gallons in 1982 to 11.7 million in 1985, with virtually no advertising. At the end of the fourth year VMCO could no longer deny that it was under pressure: Heineken's market share had dropped to 29 per cent in 1986, from over 38 per cent four years earlier.

Van Munching pointed out that, although Heineken's leadership had become less assured, sales were still growing on the back of the import market's overall growth. And he argued that this unprecedented loss of market share was largely caused by the weakness of the dollar against the Dutch guilder, which triggered a 20 per cent price increase in September 1986. But in fact the currency slide destroyed VMCO's margins: since Heineken invoiced exports in Dutch guilders, the importer's margins were largely dependent on the exchange rate.

In 1987 Corona had started moving east and begun distribution in New York, competing directly in Heineken's prime market. By the end of the year Heineken's share in the import market had shrunk further, to 24 per cent. It was not so far ahead of Corona, which had blazed past Molson and Beck's to reach a share of nearly 17 per cent. At this rate Corona might close the gap in a matter of months.

Van Munching's counter-attack finally came in April 1988, with a batch of snappy commercials aimed at the young that spoofed the trendiness of Corona and Foster's. The ten- to fifteen-second ads showed a rambling yuppie posing with a long-necked bottle: 'Check me out! If it's happening, I'm there! I live in the city but my clothes say: safari! Answering machine for my car phone! Foreign films! Mousse in my hair! Tanning salon every Thursday! My beer: so hip, with a twist ...' Then he was pushed off the screen by a green-and-white can and the calming message: 'When you're done kidding around, Heineken.'

As Van Munching had predicted somewhat prematurely, Corona lost impetus. It was dogged by a false yet persistent rumour that the beer was contaminated – with urine. Barton Beers traced the rumour back to a beer distributor in Reno, Nevada, who sold Heineken. They filed a $3 million lawsuit against the agent in the US District Court of Reno in June 1987 and engaged in a risky media campaign to quash the rumours. After an out-of-court settlement the agent stated publicly that

Corona was 'free of any contamination', but the brand had been tarnished, at least temporarily.

The Corona craze subsided, removing the imminent threat to Heineken's import market leadership. However, the sudden collapse of Corona's sales in these years marked the beginning of another unsettling trend: the decline of the import segment, to the benefit of micro-breweries and domestic super-premiums. In 1989, for the first time in more than twenty years, Heineken reported a declining volume – and this time many of the foreign brews felt the squeeze.

By the late 1980s Anheuser-Busch had emerged victorious from its megabucks duel with Miller's, the Milwaukee challengers. Steered by August Busch III, its steely CEO, the St Louis company invested heavily in scores of bright executives and its distribution network. But at the same time Anheuser-Busch effectively blocked Miller's ascent by throwing hundreds of millions of dollars into the market-place. Asked why Miller's never succeeded in topping Budweiser, one former St Louis executive smugly replied: 'We would not let them.'

To frustrate their rivals, Busch's men introduced an extremely fast and hard-hitting form of business warfare, which became known as 'guerrilla marketing'. Americans were treated to an orgy of Budweiser propaganda, with annual advertising budgets of up to $250 million. 'This Bud's for you', the advertisers said, and the consumers eagerly grabbed it. While Miller's market share remained flat at about 22 per cent, Anheuser-Busch was moving toward Busch's target to hold squarely half of the American beer market. In the late '80s the Budweiser brand alone made up about 27 per cent of the market.

The war against Miller's kept August busy throughout the '70s. With a share of less than 2 per cent of the entire American beer market, Heineken and other imports were a mere irritant. However, once the market for imports and other small beers began to rise more rapidly in the '80s, Anheuser-Busch started to take more notice. There were several ways for the larger American brewers to thwart the expansion of their imported counterparts: they could continue to swamp the market with advertising, put pressure on the beer wholesalers (most of them sold at least one of the largest American beer brands) or push their own beers at the upper end of the market. Anheuser-Busch did all three.

Heineken, Corona and Molson aside, Anheuser-Busch was irritated in the early '90s by the surge of craft breweries. The small outfits making supposedly artisanal beers appealed to the swathes of consumers who were beginning to tire of drinking the same beer as everyone else. By far the most successful of them was the Boston Beer Company, headed by the feisty Jim Koch, the maker of Samuel Adams beer. The small brewery was able to sell Samuel Adams Triple Bock at $100 a crate, because it had to ripen for six months in oak barrels that previously contained Jack Daniels whiskey. To protect their market share, the American mega-brewers latched on to the trend by turning out yet more super-premiums and gimmicky drinks, with sometimes colloquial names.

This strategy was deployed with particular shrewdness by John 'Jack' MacDonough. He was known as the inventor of Budweiser's guerrilla marketing and widely regarded as one of Anheuser-Busch's smartest managers. But in 1992 MacDonough sent a massive shock wave through the Anheuser-Busch ranks by walking over to Miller's. In the merciless war between the US beer behemoths, this was tantamount to treason.

Once he'd settled into the chief executive's seat in Milwaukee, MacDonough tried to make up for the relative weakness of the Miller name by launching a flurry of faddish brands, from offshoots of Lite to the indefinable and quirky Red Dog. To share in the much-publicised success of the micro-brews, he marketed Red Dog as a product of the 'Plank Road Brewery'. This was supposedly a tiny outfit, something like a garden shed with an old man stirring the brew in patched-up tubs. In reality, Plank Road is the location of Miller's brewery in Milwaukee, a massive beer factory.

Plank Road Brewery, Michelob Dry by Anheuser-Busch, Miller Genuine Draft, Coors Extra Gold, Samuel Adams and a gaggle of much smaller brews put an end to the rapid rise of the import category. Heineken was holding up relatively well, but the market pressures were playing on Dutch nerves. Stuck with the exclusive deal it had sealed with Leo van Munching Sr back in the early '60s, Heineken could only watch the evolution of its brand from the sidelines, in the world's largest beer market and the most important one for Heineken's brand reputation. The tension was becoming unbearable.

To get a foot in Van Munching's door, Heineken needed a diplomat, a low-key executive who was bright and tactful enough to tighten Heineken's grip on its American business slowly without inciting Van Munching's fury. Van Munching Sr and his son had always kept Heineken at arm's length, running their business with American recruits. What Heineken needed was a semi-independent operation in New York to find out what was happening in the American market and in Van Munch-ing's kitchen. This unenviable task was assigned to Weijer de Ranitz, a former export employee (and incidentally, a youngster from a family of diplomats), who was detached to the United States in 1981.

'The thought behind this move was that Heineken would be at a loss in America if anything happened to Van Munching', said one of the executives involved at Heineken. 'Previously, order sheets were the only pieces of information that Heineken in the Netherlands ever received from Van Munching.' And considering that in the '80s Heineken's American business was estimated to account for about half of the brewery's operating profits, this complete lack of insight made them understandably nervous.

Leo van Munching Sr would probably have regarded the appointment of Heineken's envoy as an intolerable intrusion into his business. Leo Jr, in charge since 1980, was slightly less hostile to collaboration: he even agreed to lead the official opening of the office on Madison Avenue, just yards away from VMCO's headquarters on the Avenue of the Americas. Yet De Ranitz needed all his diplomatic skills to convince Van Munching that he was there to help – and not (only) to spy on VMCO in preparation for a takeover. While the offices were located a stone's throw from each other, Van Munching and those in charge at Heineken USA scarcely met. De Ranitz gathered most of his information from Vincent de Michele, VMCO's logistics manager, who agreed to meet him for informal lunches. But it was only with a full change of guard that Heineken could get a firm grip on its American business.

Leo van Munching Sr, the man who had made Heineken's name in the United States, died in April 1990. Eight months later, his son and the Heineken brewery signed an agreement for a Dutch takeover of VMCO. The pressure on Van Munching Jr to sell was predominantly financial: owing to the enormous level of inheritance tax in Connecticut, he was faced with a 'death tax' bill of nearly $53 million. Van Munching agreed to stay on for another three years to help with the transition. Christopher and Philip, two of his sons who worked at VMCO, were to be given 'every opportunity of advancement'.

For about two years the company operated more or less as before. Van Munching's strategy was to rise above the scrum of what he regarded as faddish imports and craft beers by continuing to trade on Heineken's class. The company's largest advertising campaign, by Warwick Baker & Fiore, trumpeted Heineken's superiority in the same way: 'No holiday sweepstakes. No blimp with our name on it. No racing team. None of that is what made Heineken the number-one imported beer in America', it said, before concluding that 'Just being the best is enough.'

VMCO employees were nervous about their prospects after Van Munching's departure at the end of 1993. They were somewhat perplexed to hear that head office had picked the Irishman Michael Foley to head up their biggest business outside the Netherlands. While Van Munching was still clearing his desk, Foley settled into a small office at VMCO and started learning about the market. Some employees grew more comfortable with the Irishman when they saw that he seemed to listen to and value Van Munching's input. At the importer's farewell dinner Foley hailed him as 'an incredibly tough act to follow'.

But when he took charge, Foley had his diagnosis ready. He told *Modern Brewery Age* that VMCO was 'probably a bit complacent' and paralysed by 'a certain distrust of modern techniques.' 'Perhaps in recent years, the company became a bit stale and not as forward-looking as it should have been', he said. The Irishman predictably advocated an overhaul of the organisation, to align it with other consumer goods companies. VMCO had been mostly a sales organisation, operating without such functions as product and marketing managers: marketing decisions were taken by Leo van Munching together with the sales staff. That job was to be filled by Chris Vuyk, a Dutchman who had long worked at Heineken's European marketing department.

While the management changes were understandable, Foley upset some of the old hands at VMCO with less tactful decisions. A few months after Foley's arrival, senior employees were confronted with a huge shift in company culture. This was the scene at the Trophy Room, a club in Houston, as described by Philip van Munching, one of Leo's sons:

> My brother, Christopher, looked at the beautiful, nearly naked blond lap dancer writhing on the seated figure of Michael Foley and came to the realization that Van Munching & Company was changing. His thought was confirmed when Foley looked over at him, smiled, and shouted above the music, 'This is fuckin' great!'

The company's chief executive had brought an entire management layer to Houston to discuss the strengths and weaknesses of the Heineken brand in the United States, and of the former Van Munching organisation. The participants had been asked to share suggestions and to vent criticism. Some of the comments had proved useful, but the entire setting, and particularly the after-dinner entertainment, unsettled many of the employees, most of whom were conservative, middle-aged men who identified strongly with the classy demeanour and impeccable behaviour advocated by Van Munching.

While personnel turnover had been almost non-existent under Van Munching's leadership, employees suddenly departed, both voluntarily and otherwise. The two Van Munching sons both left Heineken USA, the subsidiary established by Heineken.

Perhaps most importantly for the Heineken brand, Foley no longer wanted to compete as an 'imported' brand only. The Irishman suggested that Heineken could compete head-on with the speciality and American super-premium brands, because the distinction between the domestic and imported market was becoming less relevant. He even considered teaming up with American brewers. 'Consumers want quality and taste, and we don't have to be an importer to give it to them', he said. As he admitted, this was 'a major philosophical jump'.

Among many other changes, Foley's team decided to switch advertising agencies. Both the Heineken and Amstel accounts were moved to other agencies. Heineken landed with Wells Rich Greene BDDP. Again the campaign launched in 1996 was a major departure from anything that Van Munching would ever have allowed to be broadcast or printed for Heineken. The new agency organised 'Heineken Nights' and recorded conversations held at the bar. They were run as a voice-over over a single location shot. While some of them were amusing, they didn't discuss the brand's imported status or its quality. Several words had to be beeped out, and some of the print 'conversations' were just astonishing: 'What do they call people from Holland ... Holes?' *Advertising Age* thought it was an 'unusually fresh beer campaign [...] in which loose lips make great copy'. But the newspaper's own critic, Bob Garfield, could not help wondering why 'Heineken would identify itself with these unhappy, inarticulate, semiliterate, underemployed, sexually frustrated and generally embarrassing characters'.

In any case, they did not appear to be as thirst-inducing as Corona's marketing. After a brief slowdown the Mexican beer's market share started to inflate again. It was aided by the rise of the Hispanic community, but even more so by the owners' convincing efforts to sell Corona as 'the beach in a bottle'. Less than ten years after Leo van Munching Jr closed the door of VMCO behind him, Heineken had lost its top imported beer slot in the United States.

12

The Uncrowned Beer King

While Heineken was shaken by persistent hiccups, Freddy himself was starting to detach himself from the running of the brewery. After four decades at the company, he appeared increasingly eager to demonstrate his ability elsewhere. Still, he acted out the part that had come to be expected of him – the flippant and hard-headed but ultimately shrewd owner of a uniquely international beer brand.

Few drinkers in other countries realised that their beer was named after the Dutch owner's family. But Heineken earned widespread respect among other business people for his achievement: he had built up a mighty brand and guided the rise of the company in an increasingly global beer market, while holding on to the group's majority ownership. In Heineken's own country this recognition acquired almost folkloric proportions. Heineken had become 'Freddy', the uncrowned king of the Netherlands. Nearly everyone recognised the deep lines that ploughed his face, the erratic flow of his speech and the ultra-light cigarette that seemed forever glued between his fingers.

The phenomenon was all the more remarkable in an egalitarian country where wealth tended to be despised rather than respected, and where 'acting normal' is an institutionalised prerequisite for social acceptance. The country's fondness for the brewer was partly inspired by the product sold under his name, but he also endeared himself to the crowd with his irreverent attitude. The ordeal he had endured during his kidnapping only added to the warmth that the Dutch public felt for their plucky beer magnate.

Freddy's near-royal status made headlines in August 1987, when Queen Beatrix of the Netherlands was taken ill in the south of France. It emerged that she had contracted a mild form of meningitis while cruising on board *Something Cool*, Freddy's 25-metre luxury yacht. The Dutch monarch was then pampered by the beer magnate in La Garoupe, his sumptuous villa in Cap d'Antibes, otherwise known as 'Heineken on the Rocks'. Queen Beatrix often made use of Freddy's yacht while she relaxed at her holiday home in Tuscany. Her sailing trips from Porto Ercole to Cap d'Antibes became such a routine that, according to a government official, the Dutch internal security service asked Heineken to equip the bushy path from the beach to his terrace with infra-red detectors.

Dutch newspapers then reported that the Heinekens had been royal house guests since Freddy's father, Henry Pierre Heineken, had socialised with Prince Bernhard, the Queen Mother Juliana's husband. Beatrix and her husband, Claus, a jolly character himself in earlier days, seemed genuinely fond of Freddy, and the brewer happily cultivated the relationship. He used to answer royal phone calls with the teasing question: 'Well then, tired of ruling yet?' The royal family apparently tolerated his informal manner, both in private and in public. Heineken steadfastly refused to call Beatrix 'Her Majesty', arguing that it would be absurd to adopt such formal behaviour with a woman who walked around his house in a swimsuit.

Other Dutch business people were flabbergasted that, seated near the royals at official dinners, Heineken was allowed to treat the guests to smutty jokes. He even teased Beatrix about her title princess of Orange. 'What's it like for an Orange to have dinner with a Mandarin?' he supposedly asked upon her return from a trip to China.

The relationship sometimes led to irritation, as revealed by the Dutch writer Max Pam (after twenty-five years of silence, as promised). While they were having lunch at a port on the Mediterranean, Heineken told the writer that he had just received an urgent phone call from the captain of his yacht. A very special guest on board had asked for some money to go shopping. Since the person requested a substantial sum, the captain felt compelled to check if he was allowed to open the safe. Heineken had to give in (he knew that royalty do not go out and about with travellers' cheques), but he was clearly not amused.

The Dutch monarch was only one of the many royalty and other tycoons with whom Freddy consorted. He socialised with Princess Grace of Monaco and her husband, Prince Rainier. The relationship was so informal, Freddy said, that Grace simply added water to the soup when he turned up at Rocagel without warning. Some of Europe's most famous industrialists, bankers and assorted high-flyers had a drink with Freddy on the pine-shaded terrace of La Garoupe, while other guests were treated to a speedboat race. Freddy was at the wheel: wearing shorts and espadrilles, he played 'tag' with his bodyguards. Heineken liked to spend part of the summer there, only occasionally leaving the house to have lunch with his wife at Plage Keller, a famous restaurant on the peninsula. He acquired several adjacent houses over the years, for his family and other guests.

Apart from security issues, the only factor that prevented Freddy Heineken from enjoying his wealth further afield was his bizarre reluctance to fly. A friend said that the brewer, once a keen pilot and aircraft owner, was scared off airplanes for ever after the death of his friend Horatius Albarda, a former president of the Royal Dutch Airlines KLM and a member of Heineken's supervisory board. Albarda died in May 1965, when his private jet crashed in the Swiss Alps.

Some of Freddy's pedigree acquaintances were members of the Corviglia Ski Club, based at the exclusive Swiss resort of St Moritz. Founded by such personalities as Baron Philippe de Rothschild and Coco Chanel, this club boasted probably the world's wealthiest list of members: from the Aga Khan to Giovanni Agnelli (the former Fiat chairman), Heinrich Thyssen-Bornemisza, William Guinness and Stavros Niarchos. The combined fortune of those men, added to the heritage of assorted earls, counts and princes, could easily support the economy of a small European country. As Heineken remarked: 'You won't find peroxide blondes with fake tans and men with white socks around here.' They were certain to be blackballed by Corviglia's ballot committee. At one point Freddy was the club's vice-president, 'book-keeper' and beer supplier, along with the German members Heinrich and Maximilian zu Fürstenberg.

Corviglia's clubhouse, a pink chalet perched on the hills of St Moritz, exudes the stylish comfort of an old English reading-room, with creaking parquet and a stately fireplace. The walls are also embellished with the framed smiles of the 'Glamour Girls', the winners of Corviglia's female ski race. Among the sporting heiresses are Christina Onassis, Eliette von Karajan, Princess Caroline of Monaco and Charlene Heineken.

For three generations the Heinekens have spent the winter months in St Moritz. Freddy reckoned his parents made him there. Although he was hardly ever spotted on the slopes, the altitude helped to clean up his lungs when his chain-smoking habit started to cause respiratory problems. The brewer's luxury property on the outskirts of St Moritz was built in the late '70s. It was said to contain many gadgets, such as a bathroom with a sliding roof. It is situated at the top of the resort's most prestigious road, the Via Alpina. Since this also featured the villa of the Rossis, the Italian vermouth makers, it was dubbed 'Alcohol Hill'.

The residents of St Moritz had long ceased to frown upon the frolics of such wealthy visitors, but Heineken still managed to unleash a local furore. Prominent members of the community went up in arms to prevent Freddy from destroying another of his St Moritz properties, bought in 1984 for the equivalent of €3 million, an enormous villa designed by the German neo-classical architect Heinrich Tessenow.

Böhler House was built from 1916, at the request of the Austrian weapons manufacturer Heinrich Böhler. Architects regarded it as a monument of historical significance, but Heineken saw it only as 'depressing', describing it to the local press as 'a monstrous yellow colossus'. He wanted to demolish it completely and construct a thirteen-room mansion on the site as a residence for his guests and security staff, and it was to be linked to the other Heineken villa through an underground passage. He reportedly ordered his architect, Werner Wichser, to proceed with the demolition of Böhler House – illegally. 'The story of the capitalist who does not have to comply with the law did the rounds in the Grisons', reported *Weltwoche*.

To save the house, a group of prominent locals formed a protest committee. The issue was eventually subjected to a local referendum, but the protesters were powerless against Heineken. 'Just before the referendum, Heineken threw an open house party and chartered a bus to have people picked up in the village. To make the Böhler house look sinister, he closed the shutters.' And in the end Freddy had his way again. In June 1989 an overwhelming majority of the voters rejected the committee's plea to have Böhler House placed on a list of untouchable historical monuments. Shortly afterwards, the house was bulldozed.

Freddy deeply resented the accusations of architectural barbarity. Certain of his good taste, the brewer even had special business cards printed that described him as a professional architect and interior designer. And he did indeed decorate all his properties and the brewery's buildings with incredible attention to detail: he could tell you exactly where the most mundane ornaments in his office came from, down to lampshades and doorknobs. Sometimes, though, he got so carried away with his strokes of architectural inspiration that he forgot about budgetary discipline. 'Freddy often seemed penny-wise and pound-foolish', said one former assistant. 'At one stage he had five rooms refurbished for board members. Even the bombastic decoration of Yab Yum [a luxury brothel in Amsterdam] looked discreet compared with those offices. The whole works had to be demolished.'

His hotel, the Hôtel de l'Europe, was a more suitable establishment for Freddy to display his talents for interior design. He gave precise instructions to Adriaan Grandia, whom he hand-picked as manager of the hotel and restaurant, about everything from the shape of the chairs to the lighting for the art works hung on the wall. Even the inscription under the little ashtrays in the Excelsior Restaurant and Freddy's Bar was inspired by Heineken: 'Honestly stolen from Hôtel de l'Europe', it read.

To get his hands on the right accessories, Freddy would shop around. As a result, his fleet of cars often blocked the narrow

Amsterdam streets lined with antique shops. 'It was a pretty funny sight', said one friend. 'There was this huge Bentley parked in front of the shop with two other cars, one in front and one behind. Then Freddy would walk into the shop and start haggling over the price of a silver spoon.' Freddy bought paintings too. He collected about sixty art works, and found it most stimulating to deal in works by emerging talents.

Haggling was in fact one of the billionaire's favourite occupations. One former Heineken executive witnessed how Freddy even fleeced one of his few friends, Jan Timmer, the former head of the advertising department, for the sheer pleasure of wheeler-dealing. 'When Timmer asked Freddy to purchase a company car for him, Heineken drove down to a garage in Lisse and found a respectable-looking second-hand vehicle. He bought it for six thousand guilders', said Sibe Minnema, the former export manager. 'Then he returned to the office and told Timmer he had bought a beauty for "only" six and a half thousand guilders. Freddy was really chuffed about the trick, which earned him the fantastic sum of five hundred guilders.'

Trading cars continued to entertain the brewer long after he had found other means to pay for his rent. Heineken's garage featured mostly American cars, which he rarely used. His collection, which was auctioned by Christie's a few years ago, comprised cars made by Rolls-Royce, Buick (the Roadmaster, from 1947), Mercedes, Ferrari, Cadillac and more, many of them from the '70s. Among them were supposedly practical cars like a Ford Country Squire, a wood-panelled station wagon: Christie's said Heineken bought it straight from the factory in 1979 and mostly drove it to transport suitcases to his yacht in the south of France. But the car that fetched the highest price at the auction, over €272,000, was a black Bentley R-Type Continental from 1954, with a superb curvy design. Heineken had spotted it at a petrol station in Switzerland in 1977 and immediately bought it from the owner.

But the billionaire combined his costly extravaganzas with incredible miserliness. On the one hand, he was prepared to spend many thousands of guilders to replace the marble tiling in his southern French property because the red threads in the pattern were slightly too wide. But on the other, he complained about the price of a cup of coffee at the Hilton Hotel, and he argued with restaurateurs that he should be allowed to pay half the menu price if he wanted to order only half a steak. The brewer even crossed swords with the local authorities in Noordwijk to avoid payment of the dog tax for Pasha, his Dalmatian: he argued that the 60-guilder levy was justified for his two poodles, Omar Khayyam and Donna Fabiola, but that Pasha was a guard dog.

Heineken's paranoid attitude to influence and money denied him many friendships. To avoid being exploited, when he invited contacts for lunch at Excelsior, his own restaurant in the Hôtel de l'Europe, he insisted that they take turns to pay the bill, or he would arrange for the guest to pay for wine, while he paid for the food. 'Of course, the wine bill was always the biggest', sighed the journalist Ferry Hoogendijk, one of those 'guests'.

Admittedly, being wealthy is no easy job in the Calvinistic Netherlands. Both the Dutch tax regime and its social climate were bad news for billionaires. Freddy openly loathed the country's egalitarian culture and its leading promoters on the political scene, the social-democratic Partij van de Arbeid (Labour Party).

In public, Freddy Heineken studiously abstained from making any comments about politics, explaining that 'my beer has to go down red throats as well'. But in fact he went to great lengths to support his friends or thwart the politicians he didn't approve of. He abhorred the policies implemented by the Labour Party, and he consistently railed at its supporters (one of his milder pronouncements was that 'red women are always so ugly'). Before the elections, Heineken instructed his driver to attend Labour Party meetings and to ask awkward questions about party chairman Joop den Uyl's patrimony, particularly his rather comfortable house. He even orchestrated and financed a last-minute advertising campaign by the right-wing liberal party, the VVD, ahead of parliamentary elections in 1972.

While Freddy professed to stay away from politics, in Noordwijk politicians were permanently reminded of his presence as he filed suit after suit to protect his view of the North Sea. 'He meddles with the most pathetic little things', one official sighed. But the local authorities in Amsterdam were also repeatedly confronted with Freddy's grand schemes. In the '70s Heineken even promoted himself to the rank of town architect: he proposed to reshape Amsterdam's public transport network with an underground ring, intended to decongest the town centre without destroying any historical sites. Although the plan was relegated to the municipal archives, Freddy tried again. In the late '80s he came up with another project to redesign the Museum Square in Amsterdam, with a new building for the Stedelijk Museum, a gigantic fountain at the bottom and several rows of stately brick villas.

By the early '90s the restless beer magnate had moved on to another altogether mad reconstruction scheme: this time he wanted to change the face of the entire European continent by chopping it into seventy-five independent states. Apparently insensitive to the perils of such political boldness (and predictable ridicule), he sent a glossy pamphlet with this restyled European map to thousands of journalists and decision-makers. *The United States of Europe (A Eurotopia?)* was inspired by Cyril Northcote Parkinson, the British historian, and sponsored by the Amsterdam Foundation for Historical Science – an organisation established by Heineken himself. Heineken brushed off criticism, claiming that it came from less educated journalists. If he needed proof of the idea's value, George Bush Sr, former US President, congratulated Freddy on his 'innovative and intriguing' pamphlet.

Equally presumptuous was the beer magnate's songwriting. He owned a superb Steinway and said that he liked to compose songs by just 'tinkling away' on the piano. One such song supposedly came about after dinner with Herbie Hancock. The brewer said that, when they returned from the restaurant, he opened the piano and started musing about the melodic aspects of the sentence 'We had a fish in a restaurant'. It turned into the chorus of 'In a Restaurant', one of seven songs recorded on the CD *Songs by Freddy Heineken*: 'I saw a face in a restaurant, fate was a place in a restaurant, love was a face in a restaurant', the lyrics went. The songs were recorded in London, Brussels and Blaricum, played by the London Studio Orchestra. Heineken could even afford to have Toots Thielemans, one of his favourite musicians, accompany his easy-listening tunes on the harmonica.

The main piece on the CD was meant to be 'You Again', a song that Heineken wrote with Vincent Falcone, who had been Frank Sinatra's musical director for about ten years. The song was clearly intended to be sung by Sinatra himself, but Heineken was apparently unable to persuade his friend The Voice to lend his for the occasion. Instead he asked Kenny Colman, a jazz singer who described himself as one of Sinatra's long-time friends. Freddy got angry when his friends tried to tell him that the result was schmaltzy. He had a few thousand CDs manufactured and proudly offered them to friends and visitors.

Alongside these other activities, Freddy continued to guide the rise of the Heineken brand and the company in the 1980s. He still relished the deal-making required to affirm Heineken's European leadership and watched closely for anything that had to do with his name.

◉

From the comfort of his oak-panelled office, the former parlour of his parents' home, Freddy Heineken acted as the company's strategist and brand guardian. As he liked to explain, this approach was dictated by the company's family ownership: 'I don't make plans for five years. I have to think in generations.' Heineken was still very involved in day-to-day affairs, whether that meant the design of a new Heineken bicycle rack or the tiles in the staff canteen. The brewer's instructions mostly reached employees through curt memos.

As the company's owner, Heineken was able to impose his leadership far more abruptly than other chief executives in the Netherlands, where management is often collegial. 'Obedience was a highly praised quality under his leadership', said one former executive. Freddy himself put it a little less eloquently: 'I can't stand being contradicted', he admitted, and his dealings with many other managers were tinged with barely disguised disdain. He encouraged his board members to make time for undisturbed reflection, but when subordinates challenged him with the words 'Yes, but I thought that ...', he immediately interrupted them: 'Leave that to me.'

To avoid 'tiresome' contradiction, Heineken surrounded

himself with 'disciples'. 'A product can lose its reputation almost overnight', Freddy explained in *Fortune*. 'I can't afford to have anyone except disciples running the company and brewing the beer.' A disciple was meant to devote himself to Heineken in the interest of the majority shareholder – as opposed to the 'career dog' who placed his own interest above Heineken's welfare. When picking these disciples, Freddy sometimes applied rather haphazard selection criteria – such as astrological signs. He rarely failed to mention that he was a Scorpio and was apparently convinced that this influenced his personality. He identified with both the creature's instinctive and its venomous traits. ('Hide away, wait, come out all of a sudden. Sting, got you. Better watch out.') He reckoned that Leos could be particularly suitable for managerial functions, but in any case he made sure that the star signs of his board members were not incompatible.

It was important to Freddy that aspiring managers laughed at his jokes, but they should also be well built and stylish, even attractive too, if at all possible. He openly argued that frail or ugly men were less persuasive. Size mattered as well –Heineken thought that tall men had it easier in many aspects of life. 'Had I been taller, I probably wouldn't have been so funny' was one of his favourite one-liners.

Women did not come into the picture at all. Not a single woman reached the executive board under Freddy Heineken's reign (or has done since). Along with his professed interest in women went crass misogynistic remarks, and he thought it particularly unacceptable that women should want to work when they had small children.

Heineken clearly yearned for recognition, perhaps partly to make up for his lack of formal education. He sometimes prided himself on it, or even belittled employees who did hold diplomas.

'You see he has all the diplomas, but I run the company', he once said about one of his managers at an awkward lunch with partners in Sweden. But at the same time Freddy was eager to have his achievements recognised at academic level. In 1989 he accepted an honorary doctorate in law from the University of Rochester, New York.

Dressed in a ceremonial gown, he beamed with pride as he received the honour, and told the audience of Rotterdam students (the Erasmus University having a partnership with Rochester) that he had graduated from a 'more specialised business school'. Freddy told his friends they should not bother to call him 'doctor' – 'I only have a remedy for thirst', he quipped. Yet the framed certificate hung in his office, and he regularly used the title.

At that stage, however, Freddy's business acumen had been recognised far beyond the Dutch brewing community. He had been appointed to the supervisory boards of Thyssen Bornemisza SAM, the Algemene Bank Nederland (ABN), the Steenkolen Handels Vereniging (SHV) and British Petroleum Nederland. Admittedly, the brewer partly owed those positions to personal connections: leaders of the first three companies had all been, at some point, members of Heineken's supervisory board.

Heineken's managerial talent lay in his strategic outlook, stable leadership and talent for advertising beer. In fact, Heineken rarely drank it himself. He would smile and lift a glass when photographers were around, but in his own time he was much more likely to savour a glass of wine or whisky. For most Dutch brewers of the same generation, this almost disqualified him as a brewer: he was passionate about the brand because he had built it up and owned it, but he might as well have been selling pickled onions.

Indeed, Freddy never bothered to attend the monthly meetings of the Centraal Brouwerij Kantoor (CBK), which cemented the Dutch brewers' community. Frans de Groen, formerly of the Grolsch breweries, said Freddy's distant attitude and absence from the gatherings may have been part of an effort to forge a myth. They created an artificial distinction, 'like the spiritual distance between Our Lord and the Pope'. When they inquired about Heineken's absence, the brewers were told curtly that 'Freddy likes to delegate'.

Others said that Freddy's lack of interest in the community was partly motivated by contempt for smaller brewers. Paul Rutten, former chairman of the Gulpener Bierbrouwerij, remembered he once contacted the head of Heineken's domestic network to discuss the distribution of a special Gulpener beer in Heineken-controlled pubs. Freddy insisted that he wanted to attend the talks, so the three met for dinner at the Hôtel de l'Europe. 'Freddy apparently believed I had come to discuss a possible takeover', said Rutten. 'When it became clear I had no such intention, he promptly stood up and left the table to join his mates at the bar. It was dreadfully arrogant and I was extremely angry.'

Freddy Heineken's leadership of the breweries formally came to an end at the company's shareholders' meeting in April 1989. As always, the meeting in Amsterdam's plush Okura Hotel was eagerly attended – the rounds of free beer that concluded these gatherings were part of the event's attraction, as were the figures dished out by the management. The 'Freddies', as Heineken shares were sometimes called in Amsterdam, had turned into a safe investment for long-term shareholders.

◉

It would have been hard for any successor to match Freddy's panache, but the man selected did not even try. Gerard 'Gé' van Schaik was an affable economist who had steadily climbed the ladder at Heineken over four decades. He had earned great respect at Heineken for his quiet and organised leadership as well as his amiable manner, which ensured that he got along well with Heineken partners around Europe. Van Schaik made it to the executive board in 1974 and became vice-chairman several years later. But, long-time employment at the Heineken breweries aside, Freddy and his successor had almost nothing in common: 'We are not the same at all. He is much more intuitive, I think I am more systematic', as Van Schaik said himself. While Freddy composed jazzy tunes and hobnobbed with his peers, Van Schaik listened to classical music and polished his golf swing.

Under Freddy's chairmanship Heineken's management board had normally comprised three or four other members. With a spot of self-deprecation, Van Schaik once referred to the group as 'Freddy's Three Pigeons'. In the early '80s Freddy had made each of the executive board members responsible for a specific region, as well as functional discipline. This meant that the board members had to consult each other regularly and that, to prevent ruffled feathers, the Three Pigeons had to get on reasonably well.

Unrest broke out on the board after Freddy's departure mostly because others thought that Van Schaik was only an interim ruler – a seasoned, trusted veteran whose prime task was to smooth the transition period while Heineken groomed another leader for the years to come. Lacking Freddy's undisputed authority, however, Van Schaik was unable to suppress the ensuing rivalry for his own succession.

The skirmishes centred on the toxic relationship between two likely heirs. Rob van de Vijver, the former private lawyer whom Freddy parachuted straight to the executive board in 1976, was first in line to succeed Van Schaik. He combined rare intelligence with clinical coldness. The other horse champing at the bit was Alger Oostra, the brash former president of Heineken Nederland. Catapulted on to the board just before Freddy's retirement, the youngster was widely regarded as Heineken's 'favourite'. The contrast between the personalities of the two men could hardly have been more striking: Van de Vijver was a thoughtful, sphinx-like character, while Oostra was described as an impulsive and somewhat chaotic manager.

It was easy to understand Freddy's fondness of Alger Oostra, but some felt that the young manager sucked up to Freddy with unashamed servility. 'He'd shoot off like a rocket in the middle of an important meeting when Freddy called him', said one former executive of Heineken Nederland. 'He jumped on Freddy's lap at a whistle, just like a poodle.' He exploded with laughter at Freddy's jokes, trailed behind him at parties, and never missed an opportunity to sing his praises, sometimes literally.

The animosity between the two men caused huge tensions in Heineken's head office. It reached boiling point in 1990, when Oostra, the board member in charge of Asia, was accused of nearly sabotaging Heineken's partnership with Fraser & Neave. 'Alger barged in there like a bull in a china shop. He single-handedly destroyed the many decades of work that had gone into building a harmonious relationship with Fraser & Neave', said one witness. Only two years after his appointment to the executive board, in the summer of 1990, Oostra was forced to leave. Whether or not he was to blame for the clash with Fraser & Neave remains unclear, but Oostra had apparently overplayed his hand. Van de Vijver followed about a year later, in

September 1991, to return to Loeff Claeys Verbeke, a law firm in Amsterdam.

This friction in the boardroom was a particularly unwelcome distraction at a time when Van Schaik was struggling with several other problems he had inherited from Freddy. Van Schaik had barely settled into the chairman's seat when trouble erupted in the Netherlands. The ensuing shake-up and the dismissal of the entire Dutch management were met with panic. At the same time the brewery's American business was under immense pressure, and the business in France and Spain was in need of restructuring. All of this created the unfair perception that, once Freddy had left, Heineken had lost its cool.

In 1990 Van Schaik launched his counter-attack by hiring McKinsey, the management consultants. In their report they advised that Heineken should slash costs and take more advantage of their brand's global clout. To this effect, the structure of the breweries was to be reorganised up to the highest level. Freddy's unorthodox management system and the decentralised European structure were abolished. Each of the board members would now cover one discipline worldwide. Marketing efforts should be further harmonised to create a homogeneous super-premium image worldwide. This recommendation posed a particularly tricky problem in the Netherlands, where it seemed impossible to reconcile a 30 per cent market share with an upmarket profile.

The McKinsey report led to drastic changes in Heineken's Dutch marketing approach. Heineken Nederland started supporting events such as the Dutch Golf Open and overhauled its entire advertising strategy. Heineken ended its twenty-two-year collaboration with the FHV agency, which had spawned the popular ads of the '80s, arguing that it needed an agency that would cover the whole of Europe. It moved its advertising to J. Walter Thompson. But even more startlingly for Dutch beer drinkers, Heineken dropped 'Heerlijk, helder Heineken', the catchy refrain that had identified the brand since the '60s. It was replaced by the less inspired 'Bier zoals bier bedoeld is' ('Beer just like it's meant to be'). To the Dutch, it seemed that Heineken was giving up its identity, as if Coca-Cola had started using square bottles.

As chairman, Van Schaik had insisted on meeting with Freddy only once a year, at the supervisory board meetings. But at these changes Freddy, who had apparently tried his best not to interfere, lost his patience. He started searching for another chief executive who would fulfil at least two demands: bring back 'Heerlijk, helder Heineken' and agree to consult with him several times per month. And ideally he should lead the company with a little swagger, as the beer market was turning into a global battlefield.

13

The Beer Wars

August Busch III, the Anheuser-Busch chairman, was sitting contentedly in the cockpit of his shiny Falcon aircraft as he hovered above the Czech town of České Budějovice in August 1992. Over the previous months Anheuser-Busch executives had bent over backwards to make sure the chief could touch down in the military airbase of the Bohemian town. 'It was an enormously big deal', said one of them. 'A few years earlier, the only people who were allowed to land there were Russians.'

Apparently insensitive to the commotion, August III hopped out of the plush executive jet, commanding a group of slick American executives. 'There were those fat cats from St Louis, with Armani suits and gold chains dangling from their wrists, in the middle of a forlorn East European town', smirked another beer executive. 'The poor Czechs must have thought it was an invasion from outer space.'

Indeed, August III and his troops had come to raid the Budejovicky Budvar brewery, the makers of the original Budweiser Budvar, the 'Beer of Kings'. This small Bohemian outfit, a mere minnow compared to Anheuser-Busch, had been irritating the Americans for many decades by asserting their rights to market another beer named Budweiser. The two companies had been feuding since the late nineteenth century, shortly after Adolphus Busch had started brewing his own American version of Budweiser, the 'King of Beers'. Since the two companies had carved up the international market between them just before the outbreak of the Second World War, the St Louis brewers were unable to sell their Budweiser in most of Europe.

For as long as the American beer market continued to grow, Anheuser-Busch could live with the arrangement. But in the early '90s it had become far more compelling to start exploring international markets in earnest. At this point, less than 1 per cent of Anheuser-Busch's sales were outside their own market (compared with 85 per cent of Heineken's sales). The prospects of a borderless Europe and the opening up of the former Communist countries made Europe an interesting place to start.

The Missouri brewers were therefore impatient to solve their 'Czech problem' once and for all. By teaming up with Budvar, Anheuser-Busch could sell its own beers all across Europe, while the legendary Czech brand could bolster the American sales in the premium segment. Following the Velvet Revolution, all they would have to do was persuade the Czech government, which had complete control of Budvar, to sell.

The Czechs were not impressed, however, and August's visit did nothing to appease their fears. Pictures taken during the talks showed smiling faces all around, but the proud Czechs clearly had no intention whatsoever of bowing to Anheuser-Busch. Faced with stiff local resistance, Anheuser-Busch agreed to shift the talks to a trademark settlement, hoping to acquire a stake at a later stage. But after many years of talks and litigation, the two Buds were still at loggerheads.

Anheuser-Busch put on a gentle and caring face, reportedly investing $1.5 million to convince the locals that Anheuser-Busch would be a decent partner after all. This investment saw the small town of České Budějovice converted into the somewhat surreal 'Budville'. In the medieval town square Anheuser-Busch built a 'St Louis community centre'. It organised a baseball league, built a public basketball court, sponsored English classes and even offered a $50,000 grant to the local university. All of which, predictably, failed to seduce the Czechs. 'Busch is wasting his money', said one of Budvar's managers. 'He won't reach the soul of our people.'

The complete transparency of this PR effort provoked much hilarity among European brewers. The real problem, as one of them stated, was that the St Louis men were more or less aliens in the European brewing world, and not yet attuned to the continent's business culture. A European brewer pointed out in the '90s that 'if Anheuser-Busch was headquartered in New York instead of St Louis, they'd be all over the world by now'.

Still, the tussle between the two Buds marked a shift towards an increasingly global beer business. Until the early '90s, the beer market was much more fragmented than other segments of the drinks industry. Heineken was regarded as the leading international brewer at the time (with the biggest sales outside its home market), yet its slice of the global beer market was only about 5 per cent. While Coca-Cola and Schweppes alone had a share of over 70 per cent in their market, the ten best-selling beers only made up 35 per cent of the 1.25 billion hectolitres sold globally in 1995.

What Anheuser-Busch had yet to learn, Heineken had achieved many times over the previous decades. It had cracked international markets with all sorts of tactics, from outright acquisitions to licensing agreements and distribution deals.

While Anheuser-Busch was only just starting to look beyond America's borders, Heineken was active in 170 countries and owned breweries in more than fifty of them. In terms of sales Heineken ranked second behind Anheuser-Busch and was ahead of Miller Brewing, but only Carlsberg came close to Heineken's international spread.

The man picked by Freddy Heineken to lead the 'green team' in the Beer Wars was Karel Vuursteen. A lanky executive with a brash demeanour, he had spent the previous two decades at Philips, the Dutch electronics group, in several European countries as well as North America. Freddy was attracted both by Vuursteen's extrovert personality and by his insights into marketing. In 1991 Vuursteen was hired as a board member in charge of marketing; two years later he jumped into the chief executive's chair. *Het Financieele Dagblad*, the financial daily, was so impressed by Vuursteen's cool act that it dubbed him 'the Dutch 007' – an executive version of Roger Moore, presumably with a Heineken beer bottle in his breast pocket. His wife and daughters thought he looked more like Peter O'Toole in *Lawrence of Arabia*.

At Heineken some employees abhorred Vuursteen's colloquial manner, his roaring laugh and straightforwardness. They regarded it as a lack of refinement. He was easily angered, which almost instantly turned his neck red. Despite, or perhaps in part as a result of all this, Vuursteen was undeniably cut out for the job.

Under Vuursteen, Heineken continued to function as a family-owned firm. The chief executive was regularly summoned 'for tea' with Freddy Heineken, who preached a conservative approach. 'Don't do anything crazy with this company. My name is on it', he kept reminding the chief executive. Vuursteen was instructed to respect the company's family heritage down to the outdated décor in the boardroom. 'When I got here Mr Heineken told me: "this room was good enough for my grandfather. It was good enough for my father. And it was even good enough for me." In other words, I should leave things just as they were', Vuursteen said.

The chief executive could take advantage of the company's family-owned structure to resist pressure from minority shareholders focused on short-term earnings. With Freddy Heineken's full backing, Vuursteen was unapologetic about this approach. 'I run a company. I don't manage the stock exchange', he once told disgruntled American investors.

As instructed by Freddy Heineken, Vuursteen invested in the Heineken brand. At this point Heineken made up less than 30 per cent of the entire group's turnover, with the remainder split between Amstel and a group of smaller regional brands. The company's marketing teams constantly debated the Heineken brand's international appeal – to what extent it should be marketed and advertised along the same lines in every country. Some argued that beer remained an eminently regional product, each country having its own habits and preferences. Others countered that, as the market-place was becoming increasingly international, Heineken would benefit from a global message. The first argument won over all, but the latter was still accommodated with the appointment of more international agencies and multinational sponsorship deals, such as European football and rugby championships.

Vuursteen adopted a multi-layered strategy to move into yet more markets. To begin with, Heineken acquired popular local lager brands to build up distribution and volume. If it was appropriate, particularly in Europe, Amstel would then be introduced to replace or complement it as a middle of the range branded lager. And finally, when the country's beer market was thought to be ripe enough, Heineken would introduce its green bottles. Appealing to the local élite, they could be sold at juicy margins. Smaller specialties acquired by Heineken here and there would add a little flavour (at equally attractive margins). Again, only Carlsberg had comparable weapons at its disposal as the Beer Wars loomed.

Then again, the two companies had another important thing in common: both were likely to be held back by their ownership structures. Freddy owned only a tiny majority in the Heineken group's shares, and Carlsberg was owned by the Carlsberg Foundation. As dictated by Jacob Jacobsen's will, the foundation was to keep just over half of the Danish brewery's shares and voting rights. They would be hard-pushed in the years ahead to make large-scale acquisitions without diluting the interests of their majority shareholders. None of this applied for any of the other big brewers that were starting to look beyond their own markets. Heineken suddenly faced a gang of gutsy and deep-pocketed opponents.

The Stella Artois breweries, the market leader in Belgium, were destined to become one of the earliest targets for takeovers in the international business. With a raft of beer brands that were selling at hefty prices, Stella Artois was an appetising morsel. The ownership was splintered between about sixty shareholders from three founding families. The company's growth had inflated the worth of their shares, and surely they could be tempted to cash in. Instead, Stella Artois embarked on a stunningly bold acquisition strategy, placing it at the forefront of the Beer Wars.

Just like Heineken in the Netherlands, Stella Artois's

leadership in the Belgian market was based on the union of two breweries. The deal was signed in 1971 between Stella Artois and Piedboeuf. Stella had been owned from around the beginning of the century by Belgian aristocrats, the De Spoelberch and De Mévius families. Piedboeuf was set up a few years later by investors around Albert van Damme. At the time Stella Artois was much larger than Piedboeuf, so that the agreement of the tie-up in 1971 gave just 12.5 per cent of the joint company to the Van Dammes.

However, the shareholders omitted to tell the employees. Unlike Heineken and Amstel, the two Belgian breweries were not integrated, and the managers did not formulate any strategy for their two brands. The leading executives at Stella Artois and Piedboeuf kept their alliance secret, leaving their sales people to battle it out in the market. The duel unfolded unfavourably for Stella Artois: the far more aggressive sales people at Piedboeuf snatched hundreds of accounts for Jupiler, the brand they launched in 1966. Annual sales of the Stella Artois brand peaked in 1974, reaching more than 4 million hectolitres. Twelve years later they had shrivelled to 1.4 million, while Jupiler sales rose to over 2.7 million hectolitres.

It was only in 1987 that the shareholders of the rival breweries made their alliance public, outraging many of their employees. While the two breweries had been run separately, the set-up had become badly unproductive, with ten brewing plants around the small country. The two breweries were far less efficient, producing just three hectolitres per hour per employee, compared with Heineken's five. Once the alliance became public, their operations could finally be integrated to increase productivity – although there was much resistance from the breweries' workers.

In the early '90s, the Belgian company was renamed

Interbrew. It had grown into a much more efficient company, with an estimated 60 per cent share of the Belgian market. Profits were supplemented by growing royalties from Whitbread in the United Kingdom, as well as a few profitable operations in Africa. They even built their own plant in Guangdong, China, in 1984. However, the company's leading executives were certain that this wouldn't be enough to keep the brewery's independence in the coming years. The shareholders had to take a clear-cut decision: they could either sell at the highest price or support an all-out expansion strategy. Amazingly, the shareholders went for the risky option.

By then, the capital was spread between third- and even fourth-generation descendants of the De Spoelberch, De Mévius and Van Damme families. The Van Dammes had been unable to alter the split of shares established in 1971, which no longer looked fair now that Jupiler had become the Belgian market leader. However, Alexandre van Damme, the grandson of Piedboeuf's founding partner, succeeded in winning the support of the three families for the expansion strategy.

At this time the international brewers were snatching at breweries in Eastern Europe, where the collapse of Communist rule had triggered a rush to privatisation. The targets comprised some much-wanted brands, such as Pilsner Urquell and Budvar from the Czech Republic, but the buyers frenetically snapped up almost any beer assets put up for sale in Eastern Europe. From Heineken to Bass and Anheuser-Busch to South African Breweries, anybody who had ambitions in the international beer market learned to say 'Nazdravye'.

Interbrew started rather inconspicuously in Böcs, in the east of Hungary, where it purchased a 52 per cent share in Borsodi Sörgyàr in October 1991. Hungary was a fiercely fought battleground for the brewers: less than five years after the opening of the market, all of the country's seven largest brewers were in the hands of foreign rivals. But the purchase of the second-largest Hungarian brewer was much more significant for Interbrew: profitable almost from the start, it inspired the Belgian group's strategy for the early '90s. Instead of throwing money at Stella Artois, to try and build it into a stronger international brand, Interbrew decided to bet on national or regional market leaders. These brands would secure volume and access to local accounts. Then the real profits would flow in, with the sale of the many special brews owned by the group, such as Leffe and Hoegaarden. An added benefit of this approach was that it frustrated the international beer brands, because it prevented them from swamping the East European market with a single strategy. 'They don't like that', explained Hans Meerlo, then Interbrew's chief executive. 'It means they have to find something new in every market.'

Over the second half of the '90s Interbrew executives travelled all around Eastern Europe, from Romania to Ukraine and from Poland to Croatia. They compared notes on the most corrupt officials and the best methods for crushing cockroaches. During their travels they discovered that one of their brewing plants was operated by prisoners. At another brewery, in Donetsk, which they hoped to acquire, the general manager was shot dead just a week after Interbrew came calling. But these problems didn't hold Interbrew back: within a few years they had acquired breweries all over Eastern Europe. It often worked in Interbrew's favour that they were relatively unknown, came from a small country and pledged to support the local beers. Somewhere along the line a copywriter coined the phrase that encapsulated the strategy: 'The world's local brewer.'

Interbrew's whole Eastern Europe project lost some of its grandeur, however, when the Belgians swallowed up John

Labatt, the largest Canadian brewer, in June 1995. It was the biggest takeover by a Belgian company, and at 2.7 billion Canadian dollars, it was the biggest deal the beer industry had ever seen. Labatt had two leading brands, Blue and Rolling Rock, with distribution across Canada as well as the United States. Owing to the structure of the Canadian market, which was driven almost entirely by two mega-brewers, the business turned a reliable profit. Another interesting asset was the company's 22 per cent stake in Femsa Cerveza, the second-largest brewer in Mexico.

Heineken had been in Toronto as well, and had even stayed in the same hotel as their Belgian rivals. Interbrew had apparently won Labatt from Heineken because they were prepared to make more concessions, and to share the management with the Canadians. They were also prepared to pay more, because they recognised this as an opportunity to move into the American market with a highly profitable business. All Karel Vuursteen could do was to pick up his phone and convey his admiration about the move, in his characteristic manner: 'You've got balls', Vuursteen told Meerlo, a former colleague at Philips.

With the acquisition of Labatt, Interbrew leaped from seventeenth to fourth position in the brewers' league table, with solid footholds in both the European and the North American continents. But, most importantly, the Labatt deal marked the start of the reshuffling of the global beer business. Interbrew led the way: with Labatt, the Belgians had proved themselves capable of absorbing much larger breweries. They weren't going to stop in Canada.

While many brewery executives had discovered the airports of

Budapest, Prague and Warsaw in the '90s, others had started venturing further afield. The skirmishes between international brewers started to bubble with the rush for Eastern Europe, but the boldest of them had already set their sights further east: they were making a dash for China, which was well on its way to becoming the largest beer market in the world.

While the Chinese still only quaffed about 10 litres of beer per capita annually, their country had nonetheless grown to become the second-largest beer market behind the United States. It would only take a few extra bottles per Chinese adult to trigger an explosion in the market. China had just begun to open up a few years earlier, and even the most seasoned beer executives were flabbergasted by what they saw. 'When you travel around there, you find cities of ten million people that you've never heard of', said Johnny Thijs, who succeeded Meerlo as Interbrew's international chief. 'And none of us are there yet.'

Over the years Heineken had built up teams of multi-lingual and adaptable executives who were prepared to shift beer bottles in almost any climate, regardless of the political circumstances, but China was an altogether different kettle of fish. In the late 1980s, when Heineken started exploring the market, the workings of the Chinese government were still so arcane that it took them more than three months just to find out which minister they should cajole to get into the market. Then they faced many more months of talks that often verged on the absurd, with the two parties apparently talking a different language. But the mouths of the Dutch executives really fell open once they had struck their deal and discovered local beer-selling techniques. 'For the Chinese sales manager, marketing means that consumers who want beer come and pick it up at the brewery themselves', one of them told a Dutch reporter. It was not a joke.

The pitfalls of investing in Chinese breweries were tragically (or hilariously) captured in *Mr China*, by Tim Clissold, who was involved in the purchase of the Five Star Brewery in the 1990s. He had to deal with Madame Wu Hongbo, chief engineer of the First Light Industry Bureau of the People's Municipal Government of Beijing. Clissold was a little startled that she accused him of 'talking in dog farts' and described the dire conditions at the brewery as 'a right stir-fry of pubic hairs and garlic'. But there was nothing he could do as the investors' money disappeared, without any improvements at the brewery. Employees could not be fired, even though quality control was so appalling that some bottles wore labels describing the contents as 'soy sauce' and others were altogether empty. They ended up withdrawing, having lost most of their investment.

Another complication was that Heineken was still stuck with Fraser & Neave, the Singapore traders with whom they had teamed up about sixty years earlier. In principle, all of Heineken's investments in Asia were to go through Asia Pacific Breweries (APB), the joint venture between Heineken and Fraser & Neave, in which the Dutch held just 42.5 per cent. This partnership had proved very productive in its earlier years, as Fraser & Neave provided the Dutch with trading contacts and distribution around South-East Asia. But unfortunately for the Dutch, Fraser & Neave also had an agenda of their own: to push Tiger Beer.

While the Dutch regarded this as a regional beer, meant to elevate the prestige of the international Heineken, Fraser & Neave prized their beer as the real thing, another international premium brand. They gloated about minuscule sales in the United States and even opened up a Tiger sales office in Belgium. Heineken's men watched it all with a mixture of contempt and irritation. 'It's a thorn in our side', one of them reportedly lamented. 'Our colleagues at ABP have made sure that Heineken is almost nowhere to be found in Singapore.' At least, that was the argument they put forward to open their own sales office in the region – creating an awkward stand-off with Fraser & Neave.

Heineken repeatedly tried to alter the relationship with Fraser & Neave in the late '80s and early '90s, when it was contemplating forays into China. For such a huge market the Dutch wanted a free rein to invest rapidly and abundantly without having to share the returns with their Singapore partners, who were perceived as more timorous or downright reluctant. They worked on a number of potential compromises with Fraser & Neave. The brewery was prepared to add all its hitherto independent Asian operations (the Indonesian subsidiary and a licensing agreement with the Japanese Kirin brewery) to the communal package, in exchange for a majority share. Fraser & Neave interpreted this as a brutal attempt by Heineken to get rid of them. The proposal was swept off the table.

Heineken's opening gambit in China came in 1988 with the acquisition of a minority stake in the Shanghai Mila breweries. They were the makers of Reeb ('beer' spelt backwards), the top-selling beer in Shanghai. But over the next years the Chinese government's influence on the Mila breweries drove Heineken's managers up the wall. The company was effectively in the hands of a Communist Party member whose main preoccupation was to represent the interests of the state.

'That's the way it goes out there', sighed one brewery executive. 'The Communist Party chap sits at the head of the meeting table, with a local government representative next to him, as well as a town official. Then comes the brewery manager. If you're lucky you get a seat too. The best way to get lucky, of course, is to grease all the others.'

For all these troubles and dilemmas, Vuursteen was understandably charmed by the attractions of the Asian beer market. As he pointed out, the annual growth of the Chinese market alone in the early '90s was the same volume as the entire French beer market – Heineken's largest at that stage. By April 1994 he could let it be known that he had persuaded APB to invest about 800 million guilders in Asia over the next five years. Apart from their stake in Shanghai Mila, they had invested in Fujian Breweries (making Rong Cheng) and another plant was under construction on the island of Hainan. Heineken was the leading imported beer brand in China, but its local capacity of about 1 million hectolitres was a mere trickle compared to the 150 million produced by Chinese brewers.

Anheuser-Busch, which struggled to grasp the ways of the beer business in Europe, could hardly be expected to do much better in China. In 1993 they topped an offer from Heineken to acquire a stake of just 5 per cent in Tsingtao, then described as the largest of an estimated 800 Chinese breweries (with a market share of just 2.5 per cent). But shortly afterwards, their rivals whispered that Anheuser-Busch and Tsingtao were not even on speaking terms. 'The Chinese took Busch's dollars, said thanks and closed the door', they chuckled.

But in the second half of the '90s executives from international breweries, from Heineken to Bass and from Carlsberg to Interbrew, were increasingly likely to bump into a far less familiar rival: South African Breweries (SAB). In the apartheid years the company had been mostly confined to the South African market. It held a market share estimated at more than 95 per cent with its Castle brand. When the apartheid regime was dismantled in 1993, SAB was sitting on a huge cash pile and apparently keen to spend it.

They too started by acquiring breweries in Eastern Europe,

where they angered European competitors. They were accused of violating unwritten codes of conduct in the somewhat incestuous world of European brewing – engaged in a dogfight in one country, two competitors could work together in another, or even have a shareholding agreement. To force the South Africans to stick to such rules, other brewers allegedly cut their own prices to unviable levels in areas dominated by the South Africans.

The crafty South Africans quickly moved on to China: by the end of the '90s they owned fifteen Chinese breweries, and in 2001 their interests were enlarged with a joint venture that comprised another ten breweries. SAB was then the second-largest brewing group in China behind Tsingtao, with its forty-five brewing plants. In the next years the former South Africa brewer would move to London and become the last of the major contenders in the Beer Wars.

While all of these Chinese ventures could still be regarded as long-term investments, which would take years to yield any profits, the same protagonists were continuing to clean up the European market – splitting between them the remaining independent brewers in the larger countries. In the process Heineken and its global rivals ripped apart the British beer industry.

After several decades of rationalisation, the British beer business entered the '90s with just four major brewers controlling about 76 per cent of the beers sold in Britain. At the head of the pack was Scottish & Newcastle, the owner of brands such as John Smith's and Newcastle Brown Ale as well as Foster's European business and interests in several other countries.

Next came Bass Brewing, the owner of Carling Black Label. Whitbread, Heineken's partner in the United Kingdom, was among the top players, albeit with a share of less than 15 per cent. The smallest of the four was Carlsberg-Tetley.

Scottish & Newcastle came out swinging in March 2000. To avoid being gobbled up, the company acquired one of the most sought after players in the European beer industry: Kronenbourg, the brewing arm of Danone. It was then still the leading brewer in the French market and held interests in several other European countries, from Spain to Italy. The sale of Kronenbourg had been in the making for such a long time that it had been dubbed the 'Loch Ness Monster' (the Scottish reference was appropriate, as it turned out). Danone had made it clear that it would prefer to focus on food and drinks that were less exposed to the whims of governments and other lawmakers. Scottish & Newcastle forked out €3.74 billion to snatch the French prize.

Not quite as optimistic, Bass put its brewery division up for sale in February the same year. The brewer from Burton upon Trent still owned Carling, Britain's most popular lager. Worthington Bitter and Caffrey's Irish ale were part of the same package (while other activities, such as the chains All Bar One and Harvester, were spun off).

Just three months later, in May 2000, the sale started in earnest when Interbrew walked away with Whitbread. The Belgians bought nearly all of Whitbread's brewing activities, while the British company retained the retail and catering arms. Worth just £400 million, the deal enabled Interbrew to get its hands on the brewing unit that made and sold Stella Artois in Britain – by then the largest market for the Belgian beer. And Whitbread decided to focus on its hotels and restaurants business instead.

But the deal excluded Heineken's production in Britain.

Whitbread's managers organised an orderly transition, forming a separate unit that could continue to brew the Dutch beer until the end of the licensing contract with Whitbread, in 2004. The brewing plant in Samlesbury remained open, albeit with a reduced capacity, to take care of Heineken. Meanwhile the Dutch company finally prepared to open its own office in the UK to handle its distribution there.

Next came the takeover of Bass Brewing, in August the same year. Again the buyer was Interbrew, but the price set for the owner of Carling was considerably higher than for Whitbread, at about £2.3 billion. With 7,000 employees working in six brewing plants, Bass Brewing was said to command a UK market share in the range of 24 per cent. This would increase Interbrew's British share to roughly 32 per cent. Carlsberg had put in its own bid for Bass Brewing. Heineken was left empty-handed.

The deal with Bass triggered several months of uncertainty for Interbrew and the entire British market, as the competition authorities launched an investigation. It was all the more awkward for Interbrew that, on the back of the acquisition agreement, it had decided to float shares on the stock market for the first time in December. They were to offer about 21 per cent of the company's capital on Euronext. The price bracket set for the offering valued the entire company at up to €16 billion, making it the largest initial public offering in Belgian history.

The UK competition commission inquiry on the acquisition of Bass threatened to undermine Interbrew's entire plan, because a negative ruling would considerably reduce the scope of the brewery. At the same time investors were worried about another cloud hanging over the Belgian brewery: a probe launched by the European Commission into alleged cartel agreements between beer companies in several European countries.

Despite the worries, the Interbrew shares offered were four

times over-subscribed. But just a few days later, at the beginning of January 2001, the Competition Commission startled Interbrew's advisers with a decision to torpedo the acquisition of Bass Brewing completely. Uncharacteristically, the Commission did not even allow for remedies, such as the sale of Whitbread: the Belgians had to sell Bass entirely and within six months to an approved buyer. The decisive factor in the 262-page report was that the deal would create a virtual duopoly in the British market, between Scottish & Newcastle and Interbrew: they would command about 60 per cent of the market and own four out of the ten top beer brands in Britain.

The Financial Times pointed out that precedents of intervention in the beer business had hardly been beneficial. After the Beer Orders the number of British brewers was roughly halved. In 1997 the proposed merger between Carlsberg-Tetley and Bass was approved by the Monopolies and Mergers Commission, but then Margaret Beckett, head of the Department of Trade and Industry, had still scuppered the deal. The newspaper thought that this decision had ultimately prompted Bass to pull out of brewing. And two years later Whitbread's bid to acquire the pubs business of Allied Domecq was also thwarted by the competition authorities, which encouraged Whitbread to sell its brewing arm.

Finally, the ruling on Bass was overturned by the High Court on a technicality. The Department of Trade and Industry went on to rule in September 2001 that Interbrew should divest either Bass or Carling Brewers by the end of February 2002. They opted for Carling. It was sold to Coors Brewing, the third-largest American brewer, at $1.7 billion. After this dizzying game of musical chairs, only one of the country's largest brewers remained in British hands – though not for much longer.

The British scenario, or something along the same lines, was repeated all over Europe. Even Germany was no longer spared: among the largest deals of these years was Interbrew's acquisition of Beck's, one of the earliest international brewers, for the equivalent of €1.8 billion. It was SAB that walked away with Pilsner Urquell in 1999 (along with Radegast). Heineken contributed by buying several brands, such as Fischer and Adelshoffen, the last sizeable family breweries in France.

All over Europe beer drinkers lamented that the expansion of the larger breweries had destroyed local beers and traditions. While the buyers kept some of the speciality beers and even helped to sell them through their international operations, many others were ditched. The brewers disseminated relatively bland beers, and their financial firepower made it hard for the smaller outfits to find shelf space.

Michel Debus, the chairman of Fischer and Adelshoffen, spoke out for thousands of Alsatian drinkers who bitterly watched Heineken's advance in France, for example. In the eyes of Debus, such brewers were money-spinners who threatened to destroy the vestiges of the once glorious Alsatian beer industry. Always wearing a stylish traditional Alsatian bow at his neck, he profiled himself as the leader of the beer Resistance, a flamboyant ambassador of the region's brewing culture.

For many years Debus courageously fought off the two market leaders, Kronenbourg and Heineken. Together with his colleagues at Adelshoffen, he came up with oddball drinks such as Adelscott (beer with whisky malt) and Desperados (with tequila) that helped Fischer expand in the rewarding specialties segment. He even seduced female drinkers with a supposedly aphrodisiac, spicy beer called 3615 l'Amoureuse, to be ordered by Minitel (a French precursor of the internet).

Yet, for all his verve and talent, even Debus was powerless to halt Heineken's conquest of the French market. A minority shareholder, he was utterly dismayed when the Arbogasts and the Webers, two other families of Fischer shareholders, agreed to sell to Heineken in February 1996. Debus retired to sculpt and paint in the south of France.

Unmoved by such sentiment, the global brewers bulldozed ahead. Along with regulatory pressures, their thirst for expansion precipitated more consolidation in the '90s than had occurred in the beer business over the previous five decades. With the disappearance of characters such as Michel Debus, the European industry was losing much of its fizz – and it was about to bid farewell to its most recognisable face.

14

After Freddy

On a grey Saturday in January 2002 a small convoy wound its way to Noordwijk cemetery, a leafy resting place on the outskirts of the Dutch beach resort. Only a few people huddled around the grave, which was to be covered with a huge yet elegantly simple slab of grey stone. The cemetery was heavily guarded and entirely closed off, when Freddy Heineken was laid to rest, surrounded by a very small family circle.

The royal family sent a funeral wreath on behalf of Queen Beatrix but stayed away from the short ceremony, as requested by the family. Freddy himself had picked a spot for his grave in Noordwijk, far from his father and paternal grandparents in Amsterdam.

The intimacy of the funeral contrasted with the abundant media coverage of the brewer's death, on Thursday 3 January, at the age of seventy-eight. It made the opening of news bulletins on all the national TV channels, and covered front pages and umpteen square metres of print space over the next days and weeks, as the Netherlands celebrated the life and times of its uncrowned beer king.

The brewer's health had been deteriorating steadily over the previous decade. His breathing had become so affected that he even gave up smoking, and in the few years before his death Freddy Heineken suffered several health warnings.

Dutch newspapers attributed his death to a lung infection, and reported that he died surrounded by his family at his home in Noordwijk.

'Heineken is probably the most famous Dutch name in the world. Only [the footballer Johan] Cruyff is a serious competitor', said the news bulletin of the first Dutch national channel in its lengthy opening piece. 'Since World War Two, there has been no other businessman in the Netherlands to build his name into such a global brand. That's why Freddy Heineken was unique in his way.' Abundant tributes were paid, describing him as a businessman with a brilliant flair for advertising, 'a flamboyant, multi-faceted man', and 'a bit of a jerk sometimes, but a nice jerk'.

Miles of newspaper coverage described the dramatic days of his kidnapping, his friendships with royals, his commitment to the Heineken brand. The adjectives 'charming', 'inventive' and 'stubborn' cropped up again and again in the articles, as well as his favourite sayings, such as 'I don't sell beer, I sell conviviality'. Tejo Hollander from FHV, Kees Sietsma from the Amsterdam police and Karel Vuursteen from Heineken were among the many people who paid personal tributes to the owner of the breweries.

Heineken called for a four-day period of mourning, during which flags flew at half-mast on the red-brick building of the former Heineken breweries in Amsterdam and all of the company's office buildings. The brewery also issued a short statement. 'With the passing of Freddy Heineken, a unique man has left us', said Karel Vuursteen; 'his extensive knowledge, creativity, intuition and humour made him a multi-faceted character'. The company's chief executive had continued to pay visits to the owner several times per month and had noticed gradual changes in the brewer's behaviour. 'You could see that he was starting to bid farewell in the last few months', Vuursteen said. 'In our talks he often spoke about the past, which he rarely had before.'

⊙

In his last years Freddy found it increasingly hard to deal with the physical symptoms of ageing. 'It's awful to feel that the body refuses to work when the mind is still sharp', he lamented. He shuffled around his office in his loafers, his back increasingly hunched, and the shortest walk left him gasping for breath. It could take him several minutes to recuperate from briefly crouching down to hit the 'Start' button on the CD player in his office suite.

In public, Freddy liked to jest about growing old and approaching death. When he forgot something, in the middle of a conversation, he tapped on his knees and whistled for an imaginary dog called 'Alzheimer'. He joked that he had started to avoid public outings because people tended to treat him somewhat condescendingly, like a respectable but decaying personality. 'I get the Prince Claus treatment', he said, alluding to the husband of then Queen Beatrix, who was suffering from Parkinson's disease. And he liked to underline the relative insignificance of his being by pointing out that few people remembered the brands drunk by Egyptians when they invented beer several thousand years ago.

Freddy Heineken remained as chairman of the supervisory board at Heineken N.V. until 1995, and he was occasionally celebrated more publicly for his achievements. Such an acclaim came when he was made Advertiser of the Year at the Cannes International Advertising Festival in 1995. He said to *Lions News*, the paper linked to the awards: 'If I had not been a brewer, I would have been an ad man', adding that beer advertising was the hardest because the product has been around for several thousand years, so 'there is not much new to say about it'.

Freddy's retirement gave him more time for other activities. It sometimes bothered him that he did not have the brains to conduct scientific research or the talent to distinguish himself as an artist. 'I'm frustrated that I'm not Einstein', he said earnestly. Instead he affixed his name to scientific research by supporting several prizes and foundations. The Henry Pierre Heineken prize for biochemistry and biophysics was established in 1964 in honour of his father, who had studied chemistry. Another four prizes were named after Alfred Henry Heineken, focusing on environmental sciences, history, medicine and the arts. Heineken liked to point out that three of the Heineken award winners went on to be awarded a Nobel Prize – prompting Heineken to call himself 'Nobel Alfred'.

Heineken fancied himself an inventor as well. In 1994 he became a member of Novu, the Dutch association for inventors, and joined other members on its collective stand to display one of his own inventions at the Salon des Inventions in Geneva. 'He was absolutely fascinated by the whole phenomenon of invention and particularly chuffed that people approached him as an inventor, not as Freddy Heineken', said Wouter Pijzel, director of Novu. The invention in question, patented in 1997, was a design meant to save space in aeroplanes and public transport, with rows of staggered seats that left more room for legs as well as more privacy. 'The seats are arranged so that each successive seat is offset by a small amount from the adjacent seat, forming a zigzag pattern', read the description. Another invention, patented three years earlier, was more relevant to his business: an apparatus 'for repairing mechanical and/chemical damage to the surface of bottles destined for re-use'.

When he was in the Netherlands, the brewer spent most of his afternoons at The Pentagon, an office cum penthouse and private cinema next to Gerard Adriaan Heineken's former mansion and Heineken's head office. From the outside the building looked quite ordinary, but The Pentagon occupied three adjacent houses. Heineken had the internal walls torn down to build this space exactly as he wanted. After his kidnapping, a large chunk of the ground floor was occupied by his security staff.

His own white desk was invariably clear, which he put down to his habit of dealing with incoming issues right away. It was situated at one end of a large living-room, with plush sofas and a grand piano directly overlooking the Weteringplantsoen square. But when he didn't have anybody to impress, Heineken preferred to sit in a small room at the back of the building, presumably a former kitchen. The office, with a plain table and functional chairs, was where Heineken went about his reading and writing in the company of an imperturbable personal assistant. This preppy woman apparently got used to his whims as well as his very individual brand of humour.

In those years Freddy also started giving more public credit to his wife, Lucille, who had stuck with him for so many years despite his public philandering. He described the longevity of their marriage as an example of how he planned for the long term. Almost movingly, he boasted to his older acquaintances that she scrubbed his back in the shower and stood by the window of their home in Noordwijk every day to wave him off.

◉

Just a few months before Heineken passed away, the company's shareholding structure came under scrutiny. Freddy Heineken had placed his shares under a Swiss holding, L'Arche, in Sion, which held slightly more than half of the shares in the Heineken Holding, a listed company itself owning just over half of Heineken N.V. The adequacy of the set-up was questioned by shareholders of Heineken Holding, because the gap between the price of Heineken N.V. and Heineken Holding shares had increased significantly: the discount was usually somewhere between 10 and 15 per cent, but in August 2000 it had widened to about 36 per cent. The unhappy shareholders questioned the entire shareholding construction, and particularly the management of Heineken Holding.

Profima Belgium N.V. hired the law firm NautaDutilh to investigate the structure of Heineken Holding and what action the company could take to address the gap in the share price of the two listed companies. One option they suggested was the liquidation of Heineken Holding, which was of course out of the question for the Heinekens.

Unwilling to drop the issue, NautaDutilh demanded that it should be taken up at the shareholders' meeting in April 2001. Freddy Heineken himself, chairman and delegate member of Heineken Holding's supervisory board, had to be excused from the gathering. He had suffered another bout of ill health a few months earlier. In his absence it was Maarten Das, Heineken's lawyer and a member of the Heineken Holding board, who read out a short statement. One reason for the price gap between the Holding and N.V. shares, he explained, was that several funds had rejigged their holdings and mostly sold their shares in small and medium-sized companies. He repeated promises to attract more attention to Heineken Holding – for example, by publishing an annual report in

English – but added that the company only had limited means to reduce the discount.

Heineken Holding meetings were usually quiet and wrapped up in a matter of minutes, but this time shareholders queued to use the microphone – not to ask difficult questions but to applaud the management and the Heineken family. Das had smartly reminded them that a shareholder who invested 12,500 guilders in the company that became Heineken Holding in 1962 would have seen the value of his shares inflate to 6.6 million guilders by January 2001. Even the representative from the Dutch Association for the Protection of Shareholders had no interest in more independent management. 'Even if it sounds chauvinistic, he is pleased that Heineken is still a Dutch company, and one with a great image, a better image sometimes than the foreign affairs ministers who are meant to represent our interests', read the record of the meeting.

Unrepentant, NautaDutilh filed a request to the Enterprise Chamber in Amsterdam, in July 2001. They wanted the Chamber to appoint an investigator to conduct an inquiry into the management and business at Heineken Holding over the previous three and a half years. A public hearing took place in Amsterdam in September. After six weeks the judge threw out all of the claimant's requests. The statutes of Heineken Holding clearly stated that the company's aim was to safeguard the stability of the Heineken group, by securing the majority shareholding of the Heineken family. Shareholders in Heineken Holding mostly bought their shares for potential price increases and the dividend (received by Heineken Holding on its shares in Heineken N.V. and transferred to the shareholders of the Holding). The judges smacked Heineken Holding on the hand for not responding to NautaDutilh's questions promptly and openly enough, but still did not see that as sufficient reason to question the structure or to allow an inquiry. Nevertheless, Profima achieved what it probably wanted anyway: on the back of the commotion, the discount in Heineken Holding shares was sharply reduced.

As the beer magnate's health became increasingly fragile, it was widely speculated that Heineken's demise would trigger a sharp rise in the price of Heineken shares. The reasoning was that, once Freddy had passed away, his heirs might be more inclined to consider a takeover bid from other breweries – and appetite for the brand was undiminished. As things turned out, the price of Heineken shares did inch up after the announcement of his death, but it soon retreated again: it quickly became clear that Freddy Heineken had meticulously arranged the handover of his shares to his daughter.

On Freddy's death, Charlene duly reported her shareholding to the stock market authorities. She had inherited the entire package formerly held by the tycoon – amounting to a small majority in Heineken Holding, which itself held a tiny majority in Heineken N.V. The share structure that had protected the Heineken breweries from takeover raids while Freddy was alive would protect the company under his daughter too.

The ins and outs of the arrangements remained somewhat unclear. An important aspect of the handover was the inheritance tax due in the Netherlands – then amounting to 27 per cent on an estate of more than €800,000. The value of the Heineken share package was about €3.4 billion, so it was estimated that Dutch inheritance tax would have amounted to over €850 million. A tax bill of this size might have forced her to sell at least some of the shares and, as the family's majority was so thin, this might have meant losing the majority holding.

To avoid this situation, Heineken said that he had arranged for the handover to take place through a foundation. With the brewery in Charlene's hands, the spotlight quickly turned to her and her London-based family.

Freddy had been eager to extend the dynasty with several little Heinekens, but in the end he could only produce one heir, his daughter Charlene, and even that was 'a lot of hassle', he said. Then again, he admitted that this might have been a blessing in disguise: the absence of a plentiful progeny at least prevented dilution and the internal squabbles which he had come to recognise as the worst threat for a family company (along with the tax authorities).

The portrait that emerged of the new owner of Heineken was that of a level-headed woman who had decided not to let her father's fortune or his antics stand in the way of a harmonious family life. Aged forty-seven at the time of her father's death, Charlene de Carvalho was living in London with her husband and five children. Those who watched her invariably praised her warmth and unpretentious attitude, as well as her commitment to her children.

Charlene made it a priority to raise her children herself, in an easy-going and down-to-earth manner. Even though she ranked among the wealthiest women in Britain, she tended to avoid ostentatious displays of wealth, such as flashy jewels and designer clothes, and to stay away from high-society parties. She usually wore unfussy, elegant outfits with a pair of flat shoes, her brown hair tied back simply.

After her law studies in Leiden, Charlene de Carvalho had agreed to start learning about the beer business. She did several internships at the company and even spent time at Lowe Howard-Spink, the British advertising agency. For about two years at the start of the 1980s she worked at Heineken in Amsterdam and Zoeterwoude, as well as Strasbourg and Paris.

However, after her wedding to Michel de Carvalho in 1983, motherhood became Charlene's main occupation. Although she had grown up a single child, she clearly aspired to a busy household, with five children born within the first seven years of the marriage: the eldest, Alexander Alfred, arrived in 1984. Then came Louisa Lucille, and the twins Isabel Catherine and Sophie Charlene. The household was completed with Charles Andrew.

Freddy Heineken himself repeatedly described his daughter as 'a woman with a good set of brains' – proving that women were 'really not always inferior', he occasionally added. He would phone Charlene several times a week. He made it clear that she would inherit his shares, and there was little doubt that she would respect her father's wish to hold on to the majority stake. She was prepared to act as an intermediary, safeguarding the family's interest until her own children were old enough to take an active part in running the company – if they so wished.

In this context, the person who provoked more scrutiny after Heineken's death was Charlene's husband, Michel de Carvalho. He had been a familiar face at Heineken shareholders' meetings since 1996, when he became a board member, yet very little was known about De Carvalho in the Netherlands. Freddy Heineken had even led his own investigations into his son-in-law's background, and had apparently been unable to obtain answers about some of the most colourful aspects of his past.

⊙

When Michel de Carvalho was brought on to the Heineken board, the company described him as a banker, but it was clear to all that he owed the nomination to his other function as Charlene Heineken's husband. What was not widely discussed at the time was that De Carvalho appeared to have led several other lives, starring in films as well as sports and business.

A few years ago two Dutch reporters dug up a British certificate that supposedly recorded the birth of Michel de Carvalho on 21 July 1944 in Gerrards Cross, in Buckinghamshire. However, the name on this certificate was Michel Ray Popper, the son of Annie and Heino Popper (described elsewhere as Heinz and later Henry Popper).

It remains unclear under what circumstances the Poppers settled down in London. They were probably brought up in Germany. Henry's family was established in the leather trade, in Berlin. Like the Heinekens before them, Henry's parents, Alfred and Elly Popper, regularly stayed at the Hotel Kulm in St Moritz for several weeks in the winter in the 1930s. Probably around the same time Henry moved to England to develop his own leather trade.

Annie's father was Alfred Lisser, a banker in Hamburg. He was an influential man at the city's famous synagogue: for many years he was the representative of the liberals and the chairman of the 'Repräsentanten-Kollegium' for Hamburg's Jewish community. Annie was born in 1905, the second of three children. The Lissers moved to the Netherlands in the early '30s, apparently for business reasons. Annie later moved on to England with her younger sister, Käte, leaving behind her parents and older brother.

The Poppers married in May 1937, at the West London

After Freddy

Synagogue, the oldest Reform synagogue in Britain, with a splendid Moorish interior, which brought together the particularly liberal Jewish community that lived around Paddington and Marylebone. They were both in their early thirties. It seems that they sought temporary refuge in Buckinghamshire while Annie was pregnant with Michel, but that their permanent address was in Paddington, just across from Hyde Park.

The question of Michel's precise provenance apparently preoccupied Freddy Heineken. Max Pam, the Dutch writer, recounted how he was approached by Heineken himself, while the brewer was researching his son-in-law's parents. As Pam recalled, Freddy suspected that Michel was illegitimate. He described the supposed father as a small-time artist with a bohemian lifestyle, who was also called Max Pam. 'I started delving into the [family] papers for him. My grandfather was called Max Pam, but it could not have been him because he was officially registered as Mozes Pam. German and Austrian Pams whom Heineken had pulled out of the archives did not appear to fit with the person he was after, either', Pam wrote. In fact, the papers indicate that Annie had been married to a Max Pam before her wedding to Popper.

Regardless of his precise family situation, Michel apparently enjoyed a comfortable youth. Henry Popper was the general manager of London and Provincial Leather Processes Ltd, and, judging from its turnover, his business was thriving. While residing in London they regularly travelled, taking Michel with them. He reportedly went to a French school in London and then boarding-school in Switzerland, where he enjoyed skiing. It reflected the parents' ample means and perhaps also their desire to take their child away from the buttoned-up education of the upper classes in England.

Michel's childhood became altogether unusual when his mother's connections in the thespian world landed him a job in the film industry. Aged just ten, he adopted the pseudonym 'Michel Ray' to appear in *The Divided Heart*, an award-winning film about a boy who is adopted as a toddler by a childless German couple in the Second World War. His parents are believed dead, but after the war the ten-year-old boy is reunited with his biological mother, who is found alive in Yugoslavia, having lost her husband and other children in the war. Based on a true story, the film won generous critical acclaim. De Carvalho was apparently picked for the part not only because he was cute but also because he spoke several languages and could ski.

Michel Ray's acting was clearly convincing as well, as he was given several other prominent parts. He was twelve when *The Brave One* came out in 1956, with Michel Ray in the lead role – a young Mexican boy who tries to save his bull, Gitano, from the bullfighting arena. The film even won an Oscar for Best Story, before that award was discontinued, and received two other Oscar nominations.

Journalists who met the boy on set in Hollywood were clearly impressed. One of them hailed Michel as 'the most promising child actor to invade Hollywood since Brandon deWilde' and marvelled that he could speak five languages: English, French, German, Spanish and Italian. Another found him 'alarmingly handsome and compelling' as young Heathcliff in a play based on *Wuthering Heights*. Yet another spoke with Michel's mother and described her as 'a lovely brunette who once studied dramatics at the Reinhardt School in Vienna'. She explained that Michel just picked up the languages on the family's many business travels. While on set, he was tutored by six teachers. He told one of the reporters that he wanted to open a restaurant.

Yet the most prestigious entry in Michel Ray's record as an actor was his part in *Lawrence of Arabia*. The teenager played Farraj, one of Lawrence's two young Arab servants. The filming took almost eighteen months, but Michel de Carvalho would mostly recall the breaks which he spent with famous actors and surrounded by female admirers. 'The parties happened on rest and relaxation days in Beirut. Quite often I went with Peter O'Toole and Omar Sharif', he told the *Daily Mail*. 'They were the superstars and I was the bag carrier. But even superstars can only handle so much. And then the bag carrier ...' Back at school, the youngster said he was inundated with fan mail.

Michel's acting took him from Mexico to Spain and Jordan, among other exotic locations. His parents apparently decided that after *Lawrence of Arabia* he should call it quits and focus on his studies. The youngster spent the next years in the United States, at Harvard University and then Harvard Business School. At the same time Michel continued to socialise with his friends in Europe, and he spent as much time as possible on skis. When the snow had melted in Europe, he and his well-heeled friends would just head to South America, to ski resorts such as Bariloche in Argentina. Or they might go water-skiing in the Mediterranean.

Somewhere along the line Michel Popper changed his name to Michel de Carvalho. He explained that this was the name of his actual Brazilian father, while Henry Popper was his step-father. This Brazilian connection caused some consternation in 1967, when Michel de Carvalho wanted to take part in the following year's Winter Olympics in Grenoble, as a downhill skier. He was to be part of the British team, but some bright bureaucrat (or perhaps a rival) pointed out that De Carvalho had competed at the World Ski Championships in 1966 in Portillo, in Chile, as a member of the Brazilian team. He could therefore not compete in Grenoble as part of the British team.

The situation became so awkward that Lord Exeter, a former chairman of the British Olympic Association and vice-president of the International Olympic Committee (IOC), sought advice from the IOC's chairman, Avery Brundage. It was explained that the potential team member was in fact a British citizen and that De Carvalho was only a pseudonym. Brundage allowed De Carvalho's inclusion in the British team on the grounds that 'a false qualification should not be irrevocable'.

At a time when Olympians were still meant to be strictly amateurs, De Carvalho said that his comfortable financial situation may have helped to obtain the selection. 'It wasn't so much for my skill as for my ability to pay the plane fare', he said. He also recalled that his mother wasn't overly supportive. 'I wish I had kept the telegram she sent', he said. 'Every second word was 'bum'. It said, "From film bum to ski bum – if you make this totally stupid decision, you will be completely cut off." So I made the completely stupid decision.' De Carvalho added that he delayed taking up his place at Harvard to compete, telling the university 'a huge porkie pie'.

While there is no record of De Carvalho actually competing in Grenoble, he took part in the Winter Olympics in 1972 in Sapporo, and then in 1976 in Innsbruck too. On both occasions he competed in the two-person luge with Jeremy Palmer-Tomkinson. He had apparently come across this discipline in St Moritz and then started practising it with his friend – but only weeks before the 1972 Games. The pair seemed to have completely taken on board the idea that it's not the winning or losing that counts – it's the taking part. In Sapporo they came last, in twentieth place.

Then again, De Carvalho did not have to rely on winter sports performances for his keeps, since he had embarked on a remarkable banking career. After his stint at Harvard Business School, he started working at White Weld & Co., a relatively small London brokerage firm. He quickly moved on to N M Rothschild, switching later to a new investment bank, Credit Suisse First Boston (CSFB). This was a fairly bold move at the time, just one year after the tie-up between the Swiss Credit Suisse and the American First Boston. De Carvalho became one of the firm's partners, and he fully enjoyed the 'work hard, play hard' ethic of the '80s.

These bachelor years came to an end when Michel started getting involved with Charlene Heineken. The two supposedly got to know each other in St Moritz, where both were members of the Corviglia Club. The Heinekens could rest assured that their prospective son-in-law was not after their daughter's money. At the beginning Freddy Heineken still had a hard time accepting the relationship: the banker's self-confidence and slick appearance may have been a little too smooth for the brewer, not to mention De Carvalho's colourful background.

The wedding put an end to any unease. Charlene and Michel married in Rolle, a small town in Switzerland just a few miles away from a Heineken family residence in Perroy, on the shores of Lake Geneva. The couple later held another wedding celebration in Belgravia.

After Freddy Heineken's death, some hoped that the smooth-talking, distinguished banker would play a more prominent role at Heineken. After all, Heineken had been hard-pressed to expand with acquisitions in the previous years. With a little more active support from a shrewd deal-maker, perhaps Heineken would be able to make its own takeovers without diluting the family's majority share in the company.

The handover was formally completed at Heineken's shareholders' meeting in April 2002. This was Charlene's first appearance as majority owner of the company. She was brief and efficiently quashed any speculation that the company might be up for grabs. 'My father is part of the history of Heineken, and what he has achieved forms the basis for the future of our company', she said. 'I see Heineken not as an inheritance, but as a legacy. An exciting company with great potential. As a family, we share its ambitions and aspirations. We are part of its past, its present and its future.' She added: 'I am looking forward to fulfilling my role as family shareholder and of course my function as member of the supervisory board.'

The formalities were rapidly completed. Charlene de Carvalho was appointed as delegate member of the supervisory board at Heineken Holding, as had been planned before her father's demise, which formally placed her in charge of running daily business at the company – however little of it there was. She had already been a member of the same board since 1988. Freddy Heineken himself was replaced as chairman of Heineken Holding's board by his lawyer, Maarten Das.

Her appearance almost eclipsed another major change at the company: after nine years at the helm Karel Vuursteen was to step down as Heineken's chief executive. He would accompany the family for several more years as a board member of Heineken Holding. But his departure marked the end of an era for the company. Heineken had stood its ground in the Beer Wars under Vuursteen's leadership and Freddy's guardianship. Without either of them, the company would have to find another way to stay independent, as the beer industry was about to be stormed by fabulously bold deal-makers.

15

Last Round

Just the right mix of cool and swagger, a touch of cosmopolitan class and, above all, resolutely global appeal: these are some of the attributes that Heineken shares with Britain's most famous spy. While James Bond outwits villains around the world, Heineken profiled itself as an indispensable accessory for the stylish and worldly. At an estimated cost of €60 million to the brewer, Heineken persuaded Bond in *Skyfall* to stray from his vodka martini and slug Dutch beer (neither shaken nor stirred). Daniel Craig even made an appearance in a Heineken commercial.

Critics have argued that such adverts are eminently forgettable and could apply to scores of other brands – be it beer, jeans or aftershave. One of the common gripes is that the global target of beer advertising almost inevitably makes it blander. Frank Lowe, the director behind the 'parts' campaign, lamented that such efforts were bound to focus on 'the lowest common denominator'.

The branding meticulously established by Freddy Heineken has been tweaked in the last couple of decades to make it more globally consistent and recognisable. The once controversial red star and the 'Heineken green' have become more prominent. These symbols have come to evoke cosmopolitan fun – a fashionable product coveted by middle-class consumers, all the more so in emerging markets.

Heineken's global approach is what sets it apart from other beer brands. The most international of all brands, it reached sales of 28.1 million hectolitres in the premium market in 2013, way ahead of Budweiser, Corona, Carlsberg and the group's own Amstel brand. Every day, the equivalent of more than 23 million standard green bottles are handed across bars or lugged into shopping trolleys, across over 170 countries.

Over the years Heineken had often considered a global marketing strategy, but until a few years ago they were invariably against it. With the advent of the internet and increasing globalisation, the arguments in favour became compelling. More stringent regulations on alcohol advertising have also encouraged the company to spend more on sponsorship and product placement to link the brand with global icons, from James Bond to the UEFA Champions League and the Heineken Cup in rugby.

Heineken continues to produce local advertising and events, but 'global' has become part of the strategy as well as the message in campaigns such as Open Your World. 'You couldn't stand aloof, you had to have some connection with the local market. But consumers didn't want a local version of Heineken [for the product or the marketing]. They wanted to try the international and premium Heineken', said a former global marketing manager.

While Freddy Heineken's heirs have left the brand's advertising in the hands of slick agencies, they still made a crucial contribution to the group's global scope. Not unlike Freddy a few decades earlier, they found a clever way to spread the green bottles without losing their majority control of the company.

Several years into the international Beer Wars, Heineken had appeared a little sluggish. While the company had made a few acquisitions here and there, it shied away from the bold moves that completely reshaped the industry in those years. Rightly or wrongly, the impression arose that Heineken was too timid, held back by its ownership structure.

Things started to change in the years after Freddy Heineken passed away. Heineken's management at that time was led by Anthony 'Thony' Ruys, a former Unilever manager who had already been sitting on Heineken's executive board for several years. At long last he was able to take steps that Freddy Heineken wouldn't have approved of, such as investing in Russia. Heineken managers had watched with some frustration in the previous decade as competitors, led by Carlsberg and Interbrew, had encouraged Russians to switch from vodka to beer. Freddy Heineken probably approved the acquisition of the Bravo International brewery in Saint Petersburg, which was finalised a few weeks after his passing. But shortly thereafter the company went on a Russian buying spree, acquiring six breweries in four years.

An even more significant departure from the strategy advocated by Freddy Heineken was that the company began researching for the launch of a Heineken Light beer for the United States. This contravened one of the rules most consistently upheld by Freddy Heineken, who insisted that there should be only one Heineken. Even when the light category began to take off in the United States, he had staunchly refused to take part with the Heineken brand. He was supported by the Van Munchings as well as some of the company's global marketing managers. It was a very telling sign of the changing times that the development went ahead.

Yet, apart from the company's bold investments in Russia,

its expansion was lagging behind its bigger rivals, the share price was languishing and the owners started to worry. 'We watched the developments in the first years with some concern', De Carvalho told *FEM Business*. Ruys resigned and left Heineken in October 2005, before the end of his term. He made way for the Belgian Jean-François van Boxmeer, who had spent nearly two decades at the company.

As Van Boxmeer admitted, his Belgians friends weren't overly impressed that he had decided to head up a Dutch brewery. In fact, he had started off by peddling Stella Artois in Gabon, when he was still a student. But right after the end of his economics studies in Namur he joined Heineken, as a trainee in the Netherlands and in Cameroon. He climbed the ladder with stints in Rwanda, Congo, Poland and Italy, which helped him to learn to speak five languages fluently. Van Boxmeer made it to the executive board in 2001, and when Ruys left, the shareholders picked him, the youngest of the board's three members, to settle into the top seat. He was meant to shake up the management and radically speed up decision-making.

While the family had kept its distance in the years after Freddy Heineken's death, it built up a good working relationship with Van Boxmeer. The De Carvalhos were updated by the chief executive almost as regularly as Freddy Heineken had been a few years earlier. And the Belgian made a point of consulting the family in person on strategic decisions that involved their name: he even made the trip to London to make sure that Charlene Heineken tasted and approved Heineken Light.

But it wasn't just the new management that got Heineken to move up a gear. There was also a call from Dik Hoyer. His family had supported Gerard Adriaan when he wanted to build his brewery in Rotterdam and again helped Freddy Heineken when he struggled to regain control over the company in the late '40s. The Hoyers owed their spot on the Dutch rich list almost entirely to this loyalty. What they were now proposing was to bundle their stake of 6.81 per cent, held in the Greenfee BV holding company, with those of the Heinekens. Until then, L'Arche Holding SA, Freddy Heineken's personal holding, owned just over 50 per cent of Heineken Holding, which itself held just over half of Heineken NV. The Heinekens separately had another 1.97 per cent lodged in a holding called Lac BV. The Heinekens and Hoyers agreed to place their shares into a new joint holding, L'Arche Green NV, so that it had a larger majority of about 58.78 per cent in Heineken Holding.

The arrangement, which bore the hallmarks of the clever legal and financial engineering favoured by the Heineken family, was finalised in 2007. Without taking anything away from their ultimate control, the agreement with Hoyer gave the Heinekens more leeway for decisive acquisitions. Just a few months later Heineken was ready to strike.

Sir Brian Stewart, the chairman of Scottish & Newcastle, found out when he arrived in Helsinki for several days of meetings in October 2007. He was met in the Finnish capital by Erik Hartwall, who had joined the S&N board five years earlier, after the sale of his family's company to the British brewing group. But they had barely started talking when Hartwall's phone rang. Stewart's assistant was at the other end. The Finn hurriedly handed over the phone. 'When he hung up he just turned to me and said "Erik, there is a bid on us." He was shocked. We were all shocked', said Hartwall.

What Stewart heard that day, after several months of rumours, was that Carlsberg and Heineken had teamed up to buy S&N. The stakes were particularly high since S&N was the only large British brewer left after the shake-up triggered by the Beer Orders (although they were revoked in 2003). While others had sold out to foreign interests or, in the case of Whitbread, reinvented themselves as retailers, S&N wanted to pre-empt a takeover by expanding abroad itself. It had bought Kronenbourg in 2000 and the Hartwall group two years later. It had even invested in a major Chinese brewery in Chongqing and in an Indian drinks group. The UK made up less than half of the company's sales, which reached £4,155 millon in 2006, with an operating profit of £535 million.

Sunrise Acquisitions Limited, the vehicle formed by Carlsberg and Heineken, did not formally issue a bid for S&N in October, but they did indicate a potential price of £6.8 billion. Amounting to 720 pence per share, it was rejected as 'unsolicited and derisory'. At the heart of the ensuing dispute was one of the assets of the former Hartwall group: the acquisition had given the Brits half-ownership of Baltic Beverages Holdings (BBH), a lucrative joint venture that owned the Baltika brand in Russia and had spread to eighteen breweries around Eastern Europe. As the Russian beer market started to take off, it was estimated that S&N reaped nearly 30 per cent of its profits from its half ownership of BBH. The other half was in the hands of Carlsberg.

The deal proposed by Carlsberg and Heineken, which the Dutch internally called the 'Rainbow project', would break up the Scottish company. As well as the other 50 per cent stake in BBH, the Danes would get S&N's activities in France and Greece, and its investments in China and Vietnam. Meanwhile, Heineken would take control of the group's business in the UK, with brands such as Newcastle Brown Ale, John Smith's, Strongbow, Bulmers cider and Foster's (European rights). This would make Heineken the British market leader ahead of Carlsberg, Inbev (the former Interbrew) and Coors (which gulped Carling). The Dutch would bag further interests in Ireland, Portugal, Finland, Belgium, the USA and India.

Owing to their shared ownership of BBH, the managers of Carlsberg and S&N had been working together for several years. This made it all the more shocking, in Sir Brian Stewart's view, that the call he received in Helsinki came from Heineken – not his friends at Carlsberg. There's little doubt that this undiplomatic move contributed to the feisty spirit of the battle that ensued. The avuncular Scotsman, who had been building S&N for independence, regarded the offer as hostile. He argued, among other things, that the deal was in breach of the joint venture agreement the two companies had for BHH, which included a 'shotgun clause' designed to prevent either party from selling or seizing the other's half of the venture.

John Dunsmore, the chief executive of S&N (formally from November), was equally unsettled by Carlsberg and Heineken's approach. He heard about it while on a mid-term break in Paris with his family, when he received a call from his counterpart at Carlsberg, Jørgen Buhl Rasmussen. 'I said that I thought he was taking the shareholders for fools', Dunsmore recalled. In his eyes, Carlsberg chiefly wanted to circumvent the shotgun clause and to get its hands on the other half of BBH at an unfairly cheap price. Again as part of the joint venture agreement, neither of the parties was allowed to publicise the results of BBH, unless the other party agreed. Dunsmore was certain that the acquisition price cited by Carlsberg and Heineken did not reflect the value of BBH at that time. But he wasn't allowed to explain this in detail to the market – and Carlsberg was very well aware of that. S&N filed an arbitration case. 'We were very aggressive in getting home to the public the fact that Carlsberg's approach wasn't legitimate. It was a completely flawed and assymetrical approach', said Dunsmore. Carlsberg denounced the claims as 'spurious, without merit and a distraction'.

Over the next three months Carlsberg and Heineken had to increase their price three times. As Dunsmore explained, it was 'quite a hostile process', because for several weeks Carlsberg and Heineken refrained from making a formal bid – instead talking of a 'proposal' and turning indirectly to the share-holders in what is known as a 'bear hug'. Only in December did the Takeover Panel issue a deadline, set on 21 January, for Carlsberg and Heineken to issue a formal bid or walk away. But the former chief executive acknowledged that S&N also had at least one major advantage: 'You're dealing with a consortium bid. They always have to confer', he said. 'So if you move fast, by the time they have agreed, you are already one step ahead.' He mostly spoke with Rasmussen at Carlsberg and Van Boxmeer at Heineken, while Michel de Carvalho sometimes appeared on the sidelines to try and smooth things over.

Carlsberg and Heineken's second approach came on 15 November, at a suggested price of £7.3 billion (750 pence per share). 'The tone was a little less aggressive than last time, but still strongly dismissive', Van Boxmeer admitted. The response was much the same when Heineken and Carlsberg tried again, on 9 January 2008, this time raising the proposed price to £7.6 billion (780 pence per share). 'It's starting to become incompre-hensible', the Heineken chief executive sulked. 'We will have to wait and see if the Scots repent and hope that their shareholders force them to open talks with us.'

The pressure on S&N's management was further height-ened by shaky share prices. The British company's own shares had risen amply in the four previous years, as Stewart pushed ahead with his international drive. But towards the end of 2007 tensions in the financial markets began to transpire on stock exchanges. If the financial situation worsened any more markedly, Carlsberg and Heineken could well walk away and leave S&N shares to languish, some of the shareholders probably reasoned. Carlsberg and Heineken were offering to pay in cash, so that seemed a safer alternative. Still, the management did not cave in. 'Our intelligence was that they were absolutely determined', said Dunsmore.

It was only after Carlsberg and Heineken raised their price for the third time, on 17 January, that the board agreed to sit down. The consortium was to issue a bid of 800 pence per share, amounting to an offer of £7.8 billion. As the Dutch pointed out, it constituted a handsome earnings multiple compared with previous European beer acquisitions – far too generous, some critics thought. S&N had effectively set the price by making it clear that they would not consider talking for less. Some investors had hoped for a counter-offer; the management did hold talks with an alternative bidder, but nothing came of it.

The three months of acrimony during the takeover bid mostly pitted the Scots against the Danes. Carlsberg agreed to pay for most of the second price increase, and all of the third. More quietly, Heineken acquired a mix of operations, including brewing capacity in the United Kingdom as well as several brands that could help to diversify its business. The move into cider was most judicious, as a growing thirst for the sweeter drink was helping to make up for shrinking beer sales. Foster's was the country's second-largest lager brand after Carling.

The alliance between Heineken and Carlsberg apparently unravelled immediately after the agreement was finalised, early in the morning of 25 January after a whole night of talks. Hartwall remarked that the two parties refused to spread the news together, organising six press and analyst conferences between them on the same day. They said that Carlsberg had even flown in Danish journalists to boast about the largest ever foreign acquisition by a Danish company. Rasmussen and Van Boxmeer 'were now in a position to declare their marriage of convenience over, and the companies returned to being each other's worst competitors'.

The sell-out to the Dutch and Danes was lamented in Britain. It marked the end of two and a half centuries of brewing history, started by William Younger in Edinburgh in 1749 and the acquisition of the Tyne Brewery in Newcastle by John Barras in 1884. Commentators deplored the sale of the last sizeable independent British brewing company, describing it as 'an indictment of short-sighted regulation and government ineptitude over two decades'.

Two years after the deal, Heineken closed the Gateshead brewery making Newcastle Brown Ale and moved production to another of the plants it had bought, in Tadcaster. On the other hand, the Dutch got full control of the Caledonian Brewery in Edinburgh, whose tall chimney has become a part of the city's landscape. Van Boxmeer described the distinctive Deuchars IPA made in the open copper Edinburgh plant as his favourite. And again the Heinekens reassured staff by turning up at 'the Caley'.

The S&N takeover put an end to Heineken's ambiguous approach to the British beer market. All activities were integrated into Heineken UK. The Dutch company's relationship with Whitbread came to an end in 2003, three years after the British group's brewing activities had been snapped up by Interbrew. Heineken had then decided to just discontinue the English beer with an alcoholic strength of 3.4 per cent, known as Heineken Cold Filtered, and to sell only standard Heineken at 5 per cent. 'It was tough because there was a lot of money left on the table, but Heineken could afford it at the time', said one of the people who supported the move. 'It was just disastrous that we had this weaker beer in such a prominent market.' The move caused a collapse in volumes, from about 2 million hecto-litres down to an estimated low of 125,000. It had been one of the motives behind Heineken's eagerness to buy market leadership in the UK, as Van Boxmeer acknowledged that it would have taken years to rebuild Heineken's business in the country with imported Heineken.

The 'parts' were not forgotten, but global advertising was used in Britain as well. The country had turned into just another part of Europe for the Dutch group, selling standard Heineken (albeit imported so far) and a slew of other brands. The price was regarded as steep for assets in a sluggish market, and it weighed on the company for several years. However, it was widely under-stood that Heineken could not have afforded to let slip this opportunity to buy leadership in Europe's second-largest beer market. Over the next few years the last gaps in Heineken's global landscape were filled with two other 'must-do' deals, which safe-guarded Heineken's independence in the global market.

A sprawling city in Nuevo León, an arid province in north Mexico, Monterrey is famed for its hard-working ways. And among the most powerful clans in this industrious city are the Garza Sadas, who have built their fortune on oiling Mexican throats: they turned the village of Monterrey into an industrial powerhouse, as glass and steel manufacturers were stamped out of the ground to supply their thriving beer business.

Cervecería Cuauhtémoc Moctezuma, the family's brewing business, was just a little younger than Heineken. Started in 1890, it consisted of several mighty Mexican brands, led by Sol,

Tecate and Dos Equis. Grupo Modelo, the company behind the Corona brand, snatched the market leadership from their Monterrey rivals in the 1980s, but the brands sold by the Garza Sadas were arguably more upmarket in Mexico, where Corona was still regarded as a blue-collar beer.

It may have seemed a little alarming that the man in charge was known as 'El Diablo' ('The Devil'), but the nickname referred only to his spirited personality. José Antonio Fernández Carbajal took the helm in 1995. Married to Eva Garza Lagüera Gonda, one of the company's heirs, he transformed the family beer business into a regional drinks and retail powerhouse, named Femsa. *Harvard Business Review* hailed him as the best chief executive in Mexico.

Femsa's beer sales alone reached 41.1 million hectolitres and the equivalent of nearly €2.6 billion in 2008, about 75 per cent of that in the Mexican market (amounting to a share of 43 per cent, against an estimated 52 per cent for Grupo Modelo). An important asset was a majority stake in the Kaiser brewery in Brazil, which gave Femsa 9 per cent of the world's third-largest beer market. But Femsa had much broader activities: its Coca-Cola bottling business covered nine countries (accounting for an estimated 10 per cent of global Coke sales), and Oxxo was described as the biggest convenience store chain in Latin America.

The Heinekens got to know their way around Monterrey from 2004, when it was agreed that the Dutch group would take care of the distribution of Femsa's beer brands in the United States. Among the many things they had in common was a disastrous encounter with armed men. Eugenio Garza Sada, the grandfather of Fernández's wife, was the victim of a kidnapping attempt by suspected left-wing guerillas in the streets of Monterrey in 1973. But unlike Freddy Heineken, Garza was gunned down as he attempted to fight back.

The family ties eased discussions when it became clear that Femsa was considering a sale of its beer interests. The Mexicans were suddenly wary of remaining isolated in Latin America, without sufficient bulk to compete with their larger rivals. It may also have been a turning point in the board's deliberations that Eugenio Garza Lagüera, the chief executive's father-in-law, passed away in 2008. The auction started around the middle of the following year, and the structure of the deal offered by Heineken played strongly in its favour.

The deal unveiled in January 2010 revealed the understanding between the two families as well as the importance of the Latin American market for the Heineken group: the Dutch had agreed to pay entirely in shares. All of a sudden, the Mexicans became the second-largest shareholders in Heineken. They got a share of around 12.5 per cent in the operating company, Heineken N.V., and nearly 15 per cent in Heineken Holding. The two stakes indirectly amounted to a share of 20 per cent in Heineken, not much less than the Heinekens themselves. The all-share deal amounted to about €5.3 billion (the equity value as well as debt and other obligations), and it required a sizeable share issue by Heineken – the first time it had done so for an acquisition since it swallowed up Amstel.

Back in Monterrey, Fernández faced criticism from some Mexicans who portrayed the deal as a surrender to foreign capitalists. Others were disappointed by the price, since it had been estimated that Femsa's beer business could fetch up to $10 billion. Fernández countered that the deal was not a sale: 'We exchanged our brewery for Heineken shares', he explained. He said he took the 'toughest decision in the history of the family' after talks with the De Carvalhos. 'Would you consider us as your cousins?' Fernández had asked them. They were happy to agree, especially as Freddy's grandchildren did not have any cousins. El Diablo himself was to join Heineken's supervisory board, along with another Mexican representative.

Heineken was quick to outline the deal's virtues. It would help the company to tap Latin American markets, effervescent not only for their size but also for their profitable structure. This particularly applied to the Mexican market, which was the fifth largest in volume and lay almost entirely in the hands of just two companies. Secondly, the Heineken group could use its distribution to push the Dos Equis, Sol and Tecate brands around the world. With that, Heineken had America covered. There was only one more continent where the Dutch had never quite managed to shape their destiny.

Since their partnership with Fraser and Neave had started nearly eight decades earlier, the tensions between Heineken and its Singapore allies had hardly ever gone away. Heineken's desire to tighten its grip on its Asian business led to recurrent clashes, diplomatic disasters and face-saving efforts. Insistent offers by Heineken to buy out their partners were angrily swept off the table. They may well have been grateful in Amsterdam when an outsider broke the deadlock.

The partnership started by Pieter Feith as Malayan Breweries had turned into the most wide-ranging brewing group in Asia. The venture, renamed Asia Pacific Breweries (APB) in 1990, boasted interests in twenty-four breweries in fourteen countries, from Mongolia to New Zealand. Its sales in 2011 amounted to S$2.97 billion for an estimated 16 million hectolitres, with forty brands, led by Tiger, Anchor and Heineken. Vietnam turned into the second-largest market for the Dutch company.

However, many thought that Heineken would be able to move

much faster in Asia without F&N. The management in Singapore was regarded by some at Heineken as overly cautious. There were several countries where the partnership clearly lagged behind its rivals, most notably China, which had become the world's biggest beer market in 2002. While APB opened a brewery in Guangzhou, the two partners were frequently at loggerheads – Heineken even turned to the High Court of Singapore regarding a Chinese management appointment.

Just as frustratingly, sales of the Heineken brand itself made up just 30 per cent of the volumes sold by APB as the Singaporeans continued to push Tiger. The surge of the Asian middle class made it all the more compelling for Heineken to pull the blanket over to their side: many of the people who could suddenly afford a few extras were more likely to opt for a bottle of Heineken, with the label casually exposed.

Yet more tensions arose after the acquisition of Scottish & Newcastle in 2008. It included a promising asset in India: a 37.5 per cent stake in United Breweries, the company behind Kingfisher. India was a market with giddy prospects, meant to be part of the APB joint venture, but Vijay Mallya and his United Breweries apparently refused to work with Heineken as long as APB had competing assets in India. Heineken had to buy them out, in exchange for its Indonesian subsidiary and other assets.

Whenever they tried to buy more influence at APB, the Dutch were rebuffed. Han Cheng Fong, a former director and chief executive at F&N, later explained that the Singaporeans' stiff attitude was partly a matter of pride. 'Few know that I and my colleagues in F&N made cold calls to large shareholders to buy their Asia Pacific Breweries shares to shore up F&N's stake in it and help keep Tiger Beer Singaporean', he wrote in the *Straits Times*. 'Also, not many know that after we built F&N's holdings in APB up to an almost unassailable position, Heineken offered to buy our APB stake at twice the then market price. We turned Heineken down because we felt APB and Tiger Beer belonged to Singapore.'

As Han Cheng Fong recalled, the board was alerted in 2006 to the fact that Heineken intended to 'mount a takeover of F&N in order to extract APB'. His colleagues apparently felt 'threatened enough' to bring in a state-controlled investment fund 'as a white knight to help in this fight against Heineken'. The supposed 'white knight' went on to sell its stake of 14.9 per cent in 2010 to Kirin, the Japanese brewing group. That made the situation all the more awkward for Heineken, which had to work the Asian market with a proud partner as well as a competitor.

The battle for APB was finally unleashed in July 2012 by Charoen Sirivadhanabhakdi, the man behind the largest beer brand in Thailand. Anybody who has spent more than a few hours in Bangkok will have come across Chang and its elephant logo. Thai Bev ran three breweries in Thailand and another in China, along with more than a dozen distilleries and a large-scale soft drinks business.

The son of southern Chinese street hawkers, Charoen became the second-richest man in Thailand, with a fortune estimated by Forbes at about $5.5 billion. He was said to have left school at the age of nine and to have started in business with a small distillery making cheap, throat-burning liquor. Charoen switched to beer in the 1990s, when he teamed up with Carlsberg: from them he learned to brew lager, and his Chang brand rapidly snatched market leadership from Singha. He later moved on to soft drinks, agricultural projects and property. His plan to list Thai Bev on the stock exchange was thwarted by Buddhist monks, who staged anti-liquor protests. It was listed in Singapore instead.

When Charoen barged onto the Singaporean scene, 64.8 per cent of APB was owned by an equal joint venture between Heineken and F&N. Separately, Heineken held another stake of 9.5 per cent in APB, so its entire shareholding reached 41.9 per cent in the Asian beer company. Almost the same could be said for F&N, which held a direct stake of 7.3 per cent in APB. But Thai Bev went for the shareholdings of another party, Oversea-Chinese Banking Corp (OCBC), which held not only an 8.4 per cent share in APB but also 22 per cent in F&N. Both were interesting for Thai Bev.

Thai Bev started stirring things up on 18 July 2012, when it agreed a deal worth nearly S$2.8 billion to buy the 22 per cent stake held by OCBC in F&N. Another vehicle owned by one of Charoen's relatives snapped up the bank's 8.5 per cent in APB, with a stated ambition to mop up more on the Singapore stock exchange. The fully unexpected buys were regarded as the opening move in a high-stakes battle for the Asian beer market. 'The tanks are in the street', as one observer put it.

This time Heineken had no choice but to take the initiative publicly. Two days after Thai Bev's attack, on 20 July, the Dutch issued an offer of S$50 per share in APB held by F&N, either through their joint venture or directly. Along with the shares Heineken already owned, it would then have more than 80 per cent in APB. The offer amounted to 45 per cent more than the average price of the shares the previous month.

While F&N was weighing its options, the battle started heating up with rumours of other parties sniffing at the Singaporean company. The most likely contender was Kirin. However, few believed that F&N could back an offer from any party other than Heineken. After all, much of the venture's value resided in the Heineken brand itself, which the Dutch would be able to pull out of APB if the new owner was not to their liking.

On Friday 3 August F&N's board finally agreed to support Heineken's offer. Not to be undone, Thai Bev retaliated with another bid of S$55 per share – more than Heineken's, except that the Thai offer only covered the 7.3 per cent of APB held directly by F&N. It triggered an increased offer by Heineken on 18 August, at S$53 per share for all the APB shares held by F&N, amounting to S$5.4 billion.

The Singapore company's board again supported Heineken's offer, but Thai Bev still wouldn't walk away. At the end of August it announced that it had built up a stake of 29 per cent in F&N, by buying up shares on the market, and two weeks later an investment group owned by the Thais offered $7.2 billion for all of the remaining shares in F&N. Given the fact that the Thais had already bought 8.5 per cent in APB, gulping F&N (and its 39.7 per cent share in APB) would make them a mighty shareholder in this crucial joint brewing business.

Coffee machines overheated at banks and law offices around Singapore in the next week as Heineken and Thai Bev started talking. Just as they had done with Carlsberg in the United Kingdom four years earlier, the Dutch agreed to strike a compromise with Charoen: the Thais supported Heineken's bid for APB while Heineken refrained from bidding for F&N, allowing for Charoen's takeover of the Singapore company in 2013.

The full takeover of APB raised the share of Asia Pacific from less than 3 per cent to more than 11 per cent of Heineken's turnover in 2013. While the price of beer in China still makes it hard to turn a profit there, the Dutch rapidly increased their sales of the Heineken brand around Asia, and Singapore's Tiger started roaring more convincingly in other parts of the world.

◉

When the dust settled after these latest instalments of the Beer Wars, the global market was dominated by just four companies. They currently fill about half of all beer tanks in a market estimated by Beverage Marketing Corporation at 1,941 million hectolitres for 2012. The frenetic deals of the last decade have seen the market leaders tear down every geographic barrier. And the ensuing consolidation helped to slash costs, making up for pressure on margins as ever more drinkers opt for the couch instead of the bar.

While such concentration had been anticipated, it was eventually spurred on again by an unexpected bunch: Jorge Paulo Lemann, Marcel Telles and Carlos Alberto Sicupira, three Brazilian investors whose business credo was based on meritocracy and 'zero costs'. The partnership was driven by Lemann, a former Swiss tennis champion who made a fortune at the Garantia bank in São Paulo.

Employees at Brahma, the second-largest Brazilian brewer, with the Brahma and Skol brands, did not know what had hit them in 1989, when their company was acquired by Lemann and his acolytes. The new jeans- and sneaker-clad managers fired hundreds of people and relentlessly went through expenses. They liked to say that 'costs are like nails; they always need to be cut'. A few years later they had moved ahead of Antarctica, the market leader, and were ready to swallow it up. In 1999 Lemann and his advisers managed to convince Brazilian regulators that a combined market share of 70 per cent for Ambev, the name of the tie-up, would be judicious for the country.

The next act was even more astonishing. In 2003 Lemann began intensive talks with Alexander van Damme, described as the most active of all the family shareholders behind Interbrew in Belgium. Van Damme had an ear for the merger proposal, because he had started to map out a global strategy for Interbrew: he split the market into regional entities and targeted market leadership in each of them, potentially with a major acquisition. Ambev fitted the bill for Latin America.

Under the deal, which stunned the market in March 2004, the Brazilians held only a minority in the new entity, Inbev, but it quickly became apparent that they would have the upper hand in management. Carlos Brito, an uncompromising executive hand-picked by Lemann, became Inbev's chief executive in 2005, and several other Brazilians settled down in Leuven to cut costs furiously in the small fiefdoms built by Interbrew.

Backed by Lemann and Van Damme, it was Brito who made the call to St Louis in June 2008. This time the investors had set their sights on Anheuser-Busch, the makers of Budweiser. The St Louis company had almost entirely failed to spread its operations beyond the United States, but it was still a formidable player in the second-largest beer market. The Brazilians marvelled at the opportunities if they could get their hands on Budweiser – 'America in a bottle', as Brito put it.

By then the management of Anheuser-Busch was in the hands of August Busch IV, the eldest son of 'The Third'. The young man had made an arduous climb to the top. He struggled for many years to be taken seriously at the company, even though he did well in marketing with Budweiser's unconventional Frogs and Whassup campaigns. His father was astonishingly sparing in his support. It didn't help that 'The Fourth' had attracted the wrong kind of media attention in the '80s, most disturbingly when his Corvette crashed in Arizona, killing a twenty-two-year-old waitress. The police found Busch in his townhouse, apparently in a disoriented state. The urine sample taken from him that day reportedly vanished, and his blood sample couldn't be used as it had been put in a centrifuge. No charges were filed against him, and he denied that alcohol had played a part in the crash.

'The Fourth' finally made it to the hot seat in 2006, a

much more amenable boss than his father. Even though the Busch family only held a small minority stake in Anheuser-Busch at that stage, he vowed that it would never be bought 'on [his] watch'. He was so confident that, much to his father's annoyance, he sealed a deal with Inbev to distribute their beers in the United States – giving the Brazilians valuable insights into Anheuser-Busch's ways. A fleet of twenty planes and two helicopters, sumptuous entertainment bills and side activities such as Sea World gave them plenty of ideas.

When Brito called, 'The Fourth' hurriedly attempted to put together a cost-cutting plan of his own. He then worked on an alliance with Modelo, the Mexican owner of Corona, in which Anheuser-Busch had held a stake since 1993. The sale of the iconic American company, which unfolded amid mounting tensions in the financial markets, was ardently opposed by some staff and politicians. However, August Busch IV apparently failed to convince the board (including his own father). An improved offer of $54.8 billion was approved in July – the largest-ever all-cash acquisition of a consumer goods company.

The ensuing scenario had become familiar. Even though Anheuser-Busch was one of the most efficient brewers in the world, the Brazilians still found plenty of room to cut jobs and slash costs. Brito became the chief executive of AB Inbev, which moved its executive committee to New York. August Busch IV resigned from Anheuser-Busch's board less than three years after the deal. It was alleged in *Bitter Brew*, a book about the Busch dynasty and the fate of Anheuser-Busch, that the bright brewing heir had spiralled into drug addiction and paranoia. Friends were said to have found a stash of about 900 weapons in his house, as well as drawers and buckets full of ammunition. Busch himself acknowledged publicly that he had suffered from depression and other issues.

The AB Inbev combine wasn't just by far the world's largest brewer and the most profitable of the top players; it was also one of the ten biggest consumer goods companies after groups such as Coca-Cola and Procter & Gamble. Once it had also acquired Modelo, in 2013, AB Inbev boasted sales of 425 million hectolitres – about one of every five beers imbibed anywhere around the world.

Meanwhile, South African Breweries walked away with Miller Brewing, in a deal sealed in 2002 for $5.6 billion. The resources pumped by the former Philip Morris into the Milwaukee brewer never sufficed to undo Anheuser-Busch and its Budweiser brand. That group's sales reached some 245 million hectolitres for the year until the end of March 2014, with strongholds in Africa and the United States. SAB Miller also has 49 per cent in the joint venture China Resources Snow, which has become one of the world's largest brewing groups after the acquisition of a gaggle of Chinese breweries (including former Heineken assets in Shanghai and Jiangsu province).

After its own major acquisitions, the Heineken group has brewing plants on all continents, employing more than 85,000 people. In 2013 it sold 178.3 million hectolitres of beer (195.2 million with its share of joint ventures) and reached a group turnover of more than €21.25 billion, making it the third largest in the world. But it is less profitable than the market leader, which some attribute to family legacy – or the company's unwillingness to dismantle some of the structures put in place by the late patriarch.

The countries where Freddy Heineken built up the brand are no longer the most attractive for Heineken. The group continued to reinforce its presence in Western Europe with sizeable buys. Spain became one of Heineken's largest European markets after it snapped up a majority stake in Cruzcampo, a leading Spanish brewer based in Seville. Another gap was filled when it swallowed the Austrian Brau Union for €1.9 billion in 2003. And expansion continued unabated in Eastern Europe with acquisitions like Krušovice in the Czech Republic, as well as investments in local brands such as Żywiec in Poland. However, cost-cutting has been the order of the day for Heineken in Europe for several years as regional beer consumption has steadily declined, under pressure from smoking bans in public places and changing alcohol consumption. Another strategy to make up for the dwindling thirst for beer in Western Europe is to roll out scores of low-alcohol and even non-alcoholic drinks. Several decades earlier Heineken had already acquired a soft drinks business as well as several distilleries, which enabled it to capitalise on its distribution. The company has been investing much more in innovation in the last years, for new products as well as packaging and by-products to stimulate beer sales, such as home draught kegs.

The European beer business's promiscuity has also triggered costly anti-competition investigations – which led to a whopping fine of over €219 million for the Dutch brewer in 2007, for alleged collusion with Grolsch and Bavaria to fix prices in the Dutch market – denied by all three brewers. The EU's file described meetings that took place in hotels and bars around the country to discuss pricing in the late '90s. Interbrew was part of the talks but not fined because it acted as the whistle-blower. The EU General Court later reduced Heineken and Bavaria's fines by about 10 per cent and annulled Grolsch's fine.

Heineken remains a major employer in the Netherlands owing to its gargantuan brewery in Zoeterwoude, which is described as the largest in Europe, with an annual capacity of 12.5 million hectolitres. But the Dutch market has become almost an afterthought for the company, estimated to make up just 3 per cent of its sales in 2013, even though it markets the country's two best-selling brands. Even Heineken's branding in the Netherlands has been adjusted to other countries, with the brown bottles and yellow crates being replaced with green versions. The switch occurred in 2012 in the huge Operation Leo, named after the American importer.

The company's business in the United States is not satisfactory in every respect, and former employees at VMCO are particularly upset that Corona snatched the label of top imported beer from Heineken. 'Heineken USA chose to ignore the decades of experience it had within its employ, and to chase growth through ill-advised, ill-thought-out, and just plain dopey product extensions', said Philip van Munching. 'The Heineken brand, with a much larger (and costlier) staff behind it, along with considerably more spending, has seen nothing but a decrease in market share since my father stepped down from VMCO.'

The fate of Heineken Light seems to support the stance taken by the Van Munchings, who fully supported Freddy Heineken's decision to oppose such a beer. Heineken Premium Light was received with enthusiasm in 2006, as a low-calorie import beer that still contained 3.2 per cent alcohol. It was supported by an advertising budget estimated at no less than $50 million, but America's thirst for it was rapidly quenched. As sales started to sag, the name was changed to Heineken Light, and the company hopped from one advertising agency to another, trying five of them and as many campaigns over less than a decade. None of them had a significant impact on sales: in 2014 Heineken Light was described as one of the the fastest-declining beers in the USA. While Bud Light and Coors Light turned into the two best-selling brands in the US (ahead of Budweiser), Heineken Light was still tiny, languishing at less than 0.2 per cent of the market.

The company's US managers acknowledged that the market had been changing beyond recognition. While beers such as Yuengling and Samuel Adams have become widespread, hundreds of much smaller outfits have sprung up to quench growing thirst for distinctive craft beers. Dolf van den Brink, the youthful chief executive at Heineken USA, pointed to 'dramatic change' in the industry as the number of US breweries had soared from just fifty three decades ago to over 4,000 in 2014, and the number was still rising. Heineken is capitalising on the trend towards diversity with its multiple offering, describing Dos Equis as one of the fastest-growing beers in the country, and the same for Tecate Light in the light category.

Along with its new-found expansion in Asia and Latin America, Heineken also distinguished itself with its large-scale presence in Africa. Building on the assets it inherited from its holding company Cobra and its long-dissolved partnership with Unilever, the company has brewing plants right across Africa. The business is mostly built around the Star and Primus brands. Africa (and the Middle East) makes up about 14.5 per cent of the company's turnover, with Nigeria estimated to be the group's second-largest market after Mexico and before Vietnam. Heineken has pledged some of its most intensive social investments in Africa.

The Heineken group's size, diversity and prospects continued to whet the appetites of mighty predators in the last years. Further large-scale acquisitions in the global beer market appeared impractical, because the buyers were almost certain to be confronted with competition issues in at least some countries. But this apparently hasn't deterred AB Inbev from studying what has been described as the ultimate mega-merger in the beer industry: a tie-up between the world's two largest brewers, in which the Belgian group would gobble up SAB Miller. Rumours of such a takeover attempt have been doing the rounds for several years but they resurfaced more insistently in 2014, as AB Inbev finished digesting its acquisition of

Anheuser-Busch. It would form a beer behemoth making up more than 30 per cent of the global beer market – before likely disposals. Among SAB Miller's most interesting assets is its business in Africa, where AB Inbev has yet to make significant inroads. The company is listed on the London stock exchange.

It was Heineken that added fuel to the speculation in September 2014 by revealing that it had been approached by SAB Miller for a potential acquisition. Many were quick to interpret SAB Miller's move as a way to protect itself from a takeover attempt by AB Inbev. The *Wall Street Journal* went on to report that AB Inbev was raising funds for a potential, mammoth acquisition bid, perhaps reaching £75 billion.

Heineken promptly added that the tie-up proposed by SAB Miller was 'non-actionable' because the Heineken family wanted to 'preserve the heritage and identity of Heineken as an independent company'. L'Arche Green, the holding company of the Heineken and Hoyer families, had seen its stake in the Heineken Holding reduced from 58.78 per cent in 2007 to 50.57 per cent at the end of 2010, due to the Femsa deal, but since then L'Arche Green again slightly reinforced its shareholding to 51.48 per cent at the end of 2013. Charlene de Carvalho announced that year that she intended to spend about €100 million on Heineken Holding shares, and went on to acquire several packages in the next months.

Jean-François van Boxmeer likes to say that he and the other Heineken employees around the globe are united by the 'green blood' flowing in their veins. Yet this allegiance remains most deeply anchored in the Heineken family, which has clearly reaffirmed its grip on the company and may well continue to drive it in the years to come.

Epilogue

Alexander de Carvalho was only seventeen when his maternal grandfather passed away. Yet he had spent sufficient time with Freddy Heineken to hear some of his lectures on branding, and to acquire some of his habits. 'When I go to a supermarket, I always check that the bottles are well displayed in the fridge', he said. While his mother, Charlene Heineken, had long stayed away from the breweries, De Carvalho made his début at the shareholders' meeting in Amsterdam in April 2013, when the twenty-eight-year-old was elected a member of Heineken Holding's board of directors.

Like their mother, the De Carvalhos were brought up to be level-headed. This isn't to say that they didn't enjoy the comforts of their family home in London, the family's Candover Park estate and summer holidays in grandpa's magnificent retreat in the south of France – not to mention the chalet in St Moritz, where then Crown Prince Willem-Alexander and his bride, Máxima, began their honeymoon. Charlene de Carvalho is one of Britain's wealthiest residents, with assets estimated by *The Sunday Times* in 2014 at £6.365 billion. But she likes to say that her family is not as rich as people think, because she cannot sell her shares.

The arrangements Freddy Heineken put in place for his estate – the majority ownership of the brewery that bears his name, and which he had fought hard to regain – were particularly meticulous. While the shares are now with his daughter, before his death Freddy took measures to reduce the risk that the ownership could be diluted by his grandchildren: apparently their shares will be passed on with the condition that they may only sell to each other.

Freddy was particularly proud of Alexander, a bright, affable youngster with plenty of charm. His sheltered English childhood included an education at Eton, where he was said to be among the highest-achieving pupils. He then left the UK to attend Harvard University, another bubble of privilege and high-achievers. Among his pals were Alexander Blankfein, son of the Goldman Sachs chief executive, and Josh Kushner, whose family built its wealth on real estate. De Carvalho reportedly made it to the Porcellian Club, a group so exclusive that Franklin D. Roosevelt couldn't get membership.

After Harvard, De Carvalho started work at the small Gutmann bank in Vienna. There he met the Austrian Countess Stephanie von und zu Eltz, a distant relative of Empress Sissi, to whom he got engaged in 2012. De Carvalho moved back to London to work for Lion Capital, an investment firm with stakes in many consumer goods and retail companies. He still regularly travels to the Netherlands, where he may well use his grandfather's old office as a comfortable pied-à-terre in the centre of the capital.

Alexander appears to have inherited his grandfather's flair for publicity. When a photographer appears, he makes sure to hold his Heineken glass so that the brand name faces out. At the same time, the family's eldest son professes to be fiercely competitive, just like his father. He has said that he deliberately went to the United States at a young age, like his grandfather, and to Harvard because 'it's a meritocracy, where you really don't get judged on your background'. That suited him, he said, because he always wanted to compete and be the best he could at everything.

Like his four siblings, Alexander grew up hearing about beer on an almost daily basis, and he particularly enjoyed discussing the business with his grandfather. 'We talked a lot about the company history, passion, branding, marketing. My grandfather was twenty years ahead of the game, so there was never a surprise for him', he said. 'That was a combination of understanding very small details, understanding the people and looking forward into the future. He was always interested in inventors, academics. He broadened his understanding of so many things, and as a result he was able to move faster.'

With his brother Charles, who studied sociology and economics at Princeton, Alexander began attending management meetings a few years ago. Charles worked as a trainee at Heineken UK, peddling Heineken and Tiger beer like his grandfather before him. Alexander said he spent four months at a brewery as well – not at Heineken but at Molson in Canada, starting at five o'clock in the morning. Their three sisters appear to be less directly involved, although Louisa de Carvalho was credited as one of the co-producers of *The Magic of Heineken*, a 'documentary film' about the group, the brand and the family.

Michel de Carvalho said that it would be 'wrong' for any member of the family to lead the company, as long as it was listed. However, the De Carvalho family as a whole have become visibly more involved in the running of the company since Freddy Heineken's death. As well as concocting clever deals, Charlene and her husband regularly turn up at brewing plants to meet local employees and infuse some family spirit into the sprawling group. They like to describe themselves as 'ambassadors' for the company. They also eagerly turn up at the many sports events sponsored by the group – to hand out the Heineken Cup for rugby or to add lustre to the Holland Heineken House at the London Olympics.

As he prepared to take up his seat on the board of Heineken Holding, Alexander proudly displayed his grandfather's watch on his wrist. He insisted that his parents had never put any pressure on him to start working for the company, but it was quite clear that he never really questioned it either. 'We always talked about it at home. I don't know any better', he said. 'It's us.'

Acknowledgements

Alfred 'Freddy' Heineken was often asked when he would write down his own story. After all, he could take most of the credit for having turned his own name into one of the world's most famous brands, and the dramatic episodes in his life matched the epic aspects of the brand's trajectory. The answer wasn't promising: the Dutch billionaire said he would only consider recording his story if he got short of cash.

I became acquainted with Heineken as an Amsterdam-based contributor to several English- and French-language newspapers in the 1990s. While covering the company, I yearned to find out more about the story behind the brand and its enigmatic owner. Thousands of people shouted 'Heineken' across the bar every day, but few had any inkling of the adventures behind the product. Even fewer outside the Netherlands realised that Heineken was the name of an intriguing billionaire.

'We'll see each other in court' was his opening line when we first met, in September 1994. We were standing in the reception hall of the former Heineken brewery on the Stadhouderskade, in the centre of Amsterdam, surrounded by several other foreign correspondents. He had been told that I had begun researching a corporate biography of Heineken – the beer, the company and the family. But then, straight away he invited me 'for tea' at the Pentagon, his office and penthouse just around the corner. When I called to confirm the appointment, he said that he would slip a sleeping pill into my tea and undress me.

Heineken proudly showed me around the building, pointing to an ornament he had found in Milan and another he had unearthed in a flea market in Paris. He was often amusing, constantly engaging in wordplay and serving up incisive remarks on human society. I even got to visit the private suite behind his office, complete with four-poster bed and a shamrock-shaped jacuzzi. On the wall was a painting of a naked woman with a cat, which he crassly called 'The Woman with Two Pussies'.

All in all, I met Freddy Heineken five times, for discussions that sometimes lasted an entire afternoon. I was not allowed to tape or take notes, because these were meant to be introductory talks. In the process, he constantly switched from the most delightful observations to the most offensive remarks, and from subtle witticisms to the most utter nonsense. He avoided questions about well-documented parts of Heineken's story but talked openly about some of the most private aspects of his own life. Sometimes he would abruptly denigrate me, but the next minute he would apparently seek to charm or to impress me: for example, by casually answering a private phone call from Queen Beatrix while we were alone in his office on his birthday.

Freddy Heineken's larger-than-life personality and his somewhat flippant attitude set him apart from other captains of industry. He built up his beer brand with undeniable flair, forging an appealing identity that is recognised nearly all around the world. He also displayed remarkable strategic vision in guiding the Heineken group's international expansion. All of that made it compelling to tell the man's story, to try and explain what made him tick.

Equally interesting was the story of the Heineken brand

and the marketing phenomenon behind it. Young marketing managers in the industry will readily admit that they don't sell beer, they sell marketing. Heineken has done so most fascinatingly, persuading drinkers from San Francisco to Hanoi that they should be forking out an extra dollar to drink Heineken – even if they would be hard-pressed to distinguish the beer from any other European lager.

Freddy suggested that, if I really insisted on studying Heineken, we would 'make a nice story together'. But when it became clear to him that the corporate biography would remain independent (just as I had portrayed it when I first approached him), our relationship soured. He ignored any further queries, apparently because I refused to let him edit my manuscript. As he himself admitted, he enjoyed sharp questions but did not like being contradicted. He went to startling lengths to try and obstruct my research, making ludicrous threats and sometimes carrying them out.

Freddy Heineken's outspoken opposition to my research made it particularly arduous. Instructed by the owner, the company's sitting managers declined formal interview requests. Most of them did so out of loyalty, which is deeply ingrained at Heineken. Fortunately, many others still agreed to share their memories, documents and insights into the Heineken saga. I am enormously grateful to them, for enabling me to produce a balanced and thoroughly researched story.

Heineken celebrated its 150th anniversary this year, marked, among others, by an exhibition in the centre of Amsterdam focusing on the brewery's founder, Gerard Heineken. This appeared a fitting opportunity to update and amplify my findings for a new book on the Heineken story. In the meantime Freddy Heineken had passed away, and the ownership of the brewery had been transferred to his only daughter, Charlene de

Carvalho-Heineken. Both her family and the brewing group declined requests for formal interviews for this book, arguing that the story had been amply told already. But again, my track record and enthusiasm convinced many to share information on a personal basis.

It was David Luxton, my remarkably supportive and efficient agent, who gave the impetus for this English-language publication. Many thanks are due to all those at and around Profile Books, who provided constant encouragement and helped to get this new book into shape. Along the way I was generously supported by archivists, other journalists and friends. Some helped to dig up facts, while others allowed talk of beer at their breakfast table and provided thoughtful advice.

Perhaps most encouragingly, those I approached (again) for this book almost invariably displayed curiosity and interest. Even those who had known Freddy Heineken in his least appealing guises still admired his achievements. Whatever the length or success of their stay at Heineken, former employees, partners and competitors always shared their stories with particular relish. That, more than anything else, reaffirmed my belief that Heineken is a truly extraordinary story.

Barbara Smit
September 2014

Bibliography

Amerongen, M. van, *Het gekwelde leven van die snelgeklede, rapgekapte, fraaibesnorde, goedgebekte sherrydrinkers*, Amsterdam, 1975

Baron, Stanley Wade, *Brewed in America: A History Of Beer And Ale In The United States*, Boston, 1962

Barritt Redman, Nicholas, *The Story of Whitbread PLC, 1742–1990*, publication compiled by company archivist, London, 1990

Beek, Gert van: *Meneer Heineken, het is voorbij, hoe de politie Freddy Heineken bevrijdde,* Amsterdam, 2013

Behringer, Wolfgang, *Löwenbräu. Von den Anfängen des Münchener Brauwesens bis zur Gegenwart*, München, 1991

Boak, Jessica and Ray Bailey, *Brew Britannia: The Strange Rebirth of British Beer*, London, 2014

Bossard, J.C. and Spier, J.,*Aan d'Amstel en het Ij, 100 Jaar bouwen en brouwen. Uit de geschiedenis van de Amstelbrouwerij, 1870–1970*, Amsterdam, 1970

Janssen de Limpens, K.J.Th., *Honderd Jaar Brand, de historie van een Limburgse Brouwerij, 1871–1971*, Wijlre, 1971

Brown, Pete, *Man Walks into a Pub: A Sociable History of Beer*, London, 2010

—*Three Sheets to the Wind: One Man's Quest for the Meaning of Beer*, London, 2007

—*Hops and Glory: One Man's Search for the Beer That Built the British Empire*, London, 2009

Carlsbergfondet, *The Book of Carlsberg: Father and Son, The History of Carlsberg*, Copenhagen, 1962

Clissold, Tim, *Mr. China*, London, 2010

Cochran, Thomas, C., *The Pabst Brewing Company: The History of an American Business*, New York, 1948

Colin, Jean-Claude and Potel-Jehl, Jean-Dany, *La bière en Alsace*, Strasbourg, 1989

Cornelissen, J.F.L.M., *Het Bierboeck*, Eindhoven, 1983

Correa, Cristiane, *Dream Big: How the Brazilian Trio behind 3G Capital – Jorge Paulo Lemann, Marcel Telles and Beto Sicupira – Acquired Anheuser-Busch, Burger King and Heinz*, 2014

Dean, Martin, *Robbing the Jews: The Confiscation of Jewish Property in the Holocaust, 1933–1945*, Cambridge, 2008

Doorman, G., *De Middeleeuwse Brouwerij en de gruit*, Den Haag, 1955

Downard, W., *Dictionary of the History of the American Brewing and Distilling Industries*, Westport, 1980

Dunstan Keith, *The Amber Nectar: A Celebration of Beer and Brewing in Australia*, Ringwood (Victoria, Australia), 1987

Enbom, Sten, *The Hartwall Story*, Helsinki, 2013

Gourvish, T., and R. Wilson, *The British Brewing Industry, 1830–1980*, Cambridge, 1994

Guinness, Jonathan, *Requiem for a Family Business*, London, 1997

Habbershaw, Rodney, *El vuelo del Águila*, Madrid, 2010

Hajn, Ivo, *Budějovický Budvar, 1895–1995*, České Budějovice, 1995

Hawkins K., and C. Pass, *The Brewing Industry: A Study in Industrial Organisation and Public Policy*, London, 1979

Hernon, Peter and Ganey, Terry, *Under the Influence: The Unauthorized Story of the Anheuser-Busch Dynasty* by, New York, 1991

Jacobs, M. and Maas M., with J. van der Werf, *Heineken, 1949–1988*, Amsterdam, 1991

Jacobs, M. and Maas M., *De magie van Heineken*, Amsterdam, 2001

Korthals, H. A., *Korte geschiedenis der Heineken's Bierbrouwerij Maatschappij N.V. 1873–1948*, Amsterdam, 1948

Hoelen, H., *Een studie over de biermarkt en het verbruik van alcoholische dranken*, Amsterdam, 1952

Hoelen, H., *De economische problematiek van de biermarkt, in het bijzonder in Nederland*, Amsterdam, 1961

Jackson, M., *The World Guide to Beer*, Englewood Cliffs, 1977

Jansen, A., *Bier in Nederland en Belgie: een geografie van de smaak*, Amsterdam, 1987

Jol, G., *Ontwikkeling en organisatie der Nederlansche brouwindustrie*, Haarlem, 1933

Kistemaker, R. and Van Vilsteren, V., *Bier! Geschiedenis van een volksdrank*, Amsterdam, 1994

Knoedelseder, William, *Bitter Brew: The Rise and Fall of Anheuser-Busch and America's Kings of Beer*, New York, 2012

Lepeltak, Thomas, *Meer zeg ik niet*, Amsterdam, 2005

Lhoëst, L.P.M.H., *Honderd Vijf en Twintig jaar Gulpener Bierbrouwerij Distilleerderij en Azijnfabriek, 1825–1950*, Gulpen, 1950

Macintosh, Julie, *Dethroning the King: The Hostile Takeover of Anheuser-Busch, an American Icon*, by Julie Macintosh, Hoboken (New Jersey), 2011

Mak, Geert, *Amsterdam: A Brief Life of the City*, London, 2001

Mayle Peter, *Thirsty Work: Ten Years of Heineken Advertising*, London, 1983

Munching, Philip van, *Beer Blast: The Inside Story of the Brewing Industry's Bizarre Battles for Your Money*, New York, 1997

Reader, W. J., *Vijftig Jaar Unilever, 1930–1980*, London, 1980

Reinders, Henk and Bruggeman, W.J., *De geschiedenis van Vrumona, 1945–1993*, Bunnik, 1993

Riepl, Wolfgang, *De Belgische bierbaronnen, het verhaal achter Anheuser-Busch InBev*, Roeselare, 2009

Ritchie, Berry, *An Uncommon Brewer: The Story of Whitbread, 1742–1992*, London, 1992

Scheffer, H., *Henry Tindal. Een ongewoon heer met ongewone besognes*, Bussum, 1976

308

Scheepmaker, N. and De Groen, J., *Vakmanschap is meesterschap*, Zwolle, 1992

Schreurs, W., *Geschiedenis van de reclame in Nederland 1870–1990*, Utrecht, 1989

Schutten, Anne-Mieke, *Geef mij maar een slappe whisky, Freddy Heineken, een biografische schets*, Soesterberg, 2007

Sluyterman, Keetie and Bouwens, Bram, *Heineken: 150 jaar, Brouwerij, merk en familie*, Amsterdam, 2014

Spaendonck, C. van, *Waarom ging de Amstel Brouwerij N.V. er in 1968 toe over met de Heineken's Bierbrouwerij Maatschappij N.V. te fuseren?*, 1985

Spicer, John; Chris Thurman, John Walters and Simon Ward, *Government Intervention in the Brewing Industry*, Basingstoke, 2013

Stikker, Dirk U., *Men of Responsibility: A Memoir*, New York, 1966

—*Memoires: Herinneringen uit de lange jaren waarin ik betrokken was bij de voortdurende wereldcrisis*, Rotterdam, 1966

Voogd, Christophe de: *Geschiedenis van Nederland, Vanaf de prehistorie tot het heden*, Amsterdam, 1996

Vries, Peter R. de, *De ontvoering van Alfred Heineken*, Baarn, 1993

Wilson, C., *Unilever in de Tweede Industriële Revolutie, 1945–1965*, Den Haag, 1968

Yntema, R., *The Brewing Industry in Holland, 1300–1800*, unpublished dissertation, Chicago, 1992

Zijl, Annejet van der, *Gerard Heineken, de man, de stad en het bier*, Amsterdam, 2014

Zwaal, Peter, *Amstel, het verhaal van ons bier, 1870–heden*, Amsterdam, 2010

Sources

This book is mostly based on more than two hundred interviews conducted in the Netherlands, United Kingdom, United States, Denmark, France, Germany and Belgium. Several former Heineken employees have provided me with correspondence and internal documents, while other letters and company reports were found in public archives.

Further details and quotes are issued from newspaper articles, in *Het Financieele Dagblad, NRC Handelsblad, De Volkskrant, Het Algemeen Dagblad, De Telegraaf, Trouw, Het Parool, HP/De Tijd, Elsevier, Elan, Intermediair, Quote, FEM Business, Adformatie, The Wall Street Journal, Business Week, Fortune, Forbes, Modern Brewery Age, Beer Marketer's Insight, Impact International, The Financial Times, The Daily Telegraph, Le Monde, Libération, Les Dernières Nouvelles d'Alsace, Les Echos, Le Nouvel Economiste, Cinco Días* and *El País,* among others, as well as annual reports, company publications and press releases from the relevant companies. Heineken has also helped to publish four books about its own history.

Quotations that are not listed below are derived from interviews with people who only agreed to contribute to this book on the basis of anonymity. Quotes from discussions with Alfred H. Heineken may not be entirely verbatim, since I was not allowed to tape the conversations or to take notes.

References

Prologue

viii   'It never ceased to amaze us': interview with Marlies Ponsioen

viii   'the receptionists all had their hair done': interview with Allan van Rijn

x   'Before the presentation': Ibid

1. All or Nothing!

1   The early years of Heineken, Gerard Adriaan's family and Amsterdam in the second half of the nineteenth century were depicted colourfully in the exhibition 'Heineken's Amsterdam', at the Amsterdam city archives in 2014.

2   'With a sense of adventure': Heineken: *Korte geschiedenis*

3   'All! Or nothing!': ibid.

4   'Even the brewers': Yntema, *The Brewing Industry*

5   'No longer shall': Heineken: *Korte geschiedenis*

5   'that you will moderate': ibid.

7   'A full-bodied': *Algemeen Handelsblad*, 24 February 1870, quoted in A. Van der Zijl, *Gerard Heineken*

11   'A few years ago': *Achter de Schermen! Mevr. von B., geb. T.*, Amsterdam, 1891. The story of Willy and Hans von Barnekow is further described in: Scheffer, H., *Henry Tindal: Een ongewoon heer met ongewone besognes*

11 'when he suddenly collapsed': *NRC*, 19 March 1893

15 'Business didn't interest': *Nieuwe Revu*, 12 November 1987

15 'Everybody in our home': *HP*, 5 October 1968

15 'It was not much fun': *HP/De Tijd*, 23 December 1994

16 'Due to a poor performance': school report, Hervormd Lyceum

16 'I learned to sneeze': Sylvia Tóth, *Vakwerk, Framed Creativity:* Den Haag, 1992

17 'He won't let anything': school report Kennemer Lyceum, Bloemendaal

2. Bier soll sein!

19 'Such a balance sheet': Stikker, *Memoires*

22 'acute discomfort': ibid.

25 'There are situations': ibid.

25 'We then tried': ibid.

27 'The SS general': ibid.

28 'in an inebriated state': J. L. van der Paauw, *Guerilla in Rotterdam:* Den Haag, 1995

28 'extremely painful': unsigned letter for Dirk Stikker, dated December 1941, Heineken archive, Stadsarchief Amsterdam. Gaston-Dreyfus was seriously ill. The letter laments that the bank was liquidated after three generations and eighty-five years, during which time its reputation had remained unblemished. The letter also underlined the warm relationship between the two men and Gaston-Dreyfus's gratitude for the concern shown by Heineken.

28 'disappeared in prison': letter signed by Pieter Feith, dated 21 July 1943, summarising the findings of an envoy ('E. S.') to Marseille, Heineken archive, Stadsarchief Amsterdam

29 'because I was driving': *NRC Handelsblad*, 1 August 1992

30 'in the side-carriage': *'t Kennemer was toen zo!* (contribution of former pupil Alfred Heineken to an anniversary brochure for the Kennemer Lyceum).

30 'Fred was just': interview with Anton van Gulik

30   'The secret': interview in an unidentified and undated Dutch press
       clipping
31   'In Rotterdam, I got notes': ibid.
31   'Freddy just stayed': interview with Cees de Kruif
33   'Stikker realised': interview with Ben ter Haar
34   'He looked uglier': travel report by Dirk Stikker, June 1945,
       Heineken archive, Stadsarchief Amsterdam
35   'Your acceptance': telegram from Dirk Stikker to René Gaston-
       Dreyfus, dated February 1947, Heineken archive, Stadsarchief
       Amsterdam
36   'a stereotype': interview with Rudy de Man

3. The Dutch Beer King of Manhattan

39   'Leo would leave a case': interview with Jan Burger
40   'Snob appeal': *Het Financieele Dagblad,* 2 June 1975
42   'St Louis rowdies': *American Mercury* as quoted by P. van
       Munching, *Beer Blast*
42   'We have German enemies': Daniel Okrent, *Smithsonian
       Magazine,* May 2010
42   'the most unprincipled': Leah Rae Berk, *Temperance and
       Prohibition Era Propaganda: A Study in Rhetoric:* Essay 2004,
       Brown University Library (Providence Center for Digital
       Scholarship)
44   'I think that': *De Volkskrant,* 15 December 1990
45   'with a lot of impudence': *Het Financieele Dagblad,* 2 June 1975
45   'Only much later': ibid.
47   'That was the amazing': interview with Ben ter Haar
47   'Van Munching was hugely talented': ibid.
48   'Van Munching believed': interview with Sibe Minnema
49   'Van Munching walked': interview with John Elink Schuurman
50   'They always wanted to impress': phone interview with George
       Kahl
51   'Van Munching was like a bear': interview with Rob van Duursen
52   'this concession': interview with Sibe Minnema

313

4. Our Young Friend

5. Gulping Down Amstel

71   'The most drastic': P. Zwaal, *Frisdranken in Nederland: een twintigste eeuwse productgeschiedenis*, Rotterdam, 1993

71   'a storm in a beer glass': *Heineken 1949–1988*

74   'In a nutshell': interview with John Elink Schuurman

74   'The board was adamant': interview with Guus Avis

75   'when you thought': interview with Gregor Frenkel Frank

75   'Our position is like': *Heineken, 1949–1988*

76   'The thought of such a challenge': interview with Carel van Lookeren Campagne

76   'Egberts […] said the time had come': ibid.

77   'We knew exactly': conversation with Alfred Heineken

78   'I didn't do too badly': ibid.

79   'With a heavy heart': interview with Gregor Frenkel Frank

6. The Making of Freddy

83   'Freddy was really receptive': phone interview with Jan Blokker

84   'Heineken made a big splash': phone interview with Bob Bertina

85   'Around the time': preview of *Andere Tijden*, VPRO [TV programme], 17 October 2012

85   'The aftermath': phone interview with Fons Rademakers

86   'Look, when you order': phone interview with Jan Blokker

86   'My basic philosophy': *HP*, 5 October 1968

87   'It was a drama': *NRC Handelsblad,* April 1989

90   'Oscar ran the breweries': interview with Rob van Duursen

91   'Press the top button': conversation with Alfred Heineken

91   'The others thought': conversation with Alfred Heineken

92   'For competitors like us': interview with Raymond Boon Falleur

7. Refreshing the UK

95   'Women want a drink': The British Brewing Industry with special reference to lager, Operational Statistics Section, Economics and Statistics Department, DHR, 7 December 1961

95   'For that reason': letter from Gerard van Os van Delden, 6 December 1965, Heineken archive, Stadsarchief Amsterdam

97   'Only minor damage': Nicholas Barritt Redman notes that the brewery on Chiswell Street was probably saved from destruction by its Company Fire Brigade, which fought with 'heroic courage' in the great incendiary raid on the City in December 1940. 'When the ruins were eventually cleared, the Brewery was almost the only building left standing,' he wrote.

97   'They are interested': note about British brewing groups by J. C. Cornelis, 23 January 1961, Heineken archive, Stadsarchief Amsterdam

98   'Men like Carling': the Whitbread archive, which was transferred to the London Metropolitan Archives, includes a collection of print ads for beer brands in the UK

100   'There is little or no pressure': draft report (from Heineken UK) about 1963 turnover

100   'bursting with indignation': letter from Gerard van Os van Delden to Oscar Wittert van Hoogland, dated 22 June 1965, Heineken archive, Stadsarchief Amsterdam

102   'faced with the embarrassment': letter from Alex Bennett to Oscar Wittert van Hoogland, 1 August 1969, Heineken archive, Stadsarchief Amsterdam

102   'A few years back': from Whitbread archive

103   'Whitbread apparently has a hangover': report for Heineken's executive board regarding a meeting with Whitbread on 17 October 1969, Heineken archive, Stadsarchief Amsterdam

104   'such friendly people' and 'I do wonder': ibid.

104   'I want to follow up': letter from Alex Bennett to Oscar Wittert van Hoogland, 27 October 1969, Heineken archive, Stadsarchief Amsterdam

104   'sitting on both sides' and next quotes: ibid.

105   'It is always dangerous': letter from Alex Bennett to Oscar Wittert van Hoogland, 4 December 1969, Heineken archive, Stadsarchief Amsterdam

108   'It was fairly anarchic': interview with Michael Everett

108   'In those days': interview with Dave Trott

109 'It's just not nice' and following quotes: interview with Frank Lowe
110 'I knew that': interview with Simonds-Gooding
112 'A brief was born': ibid.
113 'three months of agony': phone interview with Terry Lovelock
114 'This Heineken campaign': dialogue as described by Frank Lowe
115 'blatant untruth' and other reactions described by P. Brown in
     Man Walks into a Pub
115 'I could do what I wanted': interview with Simonds-Gooding
116 'pretty enigmatic, three cigarettes a minute': interview with
     Simonds-Gooding
116 'It was the wrong gravity': interview with Simonds-Gooding
116 'With its whimsical, metaphorical approach': interview with Adam
     Kirby
117 'All right, Frank': as described by Frank Lowe
118 'Unlike many clients': interview with Frank Lowe
119 'We delivered to supermarkets': interview with Simonds-Gooding
119 'It was really tough': ibid.

8. Fortress Europe

122 'With a Ffr 100 million': undated and unsigned report about
     l'Alsacienne de Brasserie in Heineken archive, Stadsarchief
     Amsterdam
122 'On his desk': interview with Michel Debus
122 'due to the convergence': press release approved by Michel Hatt,
     as recorded in a telex from a banker to Alfred Heineken, dated 4
     August 1972, Heineken archive, Stadsarchief Amsterdam
123 'I felt that I was stuck': phone interview with Roland Wagner
123 'would rather be called': telex from Alfred Heineken to his
     secretary, Ms De Looper, in August 1972 (date unclear), Heineken
     archive, Stadsarchief Amsterdam
123 'I'm off for a nap': ibid.
123 'The market leaders': interview with Jean-Claude Colin
127 'massacre': *Les Dernières Nouvelles d'Alsace,* 16 January 1975
127 'The message': interview with Grégoire Champetier

9. The Kidnapping

158 'I'm a businessman': ibid.

159 'Collaborate': ibid.

159 'We made it clear': interview with Kees Sietsma

160 'rather disturbing': interview with Gert van Beek

161 'My team virtually': interview with Ed van Kerkhof

164 'I was thinking to myself': statement by Alfred Heineken

164 'Damn it, how could that be': interview with Gert van Beek

164 'That's impossible': interview with Kees Sietsma

165 'it was pure luck': interview with Gert van Beek

165 'Could you not have come': as described in an interview with Jan Baas en Rob Neve

166 'If a man breaks his word': De Vries, *De ontvoering van Alfred Heineken*

166 'I'm free': dialogue as described by Frank Lowe

167 'Everybody knows Els': *Stern*, undated clipping of lengthy feature titled '*Heineken-Entführung, Das unbekannte Leben des Bierkönigs*'

167 'About three to four': statement to the police by Elisabeth Johanna de Laat, Recherchedienst, Gemeentepolitie Amsterdam, 9 November 1983

168 'I think that mitigating': statement by Alfred Heineken

171 'half of the Amsterdam underworld': interview with Ed van Kerkhof

172 Arjo de Jong anecdote from interview in *Hoge Bomen*, a Dutch TV documentary, Pieter Jan Hagens, 2002.

172 'reminiscent of a Mafia funeral': *The Guardian*, 1 February 2003

172 'somewhat mentally disturbed': fourth hearing of Martin Erkamps, Centrale Executieve Recherche, Gemeentepolitie Amsterdam, 7 December 1983

172 'Heineken put a lot of effort': interview with Ed van Kerkhof

174 'If I feel anything': *NRC Handelsblad*, 1 August 1992

174 'The nasty aspect': statement by Alfred Heineken

175 'The nice thing about being rich': conversation with Alfred Heineken

10. Losing Its Fizz

11. Taking Over New York

202 'Mistaking it': P. van Munching, *Beer Blast*

203 'It's a very dirty business': interview with George Kahl

205 'Kronenbourg is the reason': *Het Parool,* 10 April 1982

206 'The lime kills the taste': *Adformatie,* 6 October 1988

207 Market shares of imported beers in the US market as estimated by Beverage Marketing

212 'an incredibly tough act to follow': as quoted in P. van Munching, *Beer Blast*

212 'probably a bit complacent' and 'a certain distrust': *Modern Brewery Age,* 10 July 1995

213 'Perhaps in recent years': *Business & Finance,* 04 August 1994

213 'My brother': P. van Munching, *Beer Blast.* Foley's alleged remark was not directed at Christopher van Munching personally but at a group of managers.

214 'Consumers want quality and taste': *Modern Brewery Age,* 10 July 1995

214 'unusually fresh beer campaign': *Ad Age,* May 1, 1996

214 'Heineken would identify': Bob Garfield in *Advertising Age,* 29 April 1996

12. The Uncrowned Beer King

218 Max Pam anecdote: *De Volkskrant,* 12 November 2010

219 'You won't find peroxide': *NRC Handelsblad,* 20 April 1993

220 'a monstrous yellow colossus': *De Volkskrant,* 24 May 1988, quoting an interview with Alfred Heineken in *Bündner Zeitung*

220 'The story of the capitalist': *Weltwoche,* 30 December 1993

220 'Just before the referendum': phone interview with Robert Obrist

222 'When Timmer asked': interview with Sibe Minnema

223 'Of course, the wine bill': phone interview with Ferry Hoogendijk

224 'red women are always so ugly': conversation with Freddy Heineken

224 'He meddles with': *Der Spiegel,* 5 December 1983

225 'innovative and intriguing': letter from George Bush as quoted by *The Wall Street Journal,* 1 September 1992

226 'I can't stand being contradicted': conversation with Alfred
      Heineken

227 'A product can lose': *Fortune,* 16 November 1981

227 'Hide away': *De Groene Amsterdammer,* 6 November 1996

229 'like the spiritual distance': interview with Frans de Groen

229 'Freddy apparently believed': interview with Paul Rutten sr

230 'We are not the same': *Elan,* June 1992

13. The Beer Wars

236 'Busch is wasting': phone interview with Aleš Kocvera

238 'When I got here': *Het Financieele Dagblad,* 11 December 1998

242 'They don't like that': interview with Hans Meerlo

243 'You've got balls': ibid.

244 'When you travel': interview with Johnny Thijs

244 'For the Chinese': *FEM,* 24 July 1993

245 'talking in dog farts': Tim Clissold, *Mr China*, Constable &
      Robinson, 2010

245 'It's a thorn in our side': *FEM,* 24 July 1993

14. After Freddy

255 'Heineken is probably': Nederland 1 news bulletin, 4 January 2002

256 'You could see that', *NRC Handesblad,* 4 January 2004

256 'It's awful to feel': conversation with Alfred Heineken

257 'If I had not been': *Lions News,* 22 June 1995

257 'I'm frustrated': *De Volkskrant,* 15 October 2011

257 'He was absolutely fascinated': phone interview Wouter Pijzel

257 'The seats are arranged': European Patent Office, application
      NL1001526 (C2), 1997–05–02

260 'Even if that sounds chauvinistic': minutes of the annual
      shareholders' meeting of Heineken Holding N.V. (26 April 2002)

262 'a lot of hassle': conversation with Alfred Heineken

263 'a woman with a good set of brains': *Het Parool,* 28 April 1989

265 'I started delving': *NRC Handelsblad,* 11 January 2002

266 'the most promising child': *Long Beach Independent*, 9 November 1956

266 'alarmingly handsome': *Janesville Daily Gazette*, 15 May 1958

266 'a lovely brunette': *The Raleigh Register*, 24 October 1956

267 'The parties happened': *The Daily Mail*, 10 November 2012

267 The details about the Popper and Lisser families are based on birth and marriage certificates, travel documents, American press reports and other information provided by archivists in Amsterdam and Hamburg.

268 'a false qualification': *Nouvelliste du Rhône*, 21 December 1967

268 'It wasn't so much': *The Daily Mail*, 10 November 2012

270 'My father is part': press release Heineken Holding, 25 April 2002

15. Last Round

272 'the lowest common': interview with Frank Lowe

272 The ranking of the international beer brands (counting sales outside of their home market in 2012) comes from Plato Logic as quoted by *Trends*, a Belgian magazine. Heineken published another ranking by Canadean, based on its Annual Brand Database, July 14, showing Heineken with a market share of 19 per cent in the international premium lager segment, way ahead of Corona and Budweiser with 10 per cent each. Next are Carlsberg, Modelo, Stella Artois, Beck's, Amstel, Tuborg and Tiger.

273 'You couldn't stand aloof': interview with Alan Gourdie

275 'We watched the developments': *FEM Business*, 5 May 2007

276 'When he hung up': phone interview with Erik Hartwall

278 'I said that I thought' and 'We were very aggressive': phone interview with John Dunsmore

279 'spurious, without merit': Carlsberg press release, 31 October 2007

279 'quite a hostile process' and following quotes: phone interview with John Dunsmore

279 'You're dealing with a consortium bid': ibid.

279 'The tone was a little': *NRC Handelsblad*, 16 November 2007

279 'It's starting to become': *NRC Handelsblad*, 10 January 2008

280 'Our intelligence was': phone interview with John Dunsmore

280 The Carlsberg share issue to finance the deal was made possible
     by an adjustment of the Carlsberg foundation's charter, which had
     to be approved by the Danish Ministry of Justice. It allowed the
     foundation to hold only 25 per cent of Carlsberg's shares (against
     the previous requirement of a majority) but it still has to retain 51
     per cent of the company's voting rights.

281 'were now in a position': Sten Enbom, *The Hartwall Story*

281 'an indictment of short-sighted': *The Observer*, 30 December 2007

281 'It was tough because': interview with Alan Gourdie

284 'We exchanged our brewery for Heineken shares': interview in the
     documentary film *The Magic of Heineken*

284 'Would you consider us as cousins': ibid.

284 Femsa had to commit not to sell its shares for five years (with a
     few exceptions) or increase its stake in Heineken Holding above
     20 per cent, or its stake in the Heineken group above an economic
     interest of 20 per cent.

286 'Few know that' and following quotes: *Straits Times*, 11 April 2014

288 'The tanks are in the street': Ian Shackleton from Nomura quoted
     by *De Volkskrant*, 21 July 2012

288 Global market size of 1,941 million hectolitres provided by
     Beverage Marketing Corporation, a specialist market research
     company based in New York and often used as a reference in the
     US and global beer industry.

290 'costs are like nails': Cristiane Correa, *Dream Big*

291 Arizona accident as described by Peter Hernon and Terry Ganey,
     Under the Influence

292 Alleged health issues after Anheuser-Busch's acquisition
     described by William Knoedelseder in *Bitter Brew*

294 EU fines: European Commission decision 18 April 2007 (Zaak nr.
     COMP/B-2/37.766 – Nederlandse biermarkt)

295 'Heineken USA chose': Philip van Munching in correspondence
     with the author

296 'dramatic change': video interview with *USA Today*, 7 July 2014

Epilogue

297 'When I go to a supermarket': *De Volkskrant*, 26 April 2013

298 'it's a meritocracy': *Quote*, July 2014

299 'We talked a lot': brief conversation with the author

299 'wrong': *Het Financieele Dagblad*, 7 March 2013

300 'We always talked about it': *NRC Handelsblad*, 26 April 2013

Index